The Church and Communication

The Church and Communication

Edited by
Patrick Granfield

Sheed & Ward

Sheed & Ward™ is a service of The National Catholic Reporter Publishing Company.

Library of Congress Cataloguing-in-Publication Data

The Church and communication / edited by Patrick Granfield.
      p.   cm. -- (Communication, culture & theology)
     Includes bibliographical references and index.
     ISBN 1-55612-674-3 (alk. paper)
     1. Communication--Religious aspects--Catholic Church. 2. Catholic Church--Membership. I. Granfield, Patrick. II. Series.
BX1795.C67C48 1994
261.5'2--dc20   93-46601
                                                        CIP

Published by: Sheed & Ward
                 115 E. Armour Blvd.
                 P.O. Box 419492
                 Kansas City, MO 64141

To order, call: (800) 333-7373

Contents

Introduction

The inspiration for this book came from a seminar on ecclesiology and communication that took place from September 24 to October 1, 1989, at the scenic Villa Cavalletti in the Alban Hills south of Rome. It was sponsored by the Center for Interdisciplinary Study in Communication at the Gregorian University in Rome and the Centre for the Study of Communication and Culture in London. The purpose of the seminar, according to the letter of announcement, was to "focus on current developments in ecclesiology and the significance of new conceptions and new cultural patterns of communication for ecclesiology and for the life of the Church."

Twenty-five participants, divided between theologians and communicators, were invited to the seminar. It was an international group with representatives from Europe, North America, and Latin America. Ample time was allotted for discussion—in large and small groups—and the cross-disciplinary exchange was often intense and animated. After a week of creative and at times exhausting dialogue, the participants agreed that it was a valuable experience.

At the end of the Cavalletti Seminar, it was decided that a book should be written that further examined the themes that had been discussed. I was asked to edit the volume. All the contributors—half are theologians and half are communicators—attended the seminar, with the exception of John T. Catoir. The following people translated the foreign language contributions: Edward Hughes (Ricardo Antoncich), Leslie Wearnd (Henri Bourgeois), Albert Wimmer and Andrew Wade (Klaus Kenzler and Hermann J. Pottmeyer).

A special word of appreciation is due to Robert A. White, S.J. for his role in the entire project. He had the initial vision to create the Cavalletti Seminar on Ecclesiology and Communication, and he was its chief organizer, facilitator, and tireless advocate. We have communicated regularly over the last few years about the book through personal meetings, letters, faxes, and telephone conversations. He has shown admirable patience, persistance, and dedication.

Patrick Granfield in Chapter One gives a broad analysis of the relationship between the theology of the Church and communication. He examines the meanings of communication, the difference between the Church and ecclesiology, and ten specific examples of how communication and ecclesiology interact.

Robert White in Chapter Two outlines five traditions of the theory and practice of communication, each with a distinct view of good society and of good communication: corporatist, libertarian, social responsibility, democratization, and communion. He shows why it is valuable for theologians to know the different approaches in contemporary communication research.

Peter Henrici in Chapter Three argues that if communication is important in the Church, then it requires a communication ethics that is theologically grounded. He examines the interplay between truth and power and how theology understands them. By pointing out some abuses of power and truth, he presents the main features of normatively correct ecclesial communication.

Gregor Goethals in Chapter Four broadens our view of communication with her treatment of symbolic forms. An artist, art historian, and church designer, she discusses the role of symbol, space, ritual, and myth in popular culture and high art. She concludes that a major challenge today is to reclaim the basic sacramental impulse in human experience.

Klaus Kienzler in Chapter Five gives a detailed historical and theological analysis of the Church as communion. He explains the meaning and development of the concept of *communio,* its relation to the constitution of the Church, and the connection between communion and communication as found in the Pastoral Instruction *Communio et progressio.*

Hermann J. Pottmeyer in Chapter Six analyzes dialogue as an essential aspect of *communio.* He shows the danger of neglecting dialogue, the place of reception in a dialogic community, and the exercise of authority in dialogue.

The next four chapters apply some of the ideas given earlier to four significant ecclesiological activities: ecumenism, catechesis, witness, and evangelization.

Francis A. Sullivan in Chapter Seven shows how good communication helped achieve unity in the Church of the early centuries and how failures in communication contributed to the Eastern and Western schisms. He concludes that good communication is critical in the present ecumenical quest for Christian unity.

Henri Bourgeois in Chapter Eight explains the relation between catechesis and communication, the social and cultural context of catechesis, the kinds of catechesis, and the various interactions operative in catechesis with special reference to the interaction between the catechist and the catechized.

Ricardo Antoncich in Chapter Nine addresses the role of witness in communicating the Gospel. After indicating the challenges in modern communication theory and practice, he shows how the Church can respond to them. For him witness is a privileged means of communication that is linked to the following of Christ and to the Church as a community of disciples.

Angela Ann Zukowski in Chapter Ten describes evangelization as a form of communication. She analyzes the contemporary situation and the role of evangelization, the need for authentic inculturation, the relationship between ecclesiology and communication, and some specific pastoral suggestions for the future work of evangelization.

Frances Forde Plude in Chapter Eleven presents an interdisciplinary study of communications within the Church. She gives her conceptual framework and then deals with the participative elements in communion ecclesiology and the forms of communication. She considers interactivity as an essential element in the Church and indicates how it can be institutionalized.

John T. Catoir in Chapter Twelve deals with the ecclesial status of Catholic communicators. He first presents some canonical aspects, and then discusses the mystery of Church communication, accountability, and the status of those communicators who have an official role in the Church's ecclesiastical structure.

In conclusion, these twelve articles present a comprehensive study of the relationship between the Church and communication. Using sound, scholarly methods, the authors present perceptive analyzes, innovative ideas, and exciting challenges. As far as I know, this volume is unique; no comparable work of such scope exists. The contributions reflect many of the discussions held during the Cavalletti Seminar. The same themes appear often but with different nuances. The overriding and unanimous message that all the authors give us is that ecclesiology and communication need each other. Collaboration between theologians and communicators can help make the saving Word of God better known and, by so doing, provide a service to both the Church and the wider human community.

Washington, D.C.   Patrick Granfield

The Theology of the Church and Communication

Patrick Granfield

Christianity is a religion of communication. God continues to speak to us, and we must seek to understand his message, as these words from the Epistle to the Hebrews remind us.

> At various times in the past and in various different ways, God spoke to our ancestors through the prophets; but in our own time, the last days, he has spoken to us through his Son, the Son that he has appointed to inherit everything and through whom he made everything there is (Hebrews 1:1-2).

Theology—faith seeking understanding—is replete with communication themes: revelation as the self-disclosure of God given to us through Scripture and the apostolic tradition, the trinitarian processions, Jesus Christ as the ultimate self-communication of the Father, the Holy Spirit who bestows wisdom and other gifts, and the Church as the sacrament of communion with Christ. Furthermore, theology deals with many concepts that have obvious dimensions of communication: analogy, reconciliation, reception, prayer, communion, community, *communicatio idiomatum*, and *communicatio in sacris*. In fact, it may be impossible to find any issue in theology that does not contain a reference to communication.[1]

The theology of communication, at least implicitly, goes back to earliest days of Christianity. Contemporary theologians continue to explore this theme. Yves Congar, Avery Dulles, Jacques Ellul, Bernard Lonergan, Karl Rahner, Hans Urs von Balthasar, Edward Schillebeeckx, and others have written on various aspects of communication. An extensive

---

1. For a discussion of the dialogue between theology and communication see Daniel J. Felton, "The Unavoidable Dialogue: Five Interfaces between Theology and Communication," *Media Development*, October 1989, pp. 17-23. Also see Robert Kress, *The Church: Communion, Sacrament, Communication* (New York: Paulist Press, 1985).

bibliography exists on Christian communication.[2] The official Church has also recognized the importance of communication. In 1963 the Second Vatican Council issued *Inter mirifica* (Decree on the Instruments of Social Communication). The Pontifical Council for Social Communications has published two major postconciliar pastoral instructions: *Communio et progressio* (1971) and *Aetatis novae* (1992). The Congregation for Catholic Education published the *Guide to the Training of Future Priests concerning the Instruments of Social Communication* (1986). The Code of Canon Law (1983) deals with communication in Canons 822-832. Finally, the Congregation for the Doctrine of the Faith issued the *Instruction on Social Communications and the Doctrine of the Faith* (1992) that reviewed the norms found in canon law.

In addition to numerous diocesan and national organizations dealing with the various kinds of communicative activity, there are several international groups. Chief among them are: the International Association of Catholic Radio and Television Communicators (UNDA International); the International Organization for Cinema and Audiovisual (OCIC); the International Catholic Union of the Press (UCIP); the Centre for the Study of Communication and Culture (CSCC); the World Association for Christian Commmunication (WACC); and the Associated Church Press (ACP).

My intention in this chapter is to present an overview of the relationship between the theology of the Church and communication. Later chapters will investigate in detail some of the issues that I have raised. I shall first make some observations on the meaning of communication. Second, I shall examine fundamental ideas about the Church and ecclesiology. Third, I shall discuss how communication is applicable to ten concrete ecclesiological issues.

I. The Meaning of Communication

To be human means to communicate. We cannot help but communicate, because communication touches upon all that we are and all that we do. Communication is an elemental necessity that constitutes our intersubjectivity. Through communication one becomes a full human and cultural being. Culture depends on the common sharing and participation by the members of a community. One generation communicates to another generation sets of ideas, values, moral norms, and behavioral patterns that result in a particular cultural context. No community can be established or continue to exist without communication. "Through communication," writes Bernard Lonergan, "there is constituted community and, conversely, community constitutes and perfects itself through communication."[3]

---

2. See Paul A. Soukup, *Christian Communication: A Bibliographical Survey* (New York: Greenwood Press, 1989). The section on ecclesiology is found on pp. 63-79.

3. Bernard J.F. Lonergan, *Method in Theology* (New York: Herder and Herder, 1972), p. 363.

Many kinds of communication exist: personal and interpersonal, private and public, group and organizational, mass and social, macrosocial and microsocial. We also speak of print, voice, visual, audio, and electronic media communication. Language, however, is the most sophisticated technique of communication. "There are no ideas free of the web of language," notes David Tracy."[4] But we also communicate by gestures, images, symbols, and rituals. The medieval theologian, Hugh of St. Victor, observed that "the whole sensibly perceptible world is like a book written by the finger of God."[5] The various modes of communication are interrelated even though they have different techniques, motivations, and goals, and are judged by diverse sets of criteria.

It is not easy to define communication, since it is a complex reality. It is a concept and a technique, a dynamic process that is both interactive and purposeful. The word communication comes from the Latin *communicare* and has several meanings: to make common, to share, to transmit, to inform, to unite, to impart. In its broadest sense, then, communication means sharing, interacting, participating, conversing, and exchanging information.

More precisely, communication can be defined as that dynamic and reciprocal process by which persons, individually or collectively, share messages of meaning and value with one another. Communication, as the transmission and interchange of information, is the way we share ideas, feelings, experiences, attitudes, and values with others. Since communication is a complicated and fluctuating interaction between persons, the messages that are shared have to be interpreted and evaluated. Hermeneutics, the science of interpretation, studies the various universes of discourse and proposes ways to grasp their meaning in the text and the context.

Communication is not a unilateral transfer of information from one person to another, from sender to receiver, as if it were a monologue. That understanding—sometimes called the *transportation model*—is too linear and implies that the receiver is passive and not involved in the process beyond simply receiving what is sent. By contrast, the *forum model*, holds that there is a dynamic relationship between sender and receiver. The receiver actively participates in this dialogic exchange on the basis of experience, understanding, and interpretation. Receiving involves active and creative dialogue by which the message is re-created and interpreted by the receiver. This exchange fosters full participation in meaning and value.

---

4. David Tracy, *Plurality and Ambiguity: Hermeneutics, Religion, Hope* (San Francisco: Harper & Row, 1987), p. 43.

5. Hugh of St. Victor, *De tribus diebus, Patrologia latina* 176: 814.

Communication and communion are related. St. Thomas Aquinas, for example, often used *communicatio* for *communio* and *communitas*. Communion or community is not possible without communication, since, to some extent, communion is the result of communication. Communication covers a broad spectrum. There is, for example, a great difference in intensity, quality, and duration between the casual communication of strangers and the intimate communication of friends. Yet, wherever there is communication, some kind of communion is also established, however tenuous and short-lived or cruel and exploitative it may be. Karl Rahner and Herbert Vorgrimler make this point. "Communication designates that active exchange, based on personal ability to hear and on free openness, that creates a community between the transmitter and the recipient (hearer) which is best called communion. In its very highest form, namely, self-communication, the source of the communication itself is given to the recipient."[6]

The act of communication has several dimensions. Harold D. Lasswell suggests that for a thorough analysis of the act of communication one would need to respond to the following five questions: Who? Says what? In which channel? To whom? With what effect?[7] Although these five questions are necessary, they are not sufficient. One must also ask or make explicit two further questions in order to have a more integrated view of communication. They are: For what purpose? and In what context.

II. The Church and Ecclesiology

The theology of communication is related in a special way to the Church and to ecclesiology. The Church is a worldwide communications network seeking to bring the human family into union with God. Communication of Word and Sacrament enters into the very heart of the mystery of the Church. Communication is an essential function of the Church, because it sustains Christians in their pilgrim journey toward the full realization of the Kingdom of God. Social communication, to quote *Communio et progressio*, is "an act of cooperation in the divine work of creation and conservation."[8]

---

6. Karl Rahner and Herbert Vorgrimler, *Theological Dictionary* (New York: Herder and Herder, 1965), p. 89.

7. Harold D. Lasswell, "The Structure and Function of Communication in Society," in Lyman Bryson, ed., *The Communication of Ideas* (New York: Harper & Brothers, 1948), p. 37.

8. Pontifical Commission for the Instruments of Social Communication, *Communio et progressio*. English translation in Austin, Flannery, ed., *Vatican II: The Conciliar and Post Conciliar Documents* (Northport, N.Y.: Costello, 1975), #7, p. 295.

The principal sources of Christian communication are Scripture and Tradition, which are themselves products of the Church's self-understanding and self-communication. These two sources give identity, continuity, and coherence to the Church. It is not, however, the Church's own self-understanding that is communicated, but the divine self-disclosure through its faith in God, Christ, and the Gospel. Each generation actively receives, interprets, and hands on the Gospel. We communicate not just facts or information but our living faith in Christ Jesus. The Church of Christ is "a sign and instrument of communion with God and of the unity of all mankind" (*Lumen gentium* 1).

The Church has a two-fold mission which involves commmunication. The Church gathers and sends forth. First, the Church is a gathering of persons into community membership. Most often within a parish context, the Church preaches the Word, catechizes, celebrates the sacraments, and assists the needy. Second, the Church sends forth its message to the unevangelized, to the poor, and to all who seek perduring truth and meaning in their lives. Communication is necessary for both of these missions. According to Avery Dulles, "communications is at the heart of what the Church is all about. The Church exists to bring men into communion with each other."[9]

Ecclesiology—the theology of the Church—is that discourse that studies the nature and mission of the Church. Ecclesiology is not the same as the Church; it is a reflection upon the Church, an attempt to understand and to communicate the mystery. A diversity of ecclesiologies is found both in the New Testament and in the history of Christianity, because no one ecclesiology is adequate to express the fullness of the Church. Yet in every ecclesiology communication is a critical element. No ecclesiology is effective if it cannot be communicated or if it does not sufficiently respond to the variety of contexts and experiences in which the local churches function. Today the social sciences are often conversation partners with ecclesiology.

Several types of ecclesiological reflection exist. It may be, for example, theoretical, symbolic, conceptual, apologetic. controversial, historical, pastoral, or socio-religious. Furthermore, ecclesiology may use a variety of languages: normative, idealistic, descripture, prescriptive, or applicative.

III. The Ecclesiological Application

The Church is a group of communicating persons, a network of meanings and values, where continual and multiple interactions take place.

---

9. Avery Dulles, "The Church is Communications," *IDOC International (North American Edition)*, 27 (June 12, 1971): 69.

In this section, I shall examine ten specific ecclesiological issues and show how they relate to communication. This list represents some of the major questions being discussed in contemporary ecclesiology; it does not pretend to be exhaustive. Although there are many facets to every act of communication, I will focus primarily on the sender and receiver of the message and on the direction of the communication flow. Is it, for example, unilateral or reciprocal, vertical or horizontal? I shall examine each issue first as a communicative exchange and then as an ecclesiological challenge.

1. Imaging the Church

From the beginning of Christianity, Christians sought suitable images with which to describe the Church. In the New Testament alone there are nearly one hundred images of the Church.[10] The use of images are part of our search for the meaning of the Church. Images relate to popular memory, to cultural contexts, and, especially, to our Christian heritage. All these images are vehicles of communication.

a. *The Communicative Dimension.* There are two parties in this redemptive exchange: first, God who reveals the nature of the Church through Scripture and Tradition, and, second, the believers who actively accept the message of revelation about the Church, and seek to understand it and to share it with others. Although the Church has been established once and for all and is thus a given, it is also true that each generation has to appropriate it anew. Doctrinal treasures should not be relegated to our passive memory, but must be continually rediscovered. St. James reminds us: "Humbly welcome the word that has taken root in you, with its power to save you. Act on this word. If all you do is listen to it, you are deceiving yourself" (James 1: 21-22). In a similar vein, St. Bede could say that "everyday the Church gives birth to the Church."[11]

Images help convey the meaning of the Church and provide a sense of identity and mission. A critical question is: How is the Church perceived by its own members and by others? The manner in which we and others view the Church indicates the way we understand and practice communication. If, for example, we compare the Church to a pyramid, a military organization, or a kingdom, we tend to conceive of the Church as authoritarian, rigidly controlled, highly centralized, and with limited channels of communication and collaboration among the local churches. Yet if our image of the Church is that of communion, sacrament, or People of God, then we tend to view the Church as more of a loving partnership which encourages dialogue, subsidiarity, and shared-responsibility.

---

10. These images are discussed by Paul S. Minear, *Images of the Church in the New Testament* (Philadelphia: Westminster Press, 1960).

11. St. Bede, *Explanatio Apocalypsis,* Lib. II, cap. xii, *Patrologia latina* 93: 166.

b) *The Ecclesiological Challenge.* No one image can exhaust the mystery of the Church. Neither Vatican II, nor any other Church council or magisterial document, has ever mandated one particular definition of the Church. The Church is multidimensional: human and divine, visible and invisible, institutional and spiritual. These different aspects, in the words of *Lumen gentium,* 8, "form one interlocked reality, which is comprised of a divine and a human element." The Church, therefore, is not an abstract, ahistorical, metaphysical concept, or platonic ideal suspended above the real world. The Church is an identifiable community of individuals who believe in Jesus Christ and look forward to the Kingdom of God. The Church is a socio-cultural reality that is always found in a particular time and space. A balanced ecclesiology recognizes the multidimensional character of the Church. To focus solely on the human and social aspects of the Church is to reduce the Church to just another social group. To focus solely on the divine and spiritual qualities of the Church is to exaggerate its supernatural aspects and overlook the crucial fact that its members are human beings living in the world. The Church is a human society, albeit unique because of its divine foundation, guidance, and goal.

2. Particularity and Catholicity

This issue is the ecclesiological version of the philosophical problem of the one and the many. How can there be many particular or local Churches and yet, at the same time, one universal Church? What is the relationship between the various local manifestations of the one Church? What communication system links these diverse churches?

a) *The Communicative Dimension.* The local Church (diocese, parish, religious congregation, family, basic ecclesial community) and the universal Church (the communion of local Churches) are interrelated and interdependent. In the Roman Catholic Church, for example, the local churches are in communion because they share the same Christian faith and discipline. A close organizational relationship exists among the various local churches, since it is the Pope who appoints bishops or confirms those who have been legitimately elected (Canon 377, 1). The universal Church is not a juridical federation of local churches, nor is it identical with the Church of Rome. The universal Church comes to be and is concretely present in the local churches.

In each and every local Church, according to Vatican II, "the one, holy, Catholic, and apostolic Church is truly present and active" (*Christus Dominus,* 11). The local Church is not free-standing and independent; it is in communion with its sister churches throughout the world and has a unique relationship with the Church of Rome. Since the local churches share a bond of communion, there should be dialogue between them. If there is communion, there must be communication. "Where there is one communion," wrote St. Ambrose, "there should also be common judgment and harmonious consent."[12] The gifts of one local Church benefit other local churches.

Several channels of communication exist in each local Church. Some common synodal structures in a diocese include the diocesan pastoral council, the presbyterial council, the college of consultors, the finance council, and the pastoral council. On occasion a diocese may hold a diocesan synod. Other synodal assemblies on a regional or national level are provincial and plenary councils, national or regional episcopal conferences, and national pastoral synods. In some of these assemblies there is both lay and clerical representation.

b) *The Ecclesiological Challenge.* The communion and communication within and among local churches raises several issues. First, on the local level, opportunity should exist for lay, religious, and clerical members of the community to participate in parish and diocesan consultative groups. Second, small Christian groups (e.g. ethnic parishes or basic ecclesial communities) need to maintain their link with the diocese and universal Church to avoid becoming separate, parallel churches. Third, on the national and international level, collaboration, cooperation, solicitude, and assistance should characterize the communion between local churches. Tension, at times, may develop between the central authority of the Church in Rome and the relative autonomy of the local diocesan church. The resolution of this delicate situation demands patience and charity from all parties and a judicious application of the principles of collegiality, legitimate diversity, and subsidiarity.[13] Rome should intervene in the life of a local Church as a last resort—only after other remedies have been exhausted.

3. Ministries in the Church

Ministries and charisms in the community called Church are necessary, legitimate, public, and visible gifts of the Holy Spirit given for the building up of the Church as the Body of Christ (*Lumen gentium* 4). These gifts are a participation in the ministry of Jesus Christ. They are means by which the Gospel is communicated.

a) *The Communicative Dimension.* A variety of offices, tasks, roles, and ministries exist in the Church and are exercised by clerics, religious, and laity. All of them perform a communicative function. The ordained ministries are derived from the sacrament of Orders; the lay ministries are rooted in Baptism and Confirmation. Despite sacramental and functional differences, these many ministries are united in the common work of the

---

12. St. Ambrose, *Epist.* 13, 8, *Patrologia latina* 16: 953.
13. I have analysed these themes in *The Limits of the Papacy: Authority and Autonomy in the Church* (New York: Crossroad, 1987).

Spirit (1 Cor 12:4). All ministries participate in the saving mission of the Church and seek to make Christ present in the world.

To be effective communicators of the Word, ministers have to be properly trained both in the knowledge of the faith and in the techniques of communication. Open channels of communication and collaborative ministerial activity promote unity. All ecclesial ministers are accountable to the people they serve, to both local and universal authorities, and, of course, ultimately to God.

b) *The Ecclesiological Challenge.* The role of lay ministry is of special interest today. Pius XII said that the laity do not simply belong to the Church, they are the Church.[14] Vatican II taught that the laity have a "common dignity" because of Baptism and a "true equality" regarding the building up of the Body of Christ (*Lumen gentium* 32). Lay ministry takes place both in the Church and in the world.[15] A related question is the place of women in the Church. It concerns not only the ordination of women but the greater utilization and appreciation of their many gifts for the good of the Church.

Since Vatican II, the Church in the United States has been marked by a desire for greater participation at all levels of decision making in the Church, for a more personalized faith, for a greater use of lay ministries, and for clear and convincing reasons for Church teaching. The extensive Notre Dame Study of Catholic Parish Life documented the explosion of lay ministries in the United States. It found that "beyond the pastor, 83 percent of those identified as the leadership within Catholic parishes, paid or unpaid, are laypersons."[16] The challenges for lay ministry are many: proper training, collaborative ministry between the ordained and non-ordained, and just financial compensation.

4. Liturgical Worship

The liturgy is a vivid example of religious communication. God is present and speaks to us in the celebration of the liturgy. We communicate with the divine using words, symbols, gestures, rituals, and music.

a) *The Communicative Dimension.* Liturgy is a way of communicating. According to Vatican II, the liturgy is the outstanding means for the faithful to express the mystery of Christ and the Church (*Sacrosanctum concilium* 2). Liturgical communication has several goals: worshiping God, sharing in

---

14. Pius XII, Address to New Cardinals, Feb. 20, 1946. *Acta apostolicae sedis* 38 (1946): 149.

15. See *Lumen gentium* 31, *Apostolicam actuositatem* 9, 13, and *Ad gentes* 15. John Paul II also discussed this issue in his apostolic exhortation, *Christifideles laici* in 1988. *Origins*, February 9, 1989, Vol. 18: no. 35.

16. Joseph Gremillion and Jim Castelli, *The Emerging Parish: The Notre Dame Study of Catholic Life since Vatican II* (San Francisco: Harper & Row, 1987), p. 3.

the divine gifts, and reaffirming our commitment to the triune God and to each other. The communal celebration of a shared faith combines remembrance and mission, contemplation and action, unity and diversity. The priest may "preside" at the liturgy, but it is the whole community that celebrates.

The sacraments are special forms of communication, because they are acts of Christ and the Church, involve a personal encounter with Christ, and have a strong communitarian quality. The Eucharist, for example, at which the local Church is actualized most intensely, is a powerful symbol that signifies and effects the unity of God's People. Christ is present when the Eucharist is celebrated, the Scripture is proclaimed, and the community prays and sings (*Sacrosanctum concilium* 7).

b) *The Ecclesiological Dimension.* Two issues may be mentioned. First, if the Eucharist is "the source and summit of the Christian life" (*Lumen gentium* 11), what happens to the community's sense of Church when, owing to the shortage of priests, the Eucharist is celebrated only infrequently and the liturgy of the Word becomes more common than the liturgy of the Sacrament? That scenario is already a reality in some dioceses of Europe and the United States where there are many priestless parishes with para-liturgical services in place of the Mass. How can the right of a community to the Eucharist be honored if the decline in the number of priests continues? Second, the liturgy is a sign of unity and presupposes communion. It should not create divisions or impede communication. The liturgy is the public worship of the Church. It should respect the cultural diversity of its members. A reverent celebration of the liturgy with good accompanying music and active participation by the congregation can evoke a lively sense of God's presence and a deep sense of communion.

5. *Evangelization*

The Church has the duty to communicate the core message of Christianity—the life, death, and resurrection of Jesus—to the world. Evangelization, the act of communicating the word of God, is not an abstract exercise. "To communicate the Christian message," writes Bernard Lonergan, "is to lead another to share in one's cognitive, constitutive, effective meaning."[17]

a) *The Communicative Dimension.* Evangelization, in the words of Paul VI, is "bringing the Good News into all the strata of humanity and through its influence transforming humanity from within and making it new."[18] "Faith

---

17. Bernard Lonergan, *Method in Theology*, p. 362.
18. Paul VI, Apostolic Exhortation, *On Evangelization in the Modern World* (*Evangelii nuntiandi*) (Washington: United States Catholic Conference, 1976), #18, p. 15.

comes from hearing" (Rom 10:17), and the communication of the faith takes several forms: the witness of an authentic Christian life, preaching, catechetics, the sacraments, and the utilization of the mass media. Although bishops have a special responsibility to preach the Word (*Lumen gentium* 25 and *Ad gentes* 5), "the work of evangelization is a basic duty of the People of God" (*Ad gentes* 35). No follower of Christ is exempt from this responsibility (*Lumen gentium* 17). There is also need for the re-evangelization of Christians. In one of the strongest statements of Vatican II, *Gaudium et spes* pointed out a failure in communication within the Christian community: "This split between the faith which many profess and their daily lives deserves to be counted among the more serious errors of our age" (*Gaudium et spes* 43).

b) *The Ecclesiological Challenge.* In the Catholic Church, we perhaps have sacramentalized better than we have evangelized. Vatican II urged us to seek more suitable ways to communicate the faith to our contemporaries (*Gaudium et spes* 62). To make the faith more plausible, attractive, and credible, we need to develop meaningful and convincing language, symbols, and images. Yet the witness of the Christian life remains one of the most compelling forms of evangelization. Commitment to the faith, acceptance of suffering, and charitable actions are powerful and effective means of proclaiming the Gospel. Of this "wordless witness" and "silent proclamation," Paul VI said that "all Christians are called to this witness, and in this way they can be real evangelizers."[19]

In evangelization, the communication of the mysteries of faith has to be related to concrete human experience in particular cultural settings. Inculturation is the vital relationship between faith and culture, the insertion of the Christian life into a culture, and the continuing process of reciprocal and critical interaction between them.[20] Evangelization should respect the experiences of others and understand their particular cultural and religious traditions. In the light of inculturation, missionary activity is no longer sender-oriented, as happens when the culture of the sending nation is imposed and within it the Gospel is preached. Rather it is receiver-oriented, when the Gospel is preached in the culture of the receiving nation (Cf. *Gaudium et spes* 53 ff).

6. Ecumenical Dialogue

Ecumenism is a communicative process among Christians seeking eventual reunion. Dialogue has replaced the confrontational attitude of the

---

19. Ibid., #21, p. 17.

20. On the theme of inculturation see M. deC. Azevedo, *Inculturation and the Challenges of Modernity* (Rome: Gregorian University, 1982), Robert J. Schreiter, *Constructing Local Theologies* (Maryknoll, N.Y.: Orbis Books, 1985), and Peter Schineller, *A Handbook of Inculturation* (New York: Paulist Press, 1990).

past. Vatican II considered the restoration of unity one of its major concerns and affirmed that division in Christianity "openly contradicts the will of Christ, scandalizes the world, and damages that most holy cause, the preaching of the Gospel to every creature" (*Unitatis redintegratio* 1).

a) *The Communicative Dimension.* The many bilateral consultations bring Christians together to discuss charitably and candidly the issues that unite and divide them. The hope is that dialogue will lead to progressive convergence and, eventually, to reunion. The communicative partners recognize that the bonds that unite them are more important than the differences that separate them. Christians, after all, can agree that "there is one body and one Spirit, just as you were called to the one hope of your calling; one Lord, one faith, one baptism" (Eph 4: 4-5). In our continuing ecumenical communication, openness to the truth and to the action of the Holy Spirit compel us to assume that other Christian communities have something valuable to offer us. Mutual giving and mutual receptivity are essential to the fostering of Christian unity.

Many concrete proposals for ecumenical dialogue and communication have been suggested. Joint projects in social matters, for example, allow Christians to express what already unites them and to give a common witness to Christ. The use of the media can be most beneficial to the cause of Christian unity, providing that the inappropriate manipulatory proselytizing found in some of the televangelists is avoided. The Pontifical Council for Social Communications has observed that the proper use of the mass media can foster ecumenical cooperation. "Because the mass media reach beyond the normal limits of space and time, this cooperation will be at one and the same time local, regional, and international."[21]

b) *The Ecclesiological Challenge.* An important element in the communication among the Christian churches is seen in the teaching of Vatican II that the Church of Christ transcends any one Christian communion. Roman Catholics affirm that the Church of Christ "subsists" in the Catholic Church, but it is also present in other Christian communities (*Lumen gentium* 8). It may be necessary for the churches as they move toward reunion to compromise on non-essential elements for the sake of reconciliation. Despite greater understanding of the office of the papacy, it still remains a major obstacle to reunion. Furthermore, ecumenists recognize that the expression of the Christian faith may take different forms and that unity does not require uniformity. Pope John XXIII made that clear in his address at the beginning of Vatican II. He said: "The deposit of faith is one thing; the way it is presented is another. For the truths preserved in our sacred doc-

---

21. Pontifical Council for Social Communications, "Criteria for Ecumenical and Interreligious Cooperation in Social Communications," *Origins,* November 9, 1989, Vol. 19, no. 23: 376.

trine can retain the same substance and meaning under different forms of expression."[22]

A final ecclesiological challenge is the necessity of linking spirituality and ecumenism. Church unity is a gift from God; it entails prayer, change of heart, and holiness of life. The Council reminds us that "there can be no ecumenism worthy of the name without interior conversion" *(Unitatis redintegratio* 7). The unity of Christians should be included in our private and public prayer.

7. The Church in the World

The Church and world are inextricably connected. Christians live in the world. The Church, "truly and intimately linked with mankind and its history" *(Gaudium et spes* 1), cannot live in a vacuum and be isolated from the social, political, and cultural context of the world. In the words of *Aetatis novae*, "Human history and all human relationships exist within the framework established by this self-communication of God in Christ."[23]

a) *The Communicative Dimension.* Constant communication exists between the Church and the world. Believers are joined with the rest of humanity in the process of world history. "In the name of our faith," wrote Teilhard de Chardin, "we have the right and the duty to become passionate about the things of the earth."[24] Each Christian is a sign of God's presence in the world *(Ad gentes* 15), and the laity have the special role of bringing Christian values into the temporal sphere *(Lumen gentium* 31).

The communicative relationship between the Church and the world has, however, its own dangers. Christians are a minority in the world and their values are often rejected. The Church as a "cognitive minority" in the world faces, according to Peter Berger, two unacceptable responses: cognitive defiance, which would turn the Church into a sectarian ghetto, or cognitive surrender, which would sacrifice its own unique heritage to the prevailing and often contradictory values of the world. The more acceptable response to the world, though admittedly difficult, is controlled or limited accommodation, a kind of *aggiornamento.*[25]

b) *The Ecclesiological Challenge.* The first challenge concerns the danger of ecclesiocentrism. The Church should not be turned in on itself and out of communication with the world. It may be that the common distinction between the Church *ad intra* and the Church *ad extra* is questionable. By

---

22. John XXIII, Address at the Opening of Vatican II, *Acta apostolicae sedis* 54 (1962): 792.

23. Pontifical Council for Social Communications, Pastoral Instruction *Aetatis suae, Origins,* March 26, 1992, Vol. 21, no. 42: #6, 672.

24. Pierre Teilhard de Chardin, *The Divine Milieu* (New York: Harper & Row, 1960), p. 69.

25. Peter L. Berger, *A Rumor of Angels* (New York: Doubleday, 1969), pp. 17-22.

the very coming to be of the Church in a particular place at a particular time, the Church is in the world and never apart from it. The Church is not to be viewed as an ideal, a spiritual reality totally apart from the real world. The observation of Edward Schillebeeckx is relevant. "God's action in the world and the Church is marked by the fact that it is never at work above or alongside human history, as in were in magical phenomena, but in this history itself, modestly and in a hidden way."[26]

A second challenge is the relationship between the Church and politics. The Church has no political mission as such in the world, but addresses political issues insofar as they have religious and moral ramifications. The 1971 Synod of Bishops enunciated a principle of social justice: "Action on behalf of justice and participation in the transformation of the world fully appear to us as a constitutive dimension of the preaching of the Gospel, or, in other words, of the Church's mission for the redemption of the human race and its liberation from every oppressive situation."[27]

8. Authority and Decision Making

In any community the decision-making process offers a good example of communication at work. A breakdown in communication often leads to a breakdown in communion. Failures in communication contributed to the Eastern schism and to the Protestant Reformation.

a) *The Communicative Dimension.* A multiplicity of interactions exist between the decision makers in the Church and the faithful. They differ from place to place depending on personnel, customs, and situations. Ideally, the interaction should be dialogic and participative. It is not as if bishops alone, guided by the Spirit, have the grace to teach and the faithful have only to obey passively. Rather the Holy Spirit resides in the entire Church, and gifts are distributed to all throughout the whole community. Ecclesial decision makers have the responsibility to listen to what the Spirit is saying in the Church before they make their decisions.

A cybernetic analysis of decision making in the Church emphasizes dialogue and participation and provides a helpful framework to examine the process of communication.[28] In the cybernetic model input to the decision makers occurs in the form of demands and supports; output comes from the authorities in the form of extractions (financial and service requests), distributions (spiritual, social, and educational), and symbolic actions (those dealing with faith and morals, values, cult). Subsequent feed-

---

26. Edward Schillebeeckx, *The Church. The Human Story of God* (New York: Crossroad, 1990), p. 221.

27. Synod of Bishops 1971, *Justice in the World* (Washington: National Conference of Catholic Bishops, 1972), p. 34.

28. See Patrick Granfield, *Ecclesial Cybernetics: A Study of Democracy in the Church* (New York: Macmillan, 1973).

back to the output may or may not affect future decisions. It depends on several factors: the multiplicity of the channels of communication that can reach those in authority, open and free discussion, and the willingness of the authorities to respond to legitimate requests.

The encyclical *Pacem in terris* (#12) of John XXIII and *Inter mirifica* (#47) of Vatican II stated that people have a right to information. *Gaudium et spes* encouraged honest discussion (#43) and a lawful freedom of inquiry (#62). Finally, *Communio et progressio* spoke of "a steady two-way flow of information" between ecclesiastical authorities and the faithful (#120).

b) *The Ecclesiological Challenge.* David Leege, who worked on the major study of the Church in the United States after Vatican II, concluded that "if a major purpose of Vatican II was to reinstate the sense that all Christians—lay, priests, and religious—are responsible for corporate life in the local parish, then Vatican II is succeeding in the United States. The American Church is participatory."[29]

The bishops of the United States have employed extensive collaboration and consultation in preparing their major pastoral letters. Some theologians have cautioned that a spontaneous and loosely organized dialogue with people who are not fully aware of the Christian tradition may lead to division and false expectations.[30] Discernment, therefore, has to be an essential part of consultative process. Archbishop Rembert Weakland, convinced that the Holy Spirit resides in the whole Church, urges the hierarchy to be open to what the Church says. "This does not deny the teaching role of the hierarchy," he writes, "but enhances it. It does not weaken the magisterium, but ultimately strengthens it. Discernment, not just innovation or self-reliance, becomes a part of the teaching process."[31] The dynamics of communication are also operative in the much debated issues of reception, public dissent, and the *sensus fidelium.*

Finally, it may we asked whether we have an overload of ecclesiastical documentation, which impedes communication. An avalanche of documents come from diocesan chanceries, national episcopal conferences, Vatican congregations and councils, and the Pope himself. It is difficult to read, evaluate, and assimilate so much information. It may be that the more that is written, the less that is read.

---

29. Statement of David Leege quoted in Joseph Gremillion and Jim Castelli, *The Emerging Parish*, p. 3.

30. This issue was raised by Avery Dulles, "The Church and Communications: Vatican II and Beyond," in *The Reshaping of Catholicism: Current Challenges in the Theology of the Church* (San Francisco: Harper & Row, 1988), p. 128.

31. Rembert G. Weakland, "Where Does the Economics Pastoral Stand?" *Origins,* April 26, 1984, Vol. 13, no. 46: 759.

9. Collegiality and Primacy

The Pope and the bishops form the highest level of authority in the Church. Both are symbols of unity in the Church. Since the Pope has a direct role in selecting bishops throughout the world, it is important that the relationship between the Pope and the bishops be open, honest, and supportive. How do the Pope and the bishops communicate?

a) *The Communicative Dimension.* The Pope and the bishops form a communications network. They communicate in several ways. According to Canon Law, each diocesan bishop every five years has to submit to the Pope a report on the state of his diocese and make an *ad limina* visit to Rome to see the Pope, to venerate the tombs of St. Peter and Paul, and to visit some of the Roman congregations. During 1993, the bishops of the United States made their *ad limina* visits. Every three years the Synod of Bishops is held with representatives from the various episcopal conferences. Ecumenical councils, at which all bishops are in attendance, are held irregularly. Individual bishops also correspond frequently with the various Vatican offices.

The doctrine of collegiality at Vatican II balanced the definition of papal primary at Vatican I. Collegiality refers to the world-wide solidarity of bishops who, through their sacramental consecration and hierarchical communion with one another and with their head, the Pope, possess full and supreme authority in relation to the universal Church (*Lumen gentium* 18, 22). By primacy we mean that the Roman Pontiff has ordinary, immediate, and truly episcopal jurisdiction in the entire Church; his power is full, supreme, and universal. Both the papacy and the episcopacy are of divine right. The Pope cannot abolish the episcopate, nor can the College of Bishops function without the Pope. The Pope and the bishops together form one communion.

b) *The Ecclesiological Dimension.* Vatican II did not discuss the practical consequences of collegiality for the Pope in his dealings with other bishops. For example, although the Pope is urged to consult and to be in close communication with the bishops, there is no binding legal norm that obliges him to do so. If the Pope does not consult at all, he may be acting imprudently, but he is within his legal rights. Yet the doctrines of collegiality and consultation remain an ideal and a constant reminder to Rome that dialogue with the bishops is desirable and expected. Other theological questions concerning collegiality focus on the structure and authority of the Synod of Bishops and episcopal conferences.

10. Mass Media

We live in a mass media culture which to some extent has turned the world into a "global village." The print and electronic media have a powerful impact on the Church, its faith, its community life, and its relations with the world.

a) *The Communicative Dimension.* The mass media have given rise to a new language. What may be true of interpersonal and oral communication cannot always be transferred to mass media communication. *Aetatis novae* correctly pointed out the universal quality of mass media. "Nowhere today are people untouched by the impact of media upon religious and moral attitudes, political and social systems, and education."[32] Television defines our world by shaping our ideas, values, and attitudes. In the average home in the United States the TV set is on seven hours a day and the average viewer watches TV four and a half hours a day. The mass media may present a fragmented view of the human person. They not only create reality, they also reflect what is happening in society, culture, and family.

b) *The Ecclesiological Challenge.* Mass media are a mixed blessing. First, mass communication can have great value for the Church. It enables the Church to preach the Word to vast audiences (*Christus Dominus* 13); it provides information on the missions to the faithful (*Ad gentes* 36); and it promotes universal human solidarity (*Gaudium et spes* 54). *Communio et progressio* listed three ways that the social communication media assist the Church: "They help the Church reveal herself to the modern world; they foster dialogue within the Church; and they make clear to the Church contemporary opinions and attitudes."[33] Likewise, the Congregation for the Doctrine of the Faith saw the positive value of the media when it stated that "the social communications media surely have to be counted among the most effective instruments available today for spreading the message of the Gospel."[34] For such reasons, Paul VI said in *Evangelii nuntiandi* that "the Church would feel guilty before the Lord if she did not use these powerful means that human skill is daily rendering more perfect."[35]

Second, mass media have a negative side as well. The imposition of a mass media culture may reduce the value of local churches and local ecclesiologies. Mass media may cause social conflict, ridicule genuine Judeo-Christian values, and encourage superficial thought. We live in a era in which we are more influenced by image than by abstract thought. As *Aetatis novae* puts it: "Reality, for many, is what the media recognize as real; what media do not acknowledge seems of little importance."[36]

---

32. *Aetatis novae,* #1, 669.

33. *Communio et progressio,* #125, p. 333-334.

34. Congregation for the Doctrine of the Faith, "Social Communications and the Doctrine of the Faith," *Origins,* June 18, 1992. Vol. 22, no. 6: 93.

35. Paul VI, *On Evangelization in the Modern World (Evangelii nuntiandi),* #45, pp. 30-31.

36. *Aetatis novae,* #4, p. 672.

William Kuhns in his book, *The Electronic Gospel* makes a troubling observation:

> The entertainment media has transformed the ways in which we believe and are capable of believing. An absolute kind of belief, as well as a belief in absolutes, becomes increasingly difficult as the entertainment milieu trains people to believe tentatively and with elasticity. . . . The very concept of belief—to believe in that which you cannot see and cannot understand—comes with difficulty to a generation that has depended, as perhaps no generation before, on its senses.[37]

In conclusion, communication theory and practice offers ecclesiology a profound and rich opportunity to grasp more fully the mystery of the Church. It raises intriguing challenges in a new perspective. Some of the issues discussed in this chapter will be developed by other authors from varying points of view. Our goal is to understand better the relationship between communication, the Church, and ecclesiology. It is an attempt to read "the signs of the times," as Vatican II taught us.

> The Church has always had the duty of reading the signs of the times and of interpreting them in the light of the Gospel. Thus, in language intelligible to each generation she can respond to the perennial questions when people ask about this present life and the life to come, and about the relationship of the one to the other (*Gaudium et spes* 4).

---

37. William Kuhns, *The Electronic Gospel: Religion and Media* (New York: Herder and Herder, 1969), p. 165-166. On this topic also see two books by Gregor Goethals, *The TV Ritual: Worship at the Video Altar* (Boston: Beacon, 1981), and *The Electronic Golden Calf: Images, Religion, and the Making of Meaning* (Cambridge, Mass.: Cowley Publications, 1990).

2

Communication: Meaning and Modalities

Robert A. White, S.J.

Contemporary ecclesiologists are aware of many different models of Church and different structures of ecclesial communication. Likewise, communication specialists recognize major differences in theoretical orientation and sociocultural tradition in the world of communication practice and study. Obviously our understanding of how communication is possible changes as we move from interpersonaľ to group, to community and to national society levels. Walter Ong has shown quite clearly the significance of technology shifts from oral to written, to print, and finally to electronic media.[1] Communication is not just an objective, unchanging process but depends very much on the normative conception of the good society and how communication contributes to different normatively defined societal world views. For example, if one starts with a corporatist conception of society in which a single set of values and world view are to be the basis of an integrated culture and organic society, there is likely to be acceptance of a much more "authoritarian" set of presuppositions about good communications than in a liberal, market-oriented society in which the ideal is to open up communications to many different sets of values and world views competing for acceptance.

This chapter, coming at the beginning of the book, seeks to outline five quite different traditions of communication practice and theory, each with quite different normative conceptions of the good society and "good communication."[2] Current convention in the field of communications dis-

---

1. W.J. Ong, *Orality and Literacy: The Technologizing of the Word* (London: Methuen, 1982).

2. The debate between these normative theories can be traced back through the centuries, but the more recent origin of a codification is found in a 1956 book by F.S. Siebert, T. Peterson and W. Schramm, *Four Theories of the Press* (Urbana: University of Illinois Press, 1956), inspired by one of the founders of the field of communication in the United States, Wilbur Schramm. Although the initial codification of these normative traditions—conceptions of what communications

tinguishes the following five normative traditions: 1) the *corporatist* tradition based on "metaphysical," essentialist world views, rather negatively characterized as the "authoritarian" model by liberals; 2) the dominant *libertarian* tradition, which emphasizes the rights of the individual conscience and of media owners within a free market of ideas; 3) the *social responsibility, public service* tradition, which works within the libertarian, free-market conception but subordinates individualistic goal seeking to the common good; 4) the liberation, *democratization, participation* tradition, which is highly *critical* of the inequities generated by the libertarian and social responsibility traditions and seeks a continual *liberation* from ideologies and concentration of power; and 5) the *communion, ritual* tradition, which sees all communication as forming cultural communities and which has remarkable congruence with the communitarian model put forth in the Catholic Church's official policy statement, *Communio et progressio.*[3]

Most in the field of communication, whether in practice or in academia, tend to identify, consciously or unconsciously through their formation and cultural context, with one or another of these traditions. This influences the way they define communications at all levels from interpersonal to international, the kind of conceptions of communication and areas of research and theory they think are important, and what they think are priorities for policy action. Underlying these theoretical orientations are deeper personal and sociocultural political and philosophical identifications—just as in the case of preferences for different models of Church and ecclesial communication. Virtually every conception used in the field of communication has an origin within one or other tradition and cannot be fully understood without seeing its meaning within the system of concepts of that tradition.

A presupposition of this chapter is that it is important for theologians to be aware of the contextual origins of many of the models and con-

---

should be—has been criticized because of a close linkage with dominant and opposed sociopolitical systems of the 1950s cold war period, the methodology of normative theories entered into many standard textbooks such as the widely used text, *Mass Communication Theory* (London: Sage Publications, 1987) by British sociologist of mass media, Denis McQuail. The schema used here follows a modified version of McQuail (pp. 107-134), but takes into consideration the debate between the different "paradigms" of communication found in many different subfields of communication. Cf special issue of the *Journal of Communication,* 33/3 (Summer, 1983), "Ferment in the Field."

3. Pontifical Commission for Social Communications, *Pastoral Instruction on the Means of Social Communication, Communio et progressio* (1971) in Austin Flannery, ed., *Vatican Council II. The Conciliar and Post Conciliar Documents* (Northport, N.Y.: Costello Publishing Co., 1975), pp. 293-349.

cepts in contemporary communication research. Paul Soukup has suggested, on the basis of a review of communication related theological studies,[4] that theologians, when their argument involves communication presuppositions, have tended to take one metaphor of communication and to make the logic of that metaphor the frame of reference for communication presuppositions in their argument.[5] Soukup, *starting from the perspective of theology*, finds six dominant metaphors of communication used by theologians: language systems, subjective artistic expression, interpersonal dialogue, transport of information, cultural consensus or theological conclusions about the influence of the transcendent in human communication. Even if one takes a rather generic, consensual definition of communication such as "the sharing of meaning," this definition has different interpretations depending on the presuppositions of the metaphor.

The five normative traditions discussed in this chapter, each with its particular conceptions of communication and its theories for guiding research and practice, generally describe a society-wide set of preferred communication institutions, often developed through socio-political movements that have proposed a transformation of communication structures as part of a general transformation of the society. Often what is proposed is a change in the set of values and world view governing communication so that it aims to transform the patterns of communication from the international level to the most intimate interpersonal and intra-personal communication.

I. The Corporatist Tradition of Universal Human Law

Most typologies of normative theories of communication follow a historical, evolutionary framework that begins with what strong libertarians refer to rather pejoratively as "the authoritarian theory." Explanations of the "authoritarian" tradition dwell upon the systematic repression of dissent by absolutist monarchs in the periods preceding the English, American, and French liberal revolutions, the influence of the Roman Catholic Church's definition of itself as the conserver of revealed truth and the attempts to stamp out all deviations from its own established theological-philosophical positions, and, finally, a reference to the fascist regimes of Hitler, Mussolini, and Franco. All is presented as a kind of foil for explaining how the libertarian theory emerged to introduce a new con-

---

4. P. Soukup, *Communication and Theology: Introduction and Review of the Literature* (London: World Association for Christian Communication in cooperation with the Centre for the Study of Communication and Culture, 1983).

5. P. Soukup, "Communication Theories for Theologians," Unpublished paper presented at the seminar on Fundamental Theology and Communication, Rome, The Gregorian University, 1984.

ception of social communication and correct the injustices and abuses of authoritarianism.

Nevertheless, one of the early classic codifications of the normative traditions, *The Four Theories of the Press,*[6] does recognize that the "authoritarian" tradition has been the most pervasive in theory and practice across history and cultures—especially, one might add, where there still remains some of the hierarchical structure of communication in advanced agrarian, peasant societies. These accounts also acknowledge that some of the greatest philosophical minds and most idealistic social utopians have proposed strong centralized state control of communications. The list begins with Plato, alludes to some of the great Medieval theologians and then cites Macchiavelli, Hobbes, Rousseau, and especially Hegel.[7]

If, however, one steps into the world view of those referred to rather ethnocentrically as "authoritarian," they would see themselves as proposing a well-ordered world guided by what Walter Lippmann once referred to as the universal laws of the rational order.[8] For two thousand years, argues Lippmann, social philosophers have been influenced by the idea that the rational faculties can produce a common conception of law and order which possesses a universal validity.[9] In this perspective, across the centuries of social experience and the accumulated reflection of wise people, it is possible to develop a conception of the good society which is far superior to momentary currents of public opinion and the influence of powerful demagogues. In the understanding of the good society as organic, every social role—from monarch to peasant—and every institution has its defined role of service to the integrated well-being of society. In the Christian tradition, all this has been divinely established by the creator, revealed in Jesus Christ, and upheld in its purity by the Church and its teaching.[10] One is intrinsically oriented toward fulfilling one's own personal contribution to the whole by one's rational nature, talents, social position and divine vocation. Happiness lies in harmony with one's human nature, social position and personal calling by God and in the harmony of the whole ensemble of society and creation. The best definition of communication in this organic, harmonic conception of all reality is *wisdom*, the mutual helping of all people to understand and to further the ordering of all things to their divinely established end.

---

6. F. S. Siebert, T. Peterson, W. Schramm. *The Four Theories of the Press* (Urbana: University of Illinois Press, 1956).

7. L.L. Rivers, W. Schramm, C.G. Christians, *Responsibility in Mass Communication* (New York: Harper and Row, 1980).

8. W. Lippmann, *The Public Philosophy* (Boston: Little, Brown and Company, 1955).

9. Ibid., 81.

10. S. Menache, *Vox Dei: Communication in the Middle Ages* (New York: Oxford University Press, 1990).

Perhaps the best way to briefly indicate why organic, corporatist conceptions of society—and communication—seem superior to some is to cite a few examples of how these conceptions operated in corporatist societies and still continue to operate vestigially. It was taken for granted that all major professions such as medicine and law would be exercised only by people who were licensed by legitimate authority, namely the state, in order to guarantee the public good service and protect people from charlatans.[11] Professional codes of ethics touching all public services were defined by public authority and were strictly enforced. That printing should be licensed was seen as a way to protect the public, and when Henry VIII established the custom of licensing printers, the printers were, in fact, quite pleased that business was guaranteed and that good standards could be upheld.[12] And in seventeenth and eighteenth century Europe, people were often tired of destructive religious wars and were happy to see some control put on demagogues who could stir up mobs.

During the Middle Ages, many current practices of misrepresentation, puffery and "sellerism" typically of contemporary commercial communication and advertising were not allowed within the bounds of the law.

> The craft guilds and the market towns controlled sellers and craftsmen tightly, treating them virtually as licensed public officials. The guilds . . . drew up standards of size and quality, and draftsmen who produced articles otherwise were fined, and for multiple violations were thrown out of the trade. . . . The aim was not to serve the buyer as such but to serve the entire community. The cheater was held to transgress against everyone, including his fellow workers as well as his customers, a far cry from later assumptions of the 'dog-eat-dog' competitive marketplace of nineteenth-century America.[13]

In his book on puffery in advertising, Preston's summary of how this situation changed is interesting in that it provides a normative perspective quite different from the libertarian tone found in most contemporary communication studies.

> From Protestantism and the philosophers came the notion of individualism, stating that each human being was capable of reasoning and looking out for himself. From the economists came the notion of laissez-faire, which held that merchants and their customers would arrive at fair and proper bargains through competition, without need for

---

11. A. Abbott, "Professional Ethics," *American Journal of Sociology*, 88 (1983): 886-914.

12. R. Buel, Jr, "Freedom of the Press in Revolutionary America: The Evolution of Libertarianism, 1760-1820" in B. Bailyn and J.B. Hench, eds., *The Press and the American Revolution* (Boston: Northeastern University Press, 1981), 59-97 at 64.

13. I.L. Preston, *The Great American Blow-Up: Puffery in Advertising and Selling* (Madison: The University of Wisconsin Press, 1975), 35.

regulation. All of these developments led during the seventeenth and eighteenth centuries to the significant notions that seller and buyer were equal in the marketplace, and that none of their interactions therefore need be, or should be, guaranteed.[14]

II. The Libertarian Tradition

The deep distrust that any one public institution can pretend to have a monopoly on the truth has led to the core libertarian value tenet that the ultimate criterion for truth and value must be the individual conscience. Libertarians see society as the sum of individuals seeking their own particular goals.[15] The good society will be achieved and every person can obtain the information needed for individual goals in what Oliver Wendell Holmes Jr. called "the free market of ideas." The economic, laissez-faire exchange metaphor sums up the conception of communication as essentially a process in which each is free to *sell* any ideas that the market will bear and is also free to obtain any information that one needs at a price that the market sets. By the nineteenth century freedom of expression meant, concretely, freedom of the press and was interpreted as the protection of media owners from intervention by the state or other major societal institutions.

Libertarians like to trace their intellectual tradition back to the *Areopagitica*[16] of Puritan dissenter, John Milton, attacking prior censorship and licensed printing with the argument that if the merits of any proposal are allowed to be debated freely, truth will triumph through what would today be called the "self-righting principle" of the marketplace of ideas. Another hero is John Stuart Mill with his defense in 1859 of the partiality of all knowledge and the right to be wrong.[17] In the rapidly urbanizing, pluralistic societies emerging in the nineteenth century, the reduction of ideas and information to an impersonal quantifiable monetary value seemed to bring communication into a public sphere of universal access unrestricted by particularistic criteria of social privilege, religion, ethnicity, profession or other artificial social barriers.

Not surprisingly, the focus on communication as the capacity to "sell" and overcome resistances to ideas in the marketplace was fertile ground for the development of a linear, "effects" model of source, mes-

---

14. Ibid., 50.

15. T. Glasser, "Communication and the Cultivation of Citizenship," Unpublished manuscript, 1991, to be published in *Communication*.

16. J. Milton, *Areopagitica*, originally published in 1644, Edited by George H. Sabine (New York: Appleton-Century-Crofts, 1951).

17. J.S. Mill, "Essay on Liberty," in Max Lerner, ed., *Essential Works of John Stuart Mill* (New York: Bantam Books, 1951), 249-360.

sage, channel, receiver/effects. The formulation of a "science" of communication around this model was largely an American creation in the schools of journalism that were part of the American drive toward universal professionalization but especially in the commercial research institutes that grew up to serve the audience survey needs in contracts with newspapers and radio broadcasting.[18] In the 1920s and 1930s the development of marketing science, statistical survey methods, theories of psychological motivation and methods of attitude measurement made it possible to sell expert advice and relatively precise quantified measurement of media effects to advertisers, government propaganda bureaus, political campaigns, and religious evangelists on how to penetrate the market of ideas. From these studies theories of persuasion and information flow began to emerge such as the famous "two-step flow" model which showed that information flowed from the media to community opinion leaders (more likely to follow the media) and then to ordinary people through these more authoritative interpersonal contacts.[19] This research also tended to reinforce the popular belief in the enormous power of the media.

Ironically, important developments in communication concepts in the libertarian tradition came from research stimulated by sectors of the public alarmed that the ability of the mass media to sell and persuade in the market place was going over the heads of traditional socialization—parents, clergymen, teachers—to corrupt the youth.[20] As multiple factors in a mass, urban society made traditional social controls more difficult, the mass media, believed to be so powerful, began to be blamed for a host of social problems, but especially for a perceived increase of violence, sexual licentiousness and crime.[21] Parents, teachers, and clergymen went to their political leaders and the political leaders attempted to introduce legislative controls over the mass media. The mass media, however, argued that the politicians had no objective evidence of harmful effects—meaning quantified measurements comparable to their own type of measures—and only evidence from laboratory tests or from scientific surveys could be the basis for public legislation. Thus the politicians were forced to go to researchers in university contexts, judged to be more independent and objective, to carry out the research and prepare reports as a basis of legislative action. There were major periods of study of the harmful effects of movies in the 1920s, regarding comic books and television in the 1950s and, after the assassination of M.L. King and R. Kennedy in 1968, re-

---

18. W.D. Rowland, Jr., *The Politics of Violence: Policy Uses of Communication Research* (Newbury Park, CA: Sage Publications, 1983).

19. P. F. Lazarsfeld, B. Berelson, H. Gaudet, *The People's Choice* (New York: Columbia University Press, 1948).

20. Rowland, *Politics of Violence*.

21. J. Jensen, *Redeeming Modernity: Contradictions in Media Criticism* (Newbury Park, CA: Sage Publications, 1990).

search representing investment of many millions of dollars. In each case, broadcasters were able to throw the data into question, alleging that some possible alternative cause was overlooked. Already in the 1950s, theories were proposing that media could have direct effects only in special psychological and socio-economic conditions, and by the 1970s, the classical paradigm of source, message, channel, effects was no longer dominant.

In addition to the free market emphasis, a further major value tenet of the libertarian tradition is that the individual is perfectible through education and access to information so that an increase in the *quantity* of information flows, made possible by new communication technology, contributes to the economic, social and political improvement of the society.[22] This has encouraged theories, such as those of Marshall McLuhan, and lines of research exploring the personal and social advantages that can come through progress in the more rapid transmission, greater storage capacity and more attractive display of information.

Another libertarian tenet that became important as the great push for international development began after World War II was the view that the application of media effects theories could help overcome the enormous problems of transportation and communication in less developed countries. It was taken for granted that development meant the rapid *transfer* of modern technology, social organization, and cultural values from industrialized countries to the "traditional societies." Progress was viewed as the world-wide spread of the rationality of the industrial west replacing the blind traditionalism, fatalism, religiosity, familism, etc. of these backward countries. Communication theories developed for the diffusion of agricultural innovation in American agricultural extension service were applied to methods to overcome the resistance of peasants in Latin America or India.[23]

III. The Social Responsibility Tradition

By the early twentieth century there was wide agreement that the appeal to freedom of conscience was often an excuse for great injustices—or enormous concentration of economic power over the media—and the rigidities in the so-called self-adjusting, free market of ideas made just access to information and communication channels difficult for the economically less powerful. Although personal conscience and motivations were a source of social creativity, this had to be subordinated to the common good and had to include a dimension of responsibility for developing the common good. Society is not just the sum of individual goods, but there

---

22. Rowland, *Politics of Violence*, 45.

23. E.M. Rogers in association with Lynne Svenning, *Modernization Among Peasants: The Impact of Communication* (New York: Holt, Rinehart and Winston).

exists over and above individual goal-seeking a cultural heritage, a set of common institutions. The richer the common good—for example good quality schools, libraries and broadcasting open to all in the community—the better individuals will be able to achieve their individual goals.

From this perspective flowed a series of crucial principles about public communication which were quite radically different from the libertarian tradition: 1) public communication, especially the mass media, while it might be privately owned and administered, had to be open to regulation not just in terms of the rights of individuals (against libel, etc.) but by the public, collective decision making at various levels of community; 2) the basic purpose of the public media was not to enrich the owners but to serve the common good, and work in media is not simply a job but a profession which is intrinsically oriented toward sustaining the free democratic community; 3) the public has a right to access to the media and, in our pluralistic societies, every group, region or social class sector has the right to just representation and adequate information for its needs; 4) given the fact that the public media are so central for preserving a democratic society and a democratic culture, it is a quasi-sacred institution which must be kept separate from the influence above all of government and powerful economic interests, but also separate from other powerful and possibly divisive institutions such as the churches or professional and occupational interests.

The social responsibility tradition began to come center stage at the beginning of this century just at the time when broadcasting was being introduced. Since private initiatives soon produced a cacophony of voices in the air, the technology itself seemed to demand public regulation and permitted social responsibility proponents to define the meaning of this medium much more than had been possible with the press.

The tradition of social responsibility of communication and the public media tended to emphasize different aspects in different socio-political contexts. In the United States, where there was such a strong individualistic tradition and such a profound fear of government interference or the interference of any "established" church or cultural interest, maintaining the media as a private enterprise was judged the best form of preserving independence. Public service and an orientation to the common good was introduced by a powerful drive toward internally regulated "professionalization," with its emphasis on university education and university degrees, the adoption of codes of ethics, and developing a specialized knowledge and skill based on scientific research.[24]

The ideal of the scientist who produces "objective" information which is value free but valuable for the pragmatic progress of society be-

---

24. C. Christians and C.L. Covert, *Teaching Ethics in Journalism Education* (New York: The Hastings Center, 1980).

came a kind of norm not only for people working in public media but a defining characteristic of all communication. Whereas the libertarian tradition tended to use an economic, free market metaphor, the social responsibility tradition used a more sociological metaphor of the organic system growing (progressing) and maintaining equilibrium in a changing environment through the differentiated functions of its members. Thus, the media and communication in general were to perform the functions of information supply for collective decisions and the critical discovery of problems, especially concentrations of power, that would upset the flexible process of response to internal and external change.

Whereas the libertarian tradition tended to sustain a communication research emphasis on media effects, whether these might be seen as pro or anti social, the characteristic media research approach has been "uses and gratifications" which presupposes that the media should be "serving" these individual and group needs and that the individual is educated to use the media in a rational and socially responsible manner.

The American progressive movement which sustained the drive toward professionalization, government legislation and regulation of the public service functions of the media and a more educated public, also carried a strong populist theme which echoed Walt Whitman's hope that America could develop a democratic artistic aesthetic of the common man. Thus, American attitudes toward the mass media tended to defend and appreciate the popular culture of the Broadway musical, popular music, vaudeville and its extension into radio/TV comedy, the Hollywood mass produced film and other forms of mass popular media. This came to be a kind of celebration of the tastes of the common man, an exuberant independence from elitist art, and a praise of the entertainment industry as the quintessential form of magical upward social mobility. Any kind of communication and entertainment which is widely popular must have something of the true values of American culture.[25]

In most European countries, with stronger traditions of the church and government as respected guardians of the "authentic" language, culture, religion, and artistic traditions of the country through the universities such as Oxford and Cambridge and a system of elite secondary schools, there was a much stronger emphasis on communication as "enculturation" into the national cultural tradition—very often defined by elites in the church, literary and educational circles—and as a form of sociocultural control. The closeness and competitiveness of quite different national cultures often meant that public communication and even everyday face-to-face communication was considered important for maintaining a particular national cultural tradition.

---

25. Rivers, Schramm, and Christians, *Social Responsibility*. 220-268.

Thus, when broadcasting was introduced into Britain in the mid-1920s, the idea of leaving it at the mercy of economic forces was abhorrent, and it was assimilated into the model of the university with a royal charter and governed by a group of wise citizens that attempted to make it independent of economic, political, ecclesiastical and other major institutions and that gave it the public function of preserving the national cultural heritage.[26]

The purpose of the BBC was to inform, to educate and to entertain (meaning teaching people good tastes in entertainment)—all essentially forms of enculturation into an elite-controlled culture. The radio and later the television producer in the BBC was accorded the "academic freedom" of the university don in order to stimulate cultural creativity within the tacit consensus of what is "good taste" (the term "morally right or wrong" would not be heard) within the university-like broadcasting corporation.[27]

In this context the emphasis in communications switched from effects on receivers to *content* and the *quality* of the content measured in terms of the elusive aesthetic critique of persons educated in the cultural tradition of the language and the country and fully aware of the art of various forms of expression.[28] Good communication was that which had a combination of significant content, style, form—all calculated to produce a significant aesthetic experience in the people participating in this experience. Tracey comments that an institution such as the BBC could not have come into existence without the contextual background of a Victorian conception of culture and, one might add, the Romantic literary tradition which saw in great literature a quasi religious experience that developed the fully human capacities of those exposed to it.[29] Whereas media studies in the United States were perennially concerned with pro and anti social effects or the instrumentalist "uses and gratifications," in Britain media studies never strayed too far from critical appreciation of the quality of the media and the critical appreciation of the quality of the culture as revealed in the media.

The social responsibility tradition generally has placed great emphasis on service to the cultural, educational, and other needs of different population groups. In part, this stems from the organic conception of culture and society and the maintenance of a balanced response to all aspects of human and social experience—not just what the market will bear. A communication system must insure that cultural "variety" is present. Re-

---

26. M. Tracey, *The Throne We Honor: Essays on Public Service Broadcasting* (London: Sage Publications, forthcoming).

27. C. Curran, *A Seamless Robe: Broadcasting Philosophy and Practice* (London: Collins Publications, 1979).

28. The Broadcasting Research Unit, *The Public Service Idea in British Broadcasting: Main Principles* (London: Broadcasting Research Unit, 1985).

29. Tracey, *The Throne We Honor.*

ligion, for example, is generally seen as an integral and public dimension of culture so that broadcast regulatory legislation requires a response to people's religious interests.

Many of the European countries that had established centrally controlled broadcasting systems oriented toward their national sociocultural development extended small branches of this in their colonial dependencies of Africa, Asia, and India for the expatriate and westernized native communities. The new governments usually took this over and made broadcasting an integral part of the one party governments that attempted to integrate disparate regional cultures and tribal groups into a unified nation. Most of these governments with a largely rural, peasant population also began a continual series of five-year plans and massive campaigns for improving agricultural production, teaching literacy, controlling epidemics of disease, introducing minimal knowledge of preventive medicine, and educating for family planning. In nations of small villages and interpersonal ties, the new governments created the communication of a "modern nation" with formalistic, bureaucratic "extension systems" and centrally-controlled broadcasting. This was the new "development communication" which characterized so much of the world's population: an unwieldy structure of carrying out imperfectly understood orders from a central planning office, all spliced together by an understructure of clientelistic patron-follower or other personalistic ties based on family, religion, fictive kinship and oldboy networks.

IV. The Critical and Liberating Tradition

The social responsibility tradition attempted to preserve the openness and stimulation of individual creativity of the libertarian society, but also to correct its abuses by subordinating individual initiatives to a community good and orienting the satisfaction of personal ambitions toward professional public service. Critics have pointed out, however, that the social responsibility theory has an inherent conservative, functionalist bias that prevents it from correcting the injustices inherent in the essentially economic criteria of libertarianism and, that, at times, introduces new abuses. How can social democracies firmly committed to a social responsibility tradition with a series of magnificent public service institutions still systematically justify discrimination of racial, ethnic, religious, poor and gender groups—to mention but a few of those marginalized?

A first and major problem is that any attempt to define the common good, whether through "blind market forces" or through the rational discourse, which determines contribution according to capacity and distribution according to need must, ultimately, base the common good on a selection of values and world view. No matter how effective is the social process of articulation of interests and integration of all particular goods into a common good, there must be some cultural criteria of what is good. Some cultural minorities, who may in fact be a numerical majority, often have values so far from what is defined as the common culture that their demands are defined as simply irrational and destructive of social integration. And, in pluralistic societies with rapid cultural changes, the emphasis on an organic/functionalist integration of society may introduce systematic cultural bias.

The Marxist critical tradition argues that this cultural bias is aggravated by the fact that cultural formations are inevitably linked to material, economic processes and, that where the libertarian tradition permits economic concentrations of power, this translates into a cultural definition of the common good in terms of the values and interests of economically dominant classes. Marxists such as Roland Barthes, with a background in semiotics and structuralist analysis, have pointed out that cultural definitions of the common good included a selectively constructed conception of the common history which tends to defend their existence by translating the history into a sacred myth and which give it "natural," metaphysical status, untouchable by any cultural debate. Many argue that the injustices in communication are not just in the overt patterns of concentrations of social power or in the lack of institutions of rational distribution of information and access, but are imbedded in the structure of the world view and language which defines "rationality" itself and underlies the most sacred values of our culture.

The key explanatory terms in this critical tradition have been: 1) *"ideology,"* the processes by which concentrations of power and discriminatory interests are translated into a world view and values that are simply taken for granted as the way the world is "naturally" and "theologically"; 2) *hegemony,* the processes by which people who are treated unjustly in a particular definition of the common good are nevertheless "negotiated" into accepting and supporting that definition of the common good; and 3) *alienation,* the stifling of the creativity and human potential not only among people who suffer from contexts of hegemony but also among those who perpetrate injustices. This tradition has introduced in communication studies a systematic *critical* analysis and unmasking of the forms of ideology in the culture around us.

The liberation normative discourse is closely linked with the critical tradition, but it tends to have an origin in the more existential *practice* of popular movements. A liberation language arises in a process of dialogical interaction on the basis of acceptance and respect that enables individuals and groups to discover a valued identity that is denied by the cultural context about them and to affirm the good of that depreciated cultural identity. Liberation is a communication process in so far as interaction raises to the level of conscious affirmation (*conscientization*) of the inherent human sense of value of one's own existence. The fundamental changes in the broader institutionalized patterns of communication which permit and encourage this "consciousness-raising" liberation are often referred to as the *democratization of communication.*

One model of liberating communication is the description of the stages of popular social movements that originate in "explosions" against increasing exploitation and evolve into new forms of communicative language, new participatory media, and more democratic communication institutions. Often, lower-status groups internalize the depreciative ethnic, racial, or social class images so that they come to see themselves as inferior and impotent. These destructive self-images are perpetuated in the clientelistic one-on-one dependency relationships that do not permit horizontal communication among the powerless. In a first stage of a movement, however, the less powerful begin to communicate among themselves, and one of the first processes is the development of a new language which places a positive value on their identity. Prophetic leaders of these movements similar to a Martin Luther King lead people to reaffirmation of their identity with slogans such as "black is beautiful," or the affirmations in peasant movements in the Mexican revolution that the Indian peasants are the soul and base of the nation.

This may set up vast networks of "liberating group communication" where small groups formally and informally work through their internalization of the depreciation of the dominant culture. Within the context of the small group, the powerless learn to discuss with a dialogical, participatory pattern of communication so different from the hegemonic patterns of communication and begin to lay the foundations for the democratization of communication.[30] The now widely-diffused Freirian method of "education for liberation" and "consciousness raising" is one of the best known formal methods of this form of communication.

A development important for this tradition of normative theory is the move from this new pattern and content of interpersonal communication to the level of "alternative" and "popular" media which attempts to adapt and transform the professional language and use of technology to the cultural logic and language of this minority group. At this stage, the media are used *within* the movement to reinforce the movement. For example, in Latin America, the Philippines, India, and parts of Africa those of the Catholic Church who are in contact with the rural and urban poor have provided the technical expertise to set up "peoples" radio stations, centers of communication training, networks of grassroots drama, documentation centers with libraries and the facilities to produce newsletters and newspapers and even alternative use of word processors and computers. There is a great emphasis on a new *concept* and *style* of communication in the me-

---

30. J. Martínez-Terrero, *Comunicación grupal liberadora* (Buenos Aires: Ediciones Paulinas, 1986).

dia: dialogical; participatory; horizontal; allowing the people to define the genres, formats and language; accompanying the people in their efforts at sociocultural change; responding to the historical moments of profound social change; and making public information that other media will not voice to protect those interests.

A more difficult stage is reached when the movement has gained legitimacy, has begun to change the dominant culture and conception of the common good, and may represent a significant "cultural" market. For example, at a certain point alternative or lower status musics, such as rock music, may be seen to be marketable or the "liberated woman" may be an attractive symbol for advertising.

At this point, the processes of hegemony begin to incorporate into the dominant cultural synthesis enough of the alternative symbols to enable the cultural outcasts to identify with the values of the dominant culture. For example, in the United States the formula that religion in the United States is tripartite, Protestant, Catholic, and Jewish, opened the way for the legitimacy of Catholics for public office, etc., but it also meant that Catholics came out of an alternative cultural ghetto and accepted the dominant cultural hegemony—far more secularized than the ghetto—of the United States. At this point, critical cultural scholars, who may identify with the minority movement, begin to analyze the presence of the dominant ideology in the broader culture from the perspective of their minority values, questioning the hegemonic synthesis. For example, liberation theologians and broad sectors of the Catholic Church in Latin America have questioned the dominant cultural values, as have the recent pastoral letters of the American Bishops in the United States. It is apparent that one can protect the distinctive values of a minority group now socio-politically part of the hegemonic culture only by seeking some negotiated changes in the dominant culture. And usually hegemony is a process of continual negotiation whereby one group finds within the logic of its own value tradition some basis for accepting "ecumenically" at least some elements of the outside values as long the core logic of the value tradition is respected and as long as outside groups also make some concessions.[31]

Currently, some of the most important developments in the conceptions of the critical/cultural liberation tradition are a better understanding of the processes of cultural negotiation: in the study of broadcast reception, analysis of how audiences resist, selectively accept, reinterpret in terms of their own reference groups;[32] how the creators of certain media genres have attracted audiences by incorporating the language of resis-

31. R.A. White, "Cultural Analysis in Communication for Development: The Role of Cultural Dramaturgy in the Creation of a Public Sphere," *Development*, 1990/2, 23-31.

32. J. Fiske, *Television Culture* (London: Routledge, 1987).

tance and protest into mass media, for example, women's day-time soap opera incorporating women's oral discourse;[33] how some televangelists such as Pat Robertson, with more mainstream modern American social values, have enabled people of an evangelical tradition to identify with the American mainstream.[34]

V. The Ritual Communion Normative Tradition

This most recent of the conceptual and policy traditions to gain significant acceptance represents a clear affirmation of the steady march away from an exclusively "source," vertical influence emphasis toward an emphasis on the active subject of communication. This tradition is now stimulating some of the most important current empirical theory and research. As a normative tradition, it is closest to the theological conception put forth in the opening part of *Communio et progressio*, the major document of theological-pastoral guidelines for social communication (public or mass) of the Catholic Church. *Communio et progressio* proposes that the function of mass communication in the history of salvation is the extension into time, through the Incarnation, revelation and action of Jesus Christ in establishing a Church, of the salvific will of God to bring all people to share, in some degree, the Trinitarian union of Father, Son and Holy Spirit. Although many of the main proponents of this as a model happen to share a strong humanistic, ecclesio-religious identification and there may be some common sources in our contemporary cultural imagination, the development of this tradition in the field of communication sciences is separate and parallel with the Catholic Church's position.

This communion-ritual model has emerged out of an increasing disillusionment with the essentially instrumentalist view of communication of the libertarian, social responsibility and critical traditions. For all three, communication is a *means*: obtaining effects, transport of information, personal gratifications, maintaining community integration, holding cultural power, etc. None of these traditions, it is objected, lead us to the point where human beings are actually communicating so that we can understand this process and exist as communicating human beings.

As James Carey expresses it, communication is best described as a ritual and as communion because

---

33. M.E. Brown, "Motley Moments: Soap Operas, Carnival, Gossip and the Power of the Utterance," and "Consumption and Resistance—The Problem of Pleasure" in M.E. Brown, ed., *Television and Women's Culture: The Politics of the Popular* (London: Sage Publications, 1990) 183-210.

34. S. Hoover, *Mass Media Religion: The Social Sources of the Electronic Church* (Newbury Park, CA: Sage Publications, 1988).

> . . . it is a process through which a shared culture is created, modified and transformed. . . . A ritual view of communication is not directed toward the extension of messages in space, but the maintenance of society in time; not the act of imparting information or influence, but the creation, representation, and celebration of shared beliefs. If a transmission view of communication centers on the extension of messages across geography for purposes of control, a ritual view centers on the sacred ceremony which draws persons together in fellowship and community.[35]

While the libertarian tradition has borrowed both an organizing metaphor and methods from economics, the social responsibility tradition from behavioral systems theory and the critical tradition from Marxist analysis of ideology and hegemony, the ritual-communion tradition tends to borrow more from the humanities (aesthetics, literary and textual interpretation) and from the more humanistic cultural anthropology of Clifford Geertz, Victor Turner and Mary Douglas. Again, as Carey has expressed it,

> Cultural studies...does not seek to explain human behavior, but to understand it. It does not seek to reduce human action to underlying causes or structures but to interpret its significance. It does not attempt to predict human behavior, but to diagnose human meanings. It is, more positively, an attempt to bypass the rather discrete empiricism of behavioral studies and the esoteric apparatus of formal (structuralist) theories and to descend deeper into the empirical world. The goals of communication studies as a cultural science are therefore more modest, but also more human at least in the sense of attempting to be truer to human nature and experience as it is ordinarily encountered.[36]

Here Carey cites Geertz, who refers to Max Weber, to stress one of the central unifying points of this tradition: communication is a process of construction of meaning, by definition, in social contexts, and communication science takes human culture as a text to understand the processes of constructing meaning.

> Believing with Max Weber, that man is an animal suspended in webs of significance he himself has spun, I take culture to be those webs, and the analysis of it to be therefore not an experimental science in search of law but an interpretive one in search of meaning.[37]

---

35. J.W. Carey, "Mass Communication Research and Cultural Studies: the American View," in J. Curran, M. Gurevitch & J. Woollacott, eds., *Mass Communication and Society* (London: Edward Arnold in association with Open University Press, 1977) 409-425 at 412.

36. Ibid., 418-419.

37. Ibid., 419.

Carey and others have criticized the classical methodology of the behavioral sciences because they impose the scientist's own definitions of meaning on the people. For example, studies of violence in the media have begun with a definition of violence by the analyst (usually a definition easily quantified to meet the demands of commercial broadcasters or legislators), the quantitative analysis of media content to determine the degree of violence, the quantitative amount of time viewers see violent programs and then the quantitative measurement of inclinations toward violence (or protection from violence). Critics of this approach argue that with these criteria, much of Shakespeare would be banned because its strict quantitative measures do not take into consideration the *meaning* of violence to the author, the characters in the play, or to the people (across generations and cultures) who see, interpret and re-create their own subjective means of the violence of Shakespeare.[38]

One might ask, though, what difference it makes in terms of human well-being and human society? Here, Carey goes back to the British cultural studies tradition which came out of literary and dramatic criticism.

> The British sociologist Tom Burns put this nicely when he observed that the task of art is to make sense out of life. The task of social science is to make sense out of the senses we make out of life. By such reasoning the social scientist stands toward his material—cultural forms such as religion, ideology, journalism, everyday speech—as the literary critic stands toward the novel, play or poem. He has to figure out what it means, what interpretations it presents of life, and how it relates to the senses of life historically found among a people.[39]

What Carey and others are emphasizing in this cultural studies approach is that a central task of communication studies—though not the only one—is to understand what the media and many other forms of human symbolic expression are saying as a privileged revelation of *what kind of culture we are creating*. We are then in the position, like the literary and cultural critic, to ask whether this is the kind of culture we want to create and whether we are satisfied with the agencies that are given a central task in creating it. This approach sees communication as a process of creation of cultural existence but also as a continuing process of communalistic ritual whereby we critically examine and modify but also celebrate the shared beliefs we hold.

The conceptions of anthropologist, Victor Turner[40] who studied the experience of ritual, theater and the performative arts as an experience of

38. H. Newcomb, "Assessing the Violence Profile Studies of Gerbner and Gross: A Humanistic Critique and Suggestion," *Communication Research*, 5/3 (July, 1978), 264-282; J. Phelan, *Disenchantment: Meaning and Morality in the Media* (New York: Hastings House Publishers, 1980).

39. Carey, "Cultural Studies," 413.

communitas on the threshold between time and eternity (utopia), are also widely cited by many in this tradition.[41]

Turner stressed that ritual, the performative arts and even television are a moving out of the ordinary, pragmatic, short-term commitments of life to find a space of freedom to hold in abeyance our present commitments and consider other possible values, objectives in life, ways of living. Turner and others would see the mass media as an important leisure-time experience which provides a balance between mobilization to reach established cultural goals and freedom to explore new cultural alternatives.

One of the promising lines of research in this tradition is "audience ethnography" which explores through interviews and participant observation the great range of meaning constructions that people in different social contexts and cultural backgrounds may place on the same television program. Fiske argues that the text of television is a social construction and does not really gain its full meaning until it is interpreted and discussed in a community by critics, social scientists and people of varied social and cultural backgrounds.[42] Other lines of research analyze how television writers, for example, women's day time soap opera, are able, perceptively, to incorporate many of the characteristics of women's oral discourse to create a particular form of "women's genre" in which women recognize their identity. Women, in turn, in fan and friendship networks rework the meaning of soap opera and directly or indirectly influence the turn of the soap opera narrative.[43] Thus, empirical research is showing that the linear, transport model of communication not only is not communication by definition but that it does not explain communication nearly as well as a ritual, negotiation model in which the media are, in fact, mediations between the past and present and between different sectors of society.

Another line of research-attempts to locate the role of media in a much broader social and historical context. Katz and Dayan have shown that the high points of mass media are the coronations, competitions, and funerals, all moments of ritual setting aside daily affairs to explore the

40. V. Turner, *The Ritual Process* (London: Routledge & Keegan Paul, 1969); V. Turner, *From Ritual to Theatre: The Human Seriousness of Play* (New York: Performing Arts Journal Publications, 1982).

41. H. Newcomb & R. Alley, *The Producer's Medium: Conversations with Creators of American TV* (New York: Oxford University Press, 1983); E. Katz and D. Dayan, "Media Events: On the Experience of Not Being There," *Religion* 15 (July, 1985), 305-314; B. Martin, *Sociology of Contemporary Cultural Change* (Oxford: Basil Blackwell, 1981); S. Hoover, *Mass Media Religion*.

42. Fiske, *Television Culture*.

43. M.E. Brown, *Soap Opera and Women's Talk: The Pleasure of Resistance* (Newbury Park, CA: Sage Publications, 1992).

broader meaning of life.[44] Hoover has shown how mass media personalities such as televangelists and their particular program formats are "created" by the new cultural trends and incipient religious movements, but that these televangelists, in turn, articulate what the people ready for these movements "want to hear." Case histories of people who are followers of televangelists such as Pat Robertson indicate that "effects" models do not explain this process well, but that a communion model, in which all the people in the religious movement are actively creating meaning, does explain.[45]

Congruent with the communion, ritual model at the societal level is a model at the interpersonal and group level in which communication is seen as process of cooperative creation of meaning.[46] In this model, the parties who will take part in some process of communication each begin with a different, unique perception of the situation, but, through a series of interactive approximations, their understanding of the situation *converges* until they share in some degree the same understanding. In this process of convergence of unique understandings, a *third, new* meaning comes into existence.

Conclusions

We have thought it important to present the field of communications in terms of the major normative traditions because theology tends to enter communications through its normative discourses. Theologians are reflecting on the meaning of God's action in culture and history and God's invitation to us to build this history as an expression of our union with the divine life. Theology is the "should language" of existence and life. For example, the Church document, *Communio et progressio,* uses essentially normative language, presenting a model of communitarian communication that God is inviting us to construct in society and in the church.

Communications is also an empirical science that is concerned with verification and prediction of theoretically derived hypotheses. This empirical verification may be important for theologies *of* contemporary communication and culture or for pastoral theologies of communication. For example, for developing a *communio* model of Church in concrete circumstances, it may be important to know with some certainty how conflicting groups in the community can be expected to form common, unifying sym-

---

44. Katz and Dayan, "Media Events."

45. Hoover, *Mass Media Religion.*

46. E.M. Rogers and D.L. Kincaid, *Communication Networks: Toward a New Paradigm for Research* (New York: The Free Press, A Division of Macmillan Publishing Co., 1981), 31-78.

bols. One must recognize, however, that this empirical question is likely to be posed only if communitarian communication is a value.

Awareness of the normative traditions of communication is important in order to perceive more sharply that different theological and denominational traditions are in mutual interaction with different normative communication discourses. There is a clear congruence between the libertarian tradition and classical Protestant conceptions of God, the person and society. Liberation theologies are using critical, liberation communication discourses while *communio* theologies are congruent with ritual, communion traditions in communication. Awareness of the historical normative origins of communication discourses is helpful for understanding the deeper, contextual meanings and ideological relationships of terms.

Although different normative communication traditions may have quite different underlying conceptions of the person and society, these different traditions may also be mutually complementary. For example, *Communio et progressio* stresses a *"communio"* tradition of theology from the Second Vatican Council but tends to use the "social responsibility" normative language to describe its model of public communication. The critical, liberation and ritual, communion normative communication languages were not well developed or well known to the writers and consultants formulating *Communio et progressio*. Thus, not only is there a gap between the *communio* theology and social responsibility normative language, but the critical, liberation language is almost entirely absent from both the theology and the normative communication proposals of *Communio et progressio*. Whatever the point of interaction, awareness of the richness of normative discourses in communications can be mutually beneficial to both communications and to theology.

3

Truth and Power in Ecclesial Communication

Peter Henrici, S.J.

We know the importance of communications for a correct theological understanding of the Church. The Church is a communion and needs communication. Later chapters will take up some of the basic concepts of ecclesial communication: ecumenism, catechesis, witness, and evangelization. Ecclesiology, however, cannot limit itself to merely theoretical and descriptive considerations; the normative aspect of ecclesiology is unavoidable. By explaining what the Church theologically is and does, one also defines what the concrete, historically existing Church should be and how it *should* act. The importance of communications for the very constitution of the Church implies an ecclesiastical and theologically grounded communication ethics which embraces much more than a professional code for Christian communicators. This ethics proposes a normative foundation for all ecclesiastical behavior.

This chapter will give some basic principles for an ecclesiastical communication ethics. Starting from what is normally seen as the foundational exigency of all communication ethics, namely, truthfulness, this chapter will insist on the paradoxical interplay between truth and power at all levels of human communication. The findings of a purely philosophical analysis of communication cannot be directly transposed and applied to ecclesial communications. In the Church and in ecclesiastical contexts both truth and power have a very specific theological meaning. Before we attempt to map out a typology of possible abuses, confusions and shifts between truthful and powerful communication in the Church, we must define what truth and power mean in the life of the Church. Finally, we will discuss some of the most patent abuses of power and of truth in part as a foil to distinguish more clearly the features of normatively correct ecclesial communication.

I. Communication: Truth or Power?

1. "Tell the truth." This simple imperative seems to be the most evident and basic principle for communication ethics. For ethics is concerned with the good in human acts; and the good which theoretical acts aim to achieve is truth. Communication, at a theoretical level—as a sharing of information or meaning—must, therefore, try to reach a state of truthfulness. Even for communication in a broader and more comprehensive sense (seeking to bring about the sharing of all kinds of goods), truth is normative. Communication of every kind of goods or values is *good* communication only if these are *true* goods and *true* values. To dispense a poison or drugs is surely not good communication, nor is the inculcation of bad moral principles good communication.

At a deeper level, we can affirm that any falsehood and deceit on the part of the communicator corrupts communication at its roots, even if we are dealing with cases of *effective* sharing of meaning and information and thus "good" in the sense that information is transmitted or even if some meaning is shared. The physician lying to his patient and the politician lying to his constituency may be quite "good" as communicators, but what they achieve cannot be considered *good* communication. They are able to achieve their goals, but they do not share meaning in any real sense of the term.

When we begin to examine what can be truly shared, we soon notice that only ideal, normative goods such as truth and values can be common and shared simultaneously among many people. The possession and even the use of material things can be transferred from one person to another, but they can never be held in true commonality. If one person has material goods, that logically excludes the other person from having the same thing in the same way. Even the air we breathe is appropriated by individuals in order to use it. Goods in the ideal order, on the contrary, which are based on the principles of truth and love, are really what they ought to be only insofar as they are shared by many. To aim at sharing is to aim at real truth and real love.

We can speak of communicative truth, the sharing of meaning, as a continuum from its weakest to its fullest form. At its weakest it is shared information about a situation, a "datum" or kind of "thing" that can be simultaneously possessed by many; in its fullest form sharing meaning is to share evidence as in the case of mathematical insights. The intermediate stages—for example, opinion, persuasion, and belief—can hardly be shared since they are strictly subjective and personal. Nevertheless, these diluted forms of truth constitute the main process of mediated communication. In this kind of mediated process, however, all that communication can hope to achieve is to generate in the other a *similar* point of view, not through sharing exactly the same intellectual content, that is, not sharing *truth* but sharing conviction.

Truth, then, is limited as an object or aim of communication. There are two other limits, inherent in the very nature of truth, which, consequently, can never really be overcome. Truth, firstly, must be the *entire* truth. "Only the whole is the true," Hegel stated.[1] Partial truth, by the very reason of being only partial, may be utterly untrue. This does not mean that a statement, in order to be true, must say all that can be said about a given state of things (*Sachverhalt*); it may state in quite correct terms only a single aspect of the truth. But when this statement is used to communicate, it will be true only if its context is evident, which makes clear why this is only a partial statement. In communication nothing can be more false than a partial truth. There is a famous story about a bishop arriving in New York and being asked by an impertinent reporter, "When you come to New York, do you go to a night club?" The bishop thought he had a good answer when he replied, "Are there night clubs in New York?" The next morning, a newspaper carried the headline, "Bishop's first question: Are there nightclubs in New York?" The same rule applies, as we all know, to visual communication. Nothing can be more deceptive than true images for they are by necessity always from a particular partial perspective. What a dilemma. For if it is quite impossible to ever know the whole truth, it seems still more difficult to communicate it.

And this brings us to the second limitation that affects precisely the communication of truth. Not only can the truth that I believe I know never be adequately expressed, but what I in fact communicate is not the meaning I intend but, rather, what the receiver perceives from my words or signs. It is what the *receiver* believes I intend to communicate. In order to communicate adequately "my" truth, I should know what is likely to be the receiver's interpretation of the message. And this, again, is quite impossible. All the techniques of feedback, verification, dialogue, and so forth are meant to overcome this gap. Nevertheless, the gap forever remains. We can have no insight into another's mind or heart unless the truth we communicate is so common and evident that it cannot be mistaken, as is the case, we would suggest again, with mathematical insights or pure data. All that lies in between the two extreme poles on the continuum of truth—opinion, persuasion, belief, etc.—offer no possibility of verifying definitively whether the interpretation I generate in another is actually *similar* to what I intend to tell that other.

2. The problems of truth in communication carry us back into a fundamental consideration about human communication. If the sharing of truth—or meaning—which is supposed to be the *goal* of communication is so difficult to achieve—or even to understand—perhaps it would be preferable to

---

1. Georg Wilhelm Hegel, "Preface" in *The Phenomenology of Mind*. Translated, with an introduction and notes by J.B. Baillie. Introduction to the Torchbook Edition by George Lictheim. (New York: Harper, 1967), pp. 67-130.

take a more defensible stance and focus simply on the *process* which strives toward an unreachable aim. The basic evidence about this process is, however, quite paradoxical: although the communication process tends (has the intrinsic orientation) toward perfect sharing, it is still, by its very nature, a one-sided, unilateral activity: the one who knows, possesses, or "exists" in some particular way is communicating to another who does not know, does not possess, or has a different existence. Even dialogue, which is supposedly the most perfect form of a communication process, is a two-way communication process only insofar as it is a constant interplay and alternating between two (or more) one-way communications. Sharing actually can be nothing but a *result* of many unidirectional communicative activities. The same is true for all sorts of participatory communication: participation builds up from a set of one-way communications even though these may eventually acquire new, thoroughly different characteristics through the participation process. Whatever the structure of communications, inequalities among the communicating parties are virtually unavoidable in a communication process.

That implies, in less abstract terms, that communication, in one way or another, always involves a relationship of *power*: a stronger person communicates to a weaker person. This power may be mitigated by love, but love can also make it more insistent . . . "the power of love!" Such is so often the case when parents and children, husbands and wives, fiancées, or close friends communicate. In any case, in order that communication take place at all, there must be some inequality among the communicating persons and therefore also some difference of power. A *perfectly* "powerless discussion" (*herrschaftsfreier Diskurs*), such as Habermas projects,[2] would be no communication at all, but rather sheer chatter about what all already know and about which all agree.

It is no surprise, then, that at present the main concern of communication studies is not truth but power. Communication research began with the analysis of war propaganda, electoral campaigns, and advertising, and these still remain some of the central topics. In all of these fields, the principal interest of research is not the truth of what is communicated but the effectiveness of the communication process. And, from an ethical point of view, one has to be laudatory when this effectiveness is not in the service of something bad or grossly untrue.

The fact that power structures condition and animate all communication processes is even more evident in non-speculative communication,

---

2. Jürgen Habermas introduced this neomarxist ideal of "herrschaftsfreie Diskussion" (discussion without interest in domination) in his early works (See, for example, *Der Positivismusstreit in der deutschen Soziologie*. Neuwied, 1969, p. 254). Later he brought this ideal down to a more concrete method of argumentative discourse in an ideal situation of perfect reciprocity (See *The Theory of Communicative Action*, Vol I. Boston: Beacon Press, 1984. Ch 3).

that is, in the communication of useable commodities, especially in a free-market situation. The producer and the merchant have the power to satisfy some needs by offering certain goods, and the consumer has the pecuniary power to buy them. From the interplay of these two (one-sided) positions of power originates the market. But notice that the market does not rely so much on the quality of these goods or on their use value (that is, the degree to which they provide satisfaction)—something that would be equivalent to the truth in theoretical communication—but on the *need,* often artificially created or stimulated by advertising, which creates their *value of exchange.* The need marks the weakness of the consumer and, therefore, the power of the merchant. The relation is inverted whenever one with strong purchasing power imposes on the producer the laws of production and the price for the products. In all of these more material communication processes, theoretical communication, insofar as it tries to use methods of persuasion, always plays an important intermediate role. Thus, human exchange and interaction is always an interplay of different levels of the power structure.

This affirmation, which is a commonplace for political science, economics, and social psychology, should also be a foundational insight for communications. Nevertheless, there is an essential difference between economics and political science on the one hand and psychology and communications on the other. Economics and political science are mainly interested in the *rules* of that interplay between different (human) forces; what this interplay should be good for and what (if anything) it seeks to achieve, appears only on the horizon of their analyses—if it appears at all. Psychology and communications, in contrast, are principally concerned with *persons*, and these sciences try to understand and place an interpretation on personal expression. Therefore, these sciences cannot abstract from a consideration of the realization of goals and what is good for persons. Such disciplines cannot view the interplay of power structure in a purely neutral, disinterested way. Although these sciences are not normative in the same sense as ethics, social psychology and communications cannot be concerned only with effective or less effective forms of power and interplay—in other words, they cannot refrain from distinguishing between good and bad, human or antihuman communications.

Here we encounter the root of countless distortions in communication. Since we must presuppose that the content of communication is truth and its goal to bring about sharing—and power is the law governing all communicative activity—then power should be at the service of truth. The temptation, however, to place truth at the service of power and thus, in the process of communication, to aim at domination rather than sharing, is all too obvious. Such a perversion of truth is often perpetrated in various more or less transparent ways. Sophistry is one of the more common ones. Ideology and propaganda are others. And imposition through sheer physical force is all too prevalent. The central norm of all these forms of communication is not truth but instrumental usefulness. Truth, partial truth, and distorted truth are used in these cases as long as they are effective for achieving the end that the communicator has proposed. This goal is never sharing of truth or of goods, but inculcating through persuasion or swaying opinions or provoking a certain behavioral reaction. Truth, then, becomes a mere instrument, not an end of communication, and falsehood may be just as effective or even a more effective instrument than truth. Thus, we find that power—getting power, using power, or increasing power—is transformed from a means to the central end of communications. Authoritarianism is perhaps the mildest form of this kind of distortion.

All of this analysis of the dilemmas of communication applies, with some variations, to ecclesial communication. Nevertheless, we cannot simply transpose these characteristics of communication to communication in the Church. Both truth and power, and, indeed, sharing of meaning, take on, within the ecclesial context, a new analogous meaning which is both deeper and wider than the communication of everyday life. In the next section, let us examine why this is true.

II. Truth and Power in the Church

1. "Go and teach all nations." Christ's command that has constituted the Church says much more than simply "Tell the truth." Firstly, it expresses a different kind of *imperative,* one which is not only conditioned ("Whenever you intend to speak, tell the truth.") but *absolute*: "Go and teach." The Church has no choice whether she will go and teach or not. The Church is not simply an organization constituted *by* communication—as are all organizations. The Church is constituted *in order to* communicate.

Secondly, as Christ's command implies, truth in an ecclesial context has a very specific meaning and structure. It is neither simple information nor private opinion nor is it a global truth to be searched for. It is a *message,* that is, a quite determinate truth committed to the Church by Christ in order to be transmitted to others for whom it is not only important but vital. Truthfulness to a committed message means that one must be faithful to both the content and the form of the message and to the mission to convey it. A messenger stands in the service both of the one who committed it to him and of the others for whom that truth is intended.

Thirdly, Christ's command means that the Christian message is a *powerful* message: it bears the authority of Christ who committed it to the Church, and the message has the power to save those to whom it is directed. The advertising industry may have borrowed the term "message" from Christianity in order to underline how authoritative and salvific their "messages" are. Paradoxically, the Church's message, notwithstanding the divine power bestowed on it, appears extremely weak on human grounds. It cannot claim the evidence of truth nor the obviousness of data. To those to whom it is addressed, it appears at first sight as sheer opinion. In order to communicate its message, the Church must therefore make use of power, that is, of authority, a power that seems external to the message, but which actually flows from the authority of the message itself. In biblical terms, the authority of the apostle is rooted in the authenticity of his or her message.[3]

Thus, the Church's proclamation of her powerful message unfolds in *three distinct moments*: Word, Sacrament and churchly Communion. These are suggested in the very text we quoted at the beginning of this section: "Go, therefore, make disciples of all the nations; baptize them in the name of the Father and of the Son and of the Holy Spirit, and teach them to observe all the commands I gave you" (Matthew 28:19-20). These commands are essentially the "new commandment" of brotherly love and, therefore, brotherly communion. These three moments structure the very life of the Church, the community of the faithful being itself the primary group for whom the message is intended. The acceptance of the message and its accomplishment in the everyday life of the Christian community is the prototype and the cause of all ecclesial communication. In the following pages we will therefore concentrate on the *intraecclesial* communication of the Christian message, its threefold structure, its possible distortions and its true form. It will be easy to apply our conclusions to the communicative behavior of the Church *"ad extra."*

2. Word, sacrament, and communion (or community of love), the three structuring moments of intraecclesial communication may be reduced, to parallel the terms we are using in this article, to the more secular terms of truth, power, and sharing. Regarding *truth*, there is not much that we need add to the extensive discussion above. The truth entrusted to the Church transcends herself and all her members. All are to be in the service of that truth, and no one can ever pretend to possess or master all of it. Even the hierarchy and even the Pope and a Council are but "listeners" to the Word, not different in this regard from the simple faithful. They are "judges" of the faith, a form of response to the Word, only insofar as they recognize and judge that this faith is loyally consonant with the Word and with the faith of the whole Church handed down from the Apostles. There can and must be an evolution in the *understanding* of the Christian message, but nobody may create or discover a *new* Christian truth. It is through this radical, divine "givenness" that truth has authority in the Church, an

---

3. More precisely, in God's own *dynamis*, working through the apostle. See I Cor 1:17-2:5; II Cor 4:7; 12:9-10; 13:3-4; I Thess 1:5.

authority that is rooted, in the last instance, in Christ himself who is the Truth.[4] The Magisterium has its authority precisely by its faithfulness to Christ and to his truth.

Thus, Christian truth is never separated from a context of life and love. When Christ proclaims himself to be the "Truth," he locates this word between the "Way" and the "Life" (John 14:6). Christ's life is present in the Church primarily in the *sacraments*—and from this there originates a new and specific structure of power. Administering the sacraments is a powerful communication, the most powerful and the most effective that could be. It is God's own self communication that becomes effective in the rite of the sacrament. This effectiveness passes, by necessity, through the service of a human minister, and it bestows on this minister an unequalled divine source of power. The same persons who, as members of the hierarchy are still but listeners to the Word (and, like the ordinary faithful, also need to receive the sacraments) administer these sacraments and open up a fullness of power that puts them above and beyond the reach of the "simple" faithful. If, in intraecclesial communication, there is a pre-eminent "top-down" structure, it originates inevitably from the sacramental constitution of the Church.

Thirdly, we must recognize that the hierarchical nature of this structure is mitigated and balanced by another pattern of communication: sharing of goods and *loving communion*. Communion is the central aim of all of the Church's communication. The sacramental power has, as its aim, to build up a community, grounded in Baptism and the Eucharist. Christian truth is a shared truth, shared in the one common faith. And the main task of the hierarchy is the pastoral care needed to build this community. All this implies sharing in love. Like a mother, St. Paul was to give to his communities even his life (I Thess 2:5-9), and he asks them to demonstrate their love to the other communities by sharing their material goods in a collective manner (I Cor 16:1-4; II Cor 8-9). The description of community life in the Acts: "they had all in common" (2:44; cf, 5:32-37) may be idealized, but for that very reason it is normative for all future life of the Church. By this loving sharing the Church imitates Christ, who "being rich, became poor for us, in order to enrich us by his poverty" (II Cor 8:9), "giving his life for his friends" (John 23 15).

Only in the light of sharing, may the significance and value of the structures of power in the Church be understood. Not only does this reveal that they *are in the service* of sharing (as they are in the service of truth), but it also becomes clear that the unity of hierarchical power does not consist in a pyramidal topdown organization. Its meaning is to bring the Church into unity through the loving communion of all bishops, that

---

4. John 14:6; see H.U.v. Balthasar, "The Meaning of Christ's Saying: 'I am the truth'," *Communio*, 14 (1987): 158-160.

is, the local churches, with the Church of Rome and with other Bishops. It is significant that in the action of sharing material goods in the Church, lay people do not depend on the hierarchy, but the hierarchy depends on the laity. The sustenance of priests, bishops, and even the Pope himself depends on the voluntary and loving generosity of the faithful. This ironic dependence of pastors upon their flock may be seen as a subtle pedagogy of the Spirit directed toward inculcating the correct administration of truth and power in the Church.

III. Possible Distortions of Church Communication: A Typology

Having presented the fundamental meaning of these basic structures of the Church, we are now in a position to see more clearly the deviations and the sources of the distortions. Let us map them out in a quasi-a priori typology; to each of these types correspond some very concrete experiences in the actual life of the Church that all can easily identify. Ecclesial communication is likely to be distorted whenever one of its three components—truth, power, or sharing, does not function in its expected way or one of the three is substituted for by another.

Three types of distortions are readily foreseeable. Two of these concern the right order between truth and power, and, if this right order is not present, sharing is automatically distorted. The first type is the use of truth as a means of power, and a second type is the substitution of truth by power. A third type of distortion occurs when sharing is replaced by both truth and power, distorting the true meaning of "communion."

Other distortions are less likely to happen, and many are already implicit in the three types (for example, sharing substituted by the sheer imposition of a power structure). Others occur when the right order of truth and power is inadequately expressed in the institutional order of the Church, for example, when truth attempts to substitute for power. Here, the argument is adequately sustained with a focus on the three major types.

1. Truth as Power

All can easily recognize that the concept, "knowledge is power," is a general working principle in modern societies—far beyond its original meaning in the writing of Francis Bacon!

Indeed, one of the most fundamental factors creating power today is not truth itself but *the possession of truth*, knowledge, or information. The *information rich* overpower the information poor. This principle does not, however, establish a single integrated power structure in societies or organizations because one can distinguish at least three types of concentration of power over information. First, there are those who have more information, because of their leadership positions which puts them at the center of flows of information.

A second type of information power comes from those who may not be in leadership positions at all but rather because they live in the contexts of the most numerous, mass popular sectors sharing the most typical life experiences. These are typically the "powerless," the employees, unskilled laborers, the simple masses, or those who identify most deeply with the interior of the nation (contrasted with those who identify with transnational cultures). In this context, they can begin to understand how "the common man" thinks, what are the most popular tastes, and how the mass of public opinion is formed.

Finally, there is a third group in most modern societies who have information power because it is their role to gather information and articulate in the mass media what people are trying to express. These are most typically journalists and others who work in communications. They can, at times, through their access to knowledge overpower the other two groups.

This very simple sociological model cannot be applied directly to the Church even though one can easily spot three analogous groups: the hierarchy, the faithful, and the theologians, which, *as such,* do not belong to any of the other two groups. But the "knowledge" which is available in the Church is not factual information or humanly validated experience, but divinely revealed truth. This is a truth whose "possession" confers incomparably more power that ordinary information because it is uniquely salvific. From this comes the temptation to monopolize the possession of truth, excluding other groups from access to it except through the privileged holders. In this claim to exclusiveness lies the very essence of heresy. One would not be a heretic were not the person to declare himself or herself uniquely orthodox and say that all others are heretics. Yet, is not the official ecclesiastical reaction to heresy, namely, excommunication, but an open, direct attempt to exclude a group of faithful from the possession of revealed truth?

It is the mission of the hierarchy in its magisterial function to preserve and promote the right understanding of revealed truth. This truth is not a kind of "information," the knowledge of which should be reserved to the members of the hierarchy. Indeed, the hierarchy have no more direct access to it than any of the ordinary faithful; they are but the witnesses and judges of the faith *of the Church.* From this situation, however, emerges a twofold temptation. One is to distort the role of the Magisterium so that it is transformed from a service for truth into the only source of knowledge of truth, stipulating that revealed truth can be and may be learned only from the teaching of the Magisterium. This would give the Magisterium an enormous and virtually limitless power, making it indispensable for salvation. In fact, not only some members of

the hierarchy but many of the faithful are willing victims of this temptation. They attribute to the Magisterium a power concerning truth that is
not consonant with its divine institution.

The other temptation consists in extending the charism received by
the Magisterium to many other contexts of ecclesial life, claiming infallibility for speculative statements not concerned with Revelation or for
practical pastoral decisions.

A charism meant to be a warrant of truth is then misused to protect
power structures. Strangely enough, such undue extension of infallibility
is promoted most strongly by persons who are acting outside of the
Magisterium, especially, bishops acting as individuals or ordinary parish
priests. Far too often parishes have been governed by infallible pronouncements "from the pulpit."

The processes of these temptations become much more complex,
however, in the case of the theologians. They have no magisterial
charism. Their specific function is not foreseen in ecclesiology, but nevertheless it seems indispensable for the best understanding and teaching of
revealed truth. Because of this seemingly "indispensable" role, theologians
have gained ever increasing power and importance in the life of the
Church and the misuse of this power seems ever easier. Theologians may
misuse their highly developed, specialized competence in their disciplines
(far beyond the competence of the faithful or even the bishops), a competence which has meaning only in so far as it is at the service of both the
faith of the ordinary laity and the teaching of the Magisterium. Theologians have a source of power and superiority which can tempt them to consider themselves the judges of the judges of the faith of the Church, and,
finally, establishing themselves as the judges of what is correct to believe.
They become the "dominators of the faith of the faithful" instead of being
its servants (cf. II Cor 1:24). They transform their competence in their
disciplinary science into straight ecclesiastical authority. The high esteem
that many of the laity attribute to theologians, at times giving more credit
to their statements than to the pronouncements of the Magisterium, shows
that such distortion is not a purely theoretical possibility.

The laity, too, the "simple faithful," may also misuse their participation in truth as a source of power, claiming a position which, in their own
estimation and in the views of some theologians, eclipses even the Magisterium. The temptation may be twofold. On the one hand, groups of the
laity, relying on what they have learned in catechism or from certain
preachers, may proclaim that they are the only ones who preserve the
authentic and pure faith. They accuse the theologians, the parish pastors,
the bishops, and even the Pope of infidelity to Christ's message or to the
traditional teaching of the Church. With such claims, the path to heresy is
a short and easy one.

In contrast to this sort of temptation, some, relying on the very true insight that Christian faith has its original seed in practical Christian life, proclaim their own lived experience, especially their collective experience, as a source and a norm for the knowledge of faith. In their opinion, theologians and the Magisterium have the function of simply ratifying and explaining the lived experience of these laity. Indeed, they would see the Magisterium learning from this lived experience. A true relationship—that both the Magisterium and theologians are at the service of the faith of the laity—is misinterpreted in terms of a structure of power.

Two symptoms are characteristic of all of these distortions which misuse truth as an instrument for gaining power: the reduction of truth to mere formulas and an overabundance of pronouncements. To begin with the last mentioned, an overload of often useless Church documents and magisterial pronouncements are an indication that the hierarchy tries to exert power, even oppressive power, through its mission of truth. Likewise, theologians and the laity may become overly loquacious in their striving to get power and to contest power, in a sense, trying to monopolize the truth.

The other symptom of misuse—reducing truth to formulas—is even more relevant to communication in the Church. By reducing truth to formulas and limiting the Word of God to these formulas, one renders the truth an appropriate instrument for domination. Formulas are always simplifications, and what is simplified is more manageable and more "effective", making a complex reality more easily applicable to many circumstances. Formulas are at least partially unintelligible, and this unintelligibility gives them an aura of transcendence and of mystery, adding to their force. Formulas are also impersonal; by using them, one is not directly committed to truth. One may handle them like a sword that injures the other but leaves oneself untouched. If there is no "I" or "We" to be found in pronouncements of faith, something is wrong with it from a communications point of view, just as there is something wrong from the perspective of faith itself. To be sure, formulas are meant to be clear, at least on first impression; they allow a clear distinction between those who hold to them and those who do not. Truth, whose nature is to gain consensus and to build up community, is distorted by the use of formulas to provoke dissent and to achieve separation. Let it be clear that by these formulas we mean as well catchwords of theologians or ecclesial communities, catchwords that are simply repeated, as well as unassimilated formulas of the catechism.

All of these temptations achieve what truth should not do, but what power does by its very nature: separate persons into two categories, dividing them into followers and enemies, into camps of the "orthodox" and "heretical," those who are "faith-rich" and those who are "faith-poor."

2. Power substituted for truth

A second distortion of the Church's communication is only theoretically distinct from the first one; in practice, it appears as its continuation, induced by "passing the limit." Both distortions occur when we privilege power over truth in communication, but the first does this by using truth as a kind of power while the second considers truth so weak that communication must rely on power.

In practice, the use of *truth as power* tends to reduce it to pure formulas which, being weak in themselves, become forceful only in the use that is made of them. Thus, the abuse of truth as if it were power naturally leads to its *substitution by sheer power*. The very nature of the Church allows those who hold more power to communicate in a distorted way much more easily. However, there are in the Church various spurious kinds of power which allow that virtually any member of the Church may use such a distorted form of communication. The analysis of these abuses in terms of the three major groups we have outlined—hierarchy, the laity, and the theologians—is a helpful approach.

Members of the hierarchy are endowed with sacramental and hence, with pastoral power. Their very office puts them in a true position of power in the Church. There is an obvious danger that they will make use of this sacramental, pastoral power even in their magisterial function, not content to simply propose the truth, confident in its own convincing force. Using one's power to impose or inculcate the revealed truth is always a sign of hidden unbelief. The most common case of such abuse is a misreading of what is authority. Authority in its true evangelical meaning is the force inherent in God's own word, a force that resides even in those who have the mission of announcing this word, imitating, by doing so, Christ the servant. Yet, authority has often come to assume, even in ecclesial contexts, its profane meaning, becoming a power of command over others. If authority is understood in this way, the Magisterium then *commands* the faithful to accept its pronouncements by virtue of pure obedience rather than by a loving assent to God's truth. What most characterizes this distortion is loss of transparency. By calling for obedience, members of the hierarchy exempt themselves, at least partially, from giving evidence in argument and from personal witness. While truth is transparent, power likes to hide itself. One of the most common instruments of power is the use of secrecy. Secrecy not only reserves full knowledge to a very few; it also tends to hide failures of those who exercise authority. Another instrument of power is censorship; pretending to eliminate what is untrue, it tends to conceal certain inconvenient aspects of truth under the pretext that they are not healthy for the ordinary people. Other instruments of power commonly used are disciplinary measures against dissent, the most radical of which is excommunication, a negative exercise of sacramental power. More positively, authority may demand an oath of loyalty or a statement of assent. The most bland of all instruments, but at times the most manipulative, is the distribution—or withholding—of sought after favors.

In so far as the Church is also a human society, the use of all of these instruments of power may be seen as quite legitimate, used supposedly in the service of truth and because of "human fragility." Insofar as they denote a weakness in those who have the mandate to safeguard the revealed truth, they damage the integrity of Christian witness. This applies even more strongly to those Christians who have no pastoral power but seek out some instruments of power in order to defend their own private interpretation of God's word. Today, theologians and the ordinary laity tend to be more conscious of the specific instruments of power that are at their disposal.

In the Middle Ages, theologians had a quasi-magisterial authority, at least at the level of the consensus among theologians. Theological faculties, with that of Paris holding a preeminent position, exercised a supervision of orthodoxy which is today the privilege of the Congregation for the Doctrine of Faith. Consequently there is presently little attention given to the consensus among theologians, while personal theological opinions are in high esteem. Such personal opinions are often promoted with all the available means to strengthen their own authority: interviews, promotion of bestselling books, frequent appearance on TV talkshows, and, as a last bastion of power hard to overcome, the protection afforded the professional status of theologians as university professors. The theologian as media star is today probably the most effective communicator of the Christian message. The ecclesial power of the theologian is reinforced by public opinion which hails outspokenness as a defense of the truth—or at least as more interesting and entertaining than duller forms of Magisterium. It is no wonder that the hierarchy is nowadays tempted to fight dissenting theologians with similar but not always specifically Christian arms.

The laity, in addition to the power they enjoy as the basis of public opinion in the Church,[5] have learned to use more effectively in many parts of the world a quite specific and forceful instrument of power in order to promote what they think is or should be Christian truth: the financial support they give to the Church and to the Church's institutions. Each group will support only those institutions, initiatives or movements that represent what this group thinks should be the norm of Christian truth. Naturally, doctrinal tendencies which touch the sympathies of the richer Christians become more influential than those representing the simple and the poor. Wealth, however, is not always a good criterion for authentic

---

5. See Pius XII, *La stampa cattolica e l'opinione pubblica in Discorsi e radiomesaggi*, 11 (1949/50), 363-372, and K. Rahner, *Free Speech in the Church* (New York: Sheed and Ward, 1959), pp 9-50.

evangelical values. The extreme form of financial power occurs when the
faithful simply refuse to support what they do not agree with. A recent
case is that of a Swiss diocese where the laity refused to support their
bishop to express their dissent with his views.

All the examples we have alluded to in this section show rather "un-
evangelical" features. They clearly manifest themselves as distortions of
authentic Christian communication. What these strategies bring about is
the opposite of communion in the Church. Instead, they build up an atmosphere of suspicion between the hierarchy and the faithful, between
bishops and theologians, breeding mistrust of the Magisterium and theological sciences. Everywhere there emerge tensions and divisions among
the laity, among theologians and among the bishops themselves. Power
shows its true face as a force of separation rather than of integration. Not
surprisingly, one common reaction to this situation in the history of the
Church is the quest for the utopia of an utterly powerless communication.
This is the third type of distortion, which we will consider next.

3. Sharing instead of power and truth

This third kind of distortion of the Church's communication demands less analysis than the preceding two because it deals with an ideal
rather than a reality and it is a less common abuse in the Church with all
of the rich experiences such abuses cast up. Yet for all its idealism it can
be a dangerous delusion that should be mentioned. It stresses the experience of communion in the Church in such an exclusive and radical way
that it becomes a type of evangelical anarchy.

One would think that participatory sharing would be the very essence of ecclesial life. Here, truth and power would play only subordinate
roles, gaining their ecclesial existence as byproducts of sharing. Is not
truth essentially consensus, and is not the "*consensus fidelium*" the
authentic site of the development of Christian truth? Are not the sacraments communitarian celebrations, and does not sacramental power flow
out of the delegation of the minister by the community as the presiding
officer in these celebrations? Is not collegiality the basis of hierarchical
structure in the Church, and should not bishops be elected by their dioceses? If one could characterize these ecclesiological tendencies with a
political catchword, direct participatory democracy would be the best.

We have deliberately exaggerated the formulation of these frequently
heard demands in order to reveal their ecclesiological inadequacy. It is
true that both the ministry of truth and the ministry of ecclesiastic power
have been instituted to foster communion, because communion is the essence of churchly life.

But this does not mean that communion is the only structural dimension of the Church nor is it the origin of all the other structures. God's
word given to mankind, the sacraments which are a working presence of

this word, and the "administration" (originally an ecclesiastical word if taken in its etymological meaning) of these gifts of God are even more fundamental than communion. They *bring about* communion; they do not stem from it. Henceforth, loving sharing cannot be the only norm for good communication in the Church; it has to be done in accordance with truth (namely, in accordance with the Gospel and with the Church's tradition), under the guidance of pastors who get their authority from Christ and not from the community. Pure sharing in a spirit of love may be a romantic ideal; it is not the adequate expression of churchly communion.

IV. The Right Way to Communicate in the Church

Our typology of possible distortions contains already some indications of the right way to procede. It does not consist simply in doing the opposite of what the distortions are; they are distortions because they disfigure a truth that they still contain. To find the right way, one has to single out this truth, avoiding its distortion. The last distortion we considered is also the least distorting; it comes closer to the right way. Communion is actually the essence of the life of the Church, and all ecclesial communication has to seek this as a goal. Sharing in love is indispensable for achieving this. But it cannot substitute or rule out the other two factors which are constitutive for the Church: revealed truth and sacramental power. If, as we have seen, the reduction of one of these factors to the other makes sharing difficult and *therefore* distorts ecclesial communication, the right way of communicating must consist in an interplay between the two factors that preserve both and that foster sharing. Indeed, in ecclesiological contexts, truth and power are not antagonistic but complementary, both of them originating from God's self-communication to mankind. Revealed truth is powerful by itself, and *therefore* truth is not to be abused as an instrument of power. Ecclesial power is truthful by itself and *therefore* cannot overrule truth. Both are what they are by the force of the Spirit, who animates both, being the very source and force working within all communication and communion in the Church.

1. Powerful Truth

Authentic truth is by its very nature self-evident and hence convincing. It does not need any support from an outside authority or from pressure groups. "*Veritas norma sui et falsi.*"[6] This philosophical principle, however, does not apply to Christian truth. Christian truth is revealed, precisely because it cannot be self-evident to human beings. Even where

---

6. Spinoza, *Ethica* II, prop. 43, Scholium. "Truth is the norm of itself and of falsity."

faith is concerned with so called "natural truth" (the existence of God, the precepts of natural law . . .), revelation adds an otherwise unreachable surplus of meaning and security.[7]

To gain knowledge of a truth which is not self-evident, one must come to know it by communication through another person, a process which seems, at first glance, to be very similar to the way that we get any information. Communicated information, however, is only more or less probable and "credible," while revealed truth is truth implying certainty and a special kind of "evidence."[8] The apostles and evangelists are not simply transporters of information, but *witnesses*; and witnesses are those who hand on the apostles' testimony down through the ages. The fact that Christian truth has been communicated to us through witnesses does not detract from this testimony, but adds to its convincing force.

Indeed, the revealed word is directed not only to our conviction, but also our conversion, that is, a radical change of practical attitudes and of the overall orientation of our life. It is impossible to give a purely theoretical assent to Christian truth. The witness who conveys this message must also, therefore, be a converted person. This presents to me a primary form of evidence: in receiving the message from the witness, I perceive at the same time that this message is effectively changing his life. Thus, there must be something "real" and "true" in the message. The evidence increases insofar as the conversion of this witness appears more authentic, namely, insofar as the life of the witness, as it is lived daily, is more coherent in itself and consonant with the message that is presented. Saints are the best witnesses and the most credible communicators of Christian truth.

There is still another dimension of the communication of the witness which is of profound importance: it opens up a vision of truth which transcends the witness. No witness can give witness to himself or herself; the more this witnessing is transparent to the "other," the better it is. In the case of Christian witness, this "other" is not an abstract or impersonal truth, but another person, Christ. Every Christian gives witness in his or her life to Christ, to his life, to his death and resurrection and, through all of this, to his teaching. This leads to a close identification of the Christian witness with Christ and, thus, an unusual empowerment of the witness through this union with Christ, for Christ himself was a witness and

---

7. As Vatican I clearly stated: "Not only can there be no conflict between faith and reason, they also support each other since right reason demonstrates the foundations of faith and, illumined by its light, pursues the science of divine things, while faith frees and protects reason from errors and provides it with manifold insights" (Denzinger-Schönmetzer 3019).

8. Epistemologically speaking, faith is closer to evidence than to belief, receiving from the *lumen fidei* it own specific evidence. See, for example, P. Rousselot, *The Eyes of Faith,* reprint of 1910 ed. (New York: Fordham, 1990).

presented himself as such. Far from weakening the evidence of Christian truth, this second level of mediation is strengthening and providing foundations for it. In Christ's "words and deeds,"[9] one perceives such a coherence between message and messenger that it surpasses all self-evidence of naturally known truth. Theologically speaking, this is trinitarian evidence, the evidence of Christ's identity with the totally Other. In communication terms one could say that here, and here alone, "the medium is the message."[10]

All this reveals that Christian truth is, by itself, powerful. It is brought forth by the force of witness, it tends to bring about conversion and it is transparent, in the last instance, to divine self-evidence. This is why the Scriptures, from the beginning to the end, insist on the self-imposing force of the "word."[11] A very first precept for Christian communication is, therefore, not to obfuscate or block this divine power of the message by human means or stratagems. Certainly it should not be reduced to mere formulas or opportunistic instrumentalism.

Generally speaking, all authentic Christian communication has to take the form of *witness*. If our analysis is correct, witness is not only a very important but, indeed, the primary form of Christian communication. Witness must be the foundation and model of all other forms and "mediations" for communicating Christian truth. Whoever communicates the Christian message directly and explicitly, by whatever means, has to do it as a *witness*, however imperfect that witnessing may be. This is true whether a person be a member of the hierarchy, a great preacher or a simple catechist or the ordinary lay Catholic in daily contact with believers and unbelievers. Even in indirect (mediated) and implicit communication there is always a dimension of witness, whether this is presenting symbolic figures or stories of Christian witness (for example, in film and television) or whether a communicator is presenting a very personal message. Finally, witness must be central to the communication within the Church, among Christians of different traditions and in the style of dialogue with non-Christians.

2. Truthful Power

Witness alone, however, is not sufficient if one wishes true Christian communication. A dissident theologian or a televangelist may be a powerful witness, but they are not necessarily models for Christian communication. The use they make of their power is always the test of the authenticity of their message and, indeed, this use of power may be in direct

---

9. Vatican II, *Dei Verbum*, n. 2.

10. With a much fuller meaning than in the famous slogan of M. McLuhan referred to in Ch. 1 of *Understanding Media* (New York: McGraw-Hill, 1964).

11. See, for example, Gen 1:3 ss; Is 55:10-11; I Thess 1:5; 2:13; Apoc 19:13.

contrast to the Christian message. As we have seen, Christ endowed his Church with sacramental, pastoral, and magisterial power in order to support the message and make it truly effective. Any other kind or use of power would be extraneous to or contrary to Christian truth, since it constitutes a kind of purely human "communication" parallel to the Christian witness and easily in contradiction with it. All use of power in Christian communication has to be at the service of Christian truth, and, since this truth seeks to bring about communion, at the service of love.

Here, too, an examination of Christ the witness will give us fuller insight. Christ's teaching was a powerful teaching, thanks to a source of power which was not his own but bestowed on him by the Father who gave witness to his Son and confirmed his witness with miracles (John 5:36; 10:25; Acts 2:22). This divine witness to Christ is also a person, the Spirit. Immediately after the baptism of Jesus at the Jordan and after the public manifestation of the Father's witness to his Son, Jesus is lead "by the Spirit" (Matt 4:1) to his temptations in the desert, a test of his messianic power. The test ends with a triple refusal: the refusal to use his power as his own and for his personal purposes; the refusal to ask God for more power, however useful for his mission this might seem to be; and the absolute, final refusal to accept power from a source other than God. Consequently, Jesus repeatedly warns his disciples about any abuse of power. "Anyone who wants to be great among you must be your servant, and anyone who wants to be first among you must be your slave just as the Son of Man came not to be served but to serve, and to give his life as a ransom for many" (Matt 20:27-28). Power, in an ecclesial context, has to be manifested in service.

In communication terms and as a norm for Christian communication, this authentic use of power calls for *transparency*. Transparency with regard to the source of power, making it evident that this power stems from God and avoiding all claims to power where power is not given (for example, in the case of the merely scientific authority of theologians). There must also be transparency in the use of power, avoiding unnecessary secrecy and obscure manoeuvres, making clear that power is completely at the service of truth and of loving communion. All this will pose strict limits in the use of ecclesiastical power. Transparency should also be present in the message, not imposing it by blind obedience, but allowing the message to give evidence to its own truth and value. Finally, transparency must be present in the witnessing given by those who hold positions of authority: admitting one's human fragility, recognizing one's limits and errors, ready to use one's authority in the service of love and communion. Only an authority capable of admitting and correcting its errors can be "true" authority, that is, an authority capable of growing and enabling others to *grow (augere, auctoritas)* in truth.

3. The truth of the powerless

All we have said so far about power applies only to intraecclesial communication. There is no ecclesial power *"ad extra,"* except the power of witness. Christian communicators will often find themselves as powerless as Christ chose to be. They may be communicating through Church-owned media, which are often smaller, poorer, and less powerful than commercial or state-owned media. Or they may be collaborating in some form of public or commercial media with the necessity of limiting their personal influence and the possibilities of giving public Christian witness according to the wishes and policies of these media.

It is important to recognize that this *de facto* situation may not be detrimental to Christian communication for it is consonant with the very essence: its powerlessness. Theologically speaking, the effectiveness of Christian proclamation is linked to a lack of human power that is much more than, for example, simply non-violence. Paul had to learn that divine power "is at its best in weakness" (II Cor 12:9) and in poverty. These are always the signs of authentic preaching (Matt 10:8 ff; St. Francis and St. Ignatius . . .). As Congar has noted, all reformation of the Church has to strive to make her more of a servant and more poor. This leads necessarily to the "option for the poor." In short, the martyr is the Christian witness in the fullest sense and, therefore, is also the best Christian communicator.

This does not mean, obviously, that all Christian communicators have to become martyrs. Martyrdom is a gift one cannot strive for, and a communicator who considers himself or herself a "martyr," simply because he or she opposes the "system," may not be truly a witness but only ridiculous. Nevertheless, martyrdom offers a hermeneutic key and a kind of norm for the everyday Christian experience of powerlessness. Lack of success, inadequacy in spite of efforts, lack of effectiveness due to factors beyond our control in contexts where Christians can have little power over the media and structures of communication are not necessarily negative signs for Christians. One must strive for professional competence in whatever means of proclaiming the gospel seem most effective and consonant with the gospel message itself. But having to use the less powerful means of communication often associates the Christian communicator with the poor and the powerless who are the blessed ones, the ones to whom the Kingdom is promised. By identifying oneself with the information and communication poor, the Christian communicator becomes a powerful sign for the coming of the Kingdom, which is "not of this world" (John 18:36) and does not impose itself by human means.

A final distinctive and normative feature of Christian communication is, therefore, its *alternative character*. This means alternative firstly in its use of media: the weaker, smaller, less pretentious media are normally more consonant with the Christian message than the more "powerful" and elitist. Christian communication will also be alternative in terms of the values that it promotes and the goals that it sets for itself: personal conversion and the building of communitarian communion rather than simply persuasion and effectiveness. By being faithful to its alternative mission, Christian communication may gain its own "visibility" in public communication and enrich that public communication with unexpected values.

4

Symbolic Forms of Communication

Gregor Goethals

Academicians often find themselves lost in the labyrinth of highly specialized disciplines, groping for some new evidence or insight to offer to col-
leagues. When we try, however, to examine the symbolic forms of religious
communication—myth, ritual, icon—we find that we must emerge from our
academic enclaves and join others—theologians, church historians, cultural
anthropologists, sociologists, liturgists, philosophers, art historians, and artists. The study of symbols is not the exclusive province of any single
scholarly or professional field. Nor is the view from only one perspective
sufficient in itself to encompass the richness of our sacramental experiences.

Artists and art historians look to other disciplines for philosophical
and methodological presuppositions that may broaden the discussion about
the formation and content of religious symbols. One fundamental starting
point for interdisciplinary conversation is that there is a basic sacramental
dimension to human experience—the ability to render visible or to create
signs and words that make communication possible. The anthropologist W.
E. H. Stanner called it "the metaphysical gift," one which permits self-
transcendence so that one "can stand 'outside' or 'away from' oneself, and
turn the universe, oneself, and one's fellows into objects of contemplation." Stanner, like Max Weber and others, has called attention to another
important point of departure in symbol analysis: "a 'drive' to try to 'make
sense' out human experience and to find some 'principle' in the whole human situation."[1] Weber described this as "the metaphysical needs of the
human mind as it is driven to reflect on ethical and religious questions,
driven not by material need but by an inner compulsion to understand the
world as a meaningful cosmos and to take up a position toward it."[2]

---

1. W. E. H. Stanner, "The Dreaming," *Reader in Comparative Religion, An
Anthropological Approach*,eds., William A. Lessa and Evon Z. Vogt (Evanston, IL
& Elmsford, NY: Row, Peterson and Company, 1958), p. 518.
2. Max Weber, *The Sociology of Religion* (Boston: Beacon Press, 1964), p. 117.

These two assumptions are basic to the study of symbolic forms and their meanings. "Meaning" is of course an abstract, elusive term. What humans grasp is a palpable order or pattern, concrete acts or images that locate us in both time and space. The late art historian Sir Kenneth Clark believed that "art"—especially in premodern, traditional societies—was essentially a response to the human need for meaning. To him the form-creating impulse is evident in both "fine" and "applied" art. Both are sacramental. Each attempts to give visible, tangible meaning to that which is invisible. Moreover, their value "depends on the degree to which they can be felt and accepted by others." As a historian, he observed that the sacramental character of art is "far more easily achieved when the principal objects of belief have already been given a symbolic form which is generally recognized and accepted; in other words, when there is an established mythology and iconography."[3] In earlier cultures image makers—painters, sculptors, stone masons, ceramists, architects—had to visualize an accepted immaterial order that helped make sense of personal and communal experience. Within and outside religious buildings. sculptures and pictures made visual sacred stories and presented concrete images of human history and destiny.

For some contemporary persons, however, traditional religious spaces and rituals, myths and icons have lost the power to draw them into adventures of the spirit. When people experience disenchantment, boredom, or simply become indifferent to institutional religions, what kinds of symbols seem alive and vital to them? Where do such people turn to escape the dreariness, monotony, and sometimes hopelessness of day-to-day living? Where in today's world do we find the sacramental impulse aligned with the drive for meaning? Are there multiple levels of religious symbols? How do we sort them out?

The pluralistic nature of late twentieth-century societies does not allow single or simple answers to these questions. By turning the TV dial or glancing at the morning newspaper we are readily aware of a multiplicity of worldviews, lifestyles, and conflicting ideologies communicated through various myths, icons, and rituals. The communication revolution has shown us an enormous range of habits of the heart, body, and mind that co-exist on our planet. Mainstream religious groups exist side by side with a host of others, especially in large, densely packed American cities. In a television series Joseph Campbell popularized the diversity of the religious imagination, holding PBS viewers spellbound as he recounted myriad ways in which human beings over time have sought communion with gods, goddesses, and cosmic forces. Meanwhile, in a mundane, commonplace world millions of people find mythologies and rituals in sports, mu-

---

3. Kenneth Clark, "Art and Society," in *The Nature of Art,* eds., John Glassner and Sidney Thomas (New York: Crown, 1964), pp. 62, 64.

sic, movies, the theater—indeed in all the arts. Thus, in spite of what some of us sense as a lack of interest in traditional religious forms, we live in a world teeming with all kinds of rituals and myths. I would like to explore some ways in which the sacramental impulse has manifested itself in popular and high culture.

Victor Turner and Mircea Eliade were among the first to pick up traces of myth and ritual that had, as Turner observed, migrated directly or indirectly from the religious domain into other cultural areas such as aesthetics, politics, theater and the arts.[4] Eliade discerned "survivals" and "camouflages" of myth and ritual in comic-strip characters or folklore heroes. Less attention, he noted, has been paid to the survival of ritual among the elite, especially those concerned with artistic creation. For him, today's artists and critics are caught up in a special "gnosis that has the advantage of being at once spiritual and secular in that it opposes both official values and the traditional churches."[5]

While following up the leads of these two scholars, we will maintain a cautionary view expressed by others. They argue that important distinctions may become blurred, especially when one moves from highly specialized concepts of religious rituals, based upon fieldwork data, to more loosely constructed ones. Jack Goody, for example, has protested that the concern for "secular ritual" in contemporary society introduces an inclusiveness that renders the term "ritual" meaningless.[6]

Still there are dimensions of museum and popular arts which are difficult to understand or describe without some reference to traditional forms of religious communication such as myth, ritual, icon, contemplation, or pilgrimage. One way to take Goody's concerns seriously is to note *analogical* relationships between religious and secular sacraments. Using historical forms of religious communication as analogues, we can proceed to compare and contrast contemporary symbolic expressions, pointing out both likeness and difference. At the same time, we may see how the sacramental impulse to render visible invisible values and meanings manifests itself outside of traditional congregations.

Some basic questions are these: What are some of the *residual* elements of religious symbolizations found in the visual arts? In what ways do these residues conform to or contradict the characteristics of traditional religious myths, rituals, and icons? Have some of the forms of popular

---

4. Victor Turner, "Variations on a Theme of Liminality," *Secular Ritual,* eds., Sally F. Moore and Barbara G. Myerhoff (Assen and Amsterdsm: Van Gorcum, 1977), p. 36.

5. Mircea Eliade, *Myth and Reality* (New York: Harper and Row, 1963, p. 184, 189).

6. Jack Goody, "Against 'Ritual': Loosely Structured Thoughts on a Loosely Defined Topic," *Secular Ritual,* eds., Sally F. Moore and Barbara G. Myerhoff (Assen and Amsterdam: Van Gorcum) p. 27.

and high culture appropriated and transformed—or distorted—traditional modes of religious communication? We shall look, first, at some aspects of popular culture; following that the focus will shift to high art. Finally, we will attend to the question: How do religious institutions reclaim the sacramental impulse in a secular, religiously plural society?

I. Popular Culture

1. Ritual Space as Analogue

Ritual is a multifaceted religious form, so complex that its use as an analogue for certain experiences of popular culture could take us far beyond the scope of this chapter. Thus we shall narrow the subject by choosing one aspect: ritual space. Then we want to zoom in to look more closely at some transformations of ritual space brought about by television.

Space forms a special enclosure for the enactment of myth. Sacred and extraordinary, it is set apart from the ordinary spaces of daily life; but its quality does not depend upon architectural complexity or technology. Examples come from various cultures ranging from those which have only the simplest kind of material technology, such as the Australian aborigines, to medieval Christendom, which is enormously complex in art and architectural forms. The indigenous tribes of Australia had no permanent architecture or written language. Their artifacts were extremely simple, fashioned from bark and small branches, colored with paints composed of organic materials, and textured with feathers or human hair. They shaped sacred space through elaborate ground drawings. During their rites they filled these boundaries with complex acts: mythic cycles, dance, song, myth, and simple ceremonial objects.

The cathedral at Chartres, by contrast, is one of the most elaborate ritual spaces of the western world. After a fire at the end of the 12th century, it was rebuilt with an elaborate stone masonry that continues to dazzle the mind and eye. The decades in which the northern and southern portals were built tangibly document a growing stylistic and symbolic sophistication, an increasing mastery of form. On the facades appeared a changing vision of saints, martyrs, and biblical heroes engaged in a divine mission. Yet all together the symbols within the cathedral and on its exterior tell the story of salvation.

Technology aside, however, the simple ground paintings of the Australian aborigines and the impressive space and imagery of Chartres may both be viewed on the same plane. Although radically different in form and symbol, these sacred enclosures are nonetheless similar in their function both provided space in which myths were enacted. Both defined a locale—one with complicated stone work, the other through marks on sandy ground—to accommodate patterned actions that created and celebrated an extraordinary world, one that everyday life could never offer. Throughout time, ritual spaces of varying degrees of technological sophistication have given people a place to escape the ordinariness, bewilderment, or pain of real life. Ceremonies momentarily offer a way out—or a different way of being—that cast day-to-day reality in a different light.

Throughout the United States today there are many specially bounded spaces deeply significant for those who gather there. The largest cities, for example, have major-league baseball and football teams which enjoy widespread community support. Many urban areas take pride in elaborate superdomes. Although these spaces are not identified with religion, many people look upon them as hallowed places; those who gather there are set apart and share important happenings. There they escape hum-drum routines of daily life. Reflecting on the quality of this space, a sports announcer described the stadium from he which was broadcasting as a "sanctuary from real life."

At special times and seasons important events occur—professional sports, rock concerts, political conventions. The sanctuary effect is reinforced by the cessation of "real" time within that space; temporal rhythms appropriate to particular events are created. We thus enter into a special time measured very differently from that time we spend in the office, in commuting, or in our homes. One might develop an argument that the sacred enclosures of time and space of the ancient and medieval world find their contemporary counterparts in the Super Bowl or Disneyland. In this chapter, however, we must narrow the focus, concentrating on the role of television in sensitizing us to ritual time and space and to ceremony. While most obvious in sports and entertainment, the audiovisual panoplies of TV have now become necessary in other spheres as well, especially in American politics.

2. *TV and Ritual Space*

We may gain access to many of these modern "sacred" places when we turn on the television set and tune in to special broadcasts. In a society where many mainstream religious congregations pride themselves on having "plain and simple" worship services, commercial telecasts of live events have introduced stunning visual effects and exciting dramatic movement in ceremonial space. Moreover, we have also discovered that audio-visual images seen on the tube are frequently more colorful and interesting than the ones our eyes can take in when we are aloft in the bleachers of the stadium or stuck in a crowd blocks away from where the action is. There are paradoxes here: Are we enjoying *watching*? Do we feel a genuine sense of participation? In either case, television technology has made us more sensitive to worlds created within sacred enclosures through which we transcend ourselves and the demands of everyday life.

Sports presentations prepared the way for video politics through camera techniques that introduced a wide range of spatial perceptions to TV fans. We are now accustomed to pictures of sports arenas from great distances. The viewer may "hang" from a blimp high above the playing field, looking down on the event like some indifferent, omniscient deity. This sweeping, grandiose view draws thousands of spectators, the players, and game into an abstract pictorial whole. Just as easily and quickly, however, the camera enables the fan at home to "leap" through space and suddenly be in intimate contact with quarterbacks, linemen, and tackles: inside the huddle, just behind the center as the ball is snapped, looking over the shoulder of the person holding the football for the kicker attempting a field goal, eyeballing the coach as he responds to the events on the field, or on the bottom of a massive heap of players piled up after the fumble. Thus television technology draws us into the immediacy of an extraordinary space with images that offer shifting perspectives.

Such dramatic "involvement" in space, however surrealistic, has also contributed to the formation of heroes. When their faces are framed so that they fill the space of the TV screen, the players soon develop a familiarity once reserved only for family members or close associates. Thus the technology of television allows us to penetrate so deeply and consistently into formal spaces that we "know" these sports stars in a special way. Intense TV portraits of competing athletes—detailed close-ups under stressful, decisive action—have been instructive to those responsible for political portraiture and rituals.

Throughout human history political rituals have been occasions for privileged individuals to enter into an extraordinary space. Perhaps the most significant event in the early days of television was the broadcast of the coronation of Elizabeth II. While many opposed their presence on this momentous occasion, cameras were permitted, and thousands of ordinary people, not just the nobility and aristocracy, saw their queen crowned. Even today, watching a replay of that ritual, we may sense its awesome dimensions. Cameras allowed viewers to hover above the Archbishop and watch as the crown, held high above the Princess' head, is slowed lowered and placed on her head. Then before us in full splendor is the Queen of England, Elizabeth II.

Even though American governance and politics offer no comparable ritual, still politicians and publicity firms have transformed all aspects of our democratic processes into made-for-television symbolizations of power. Conventions, campaigns, debates, election nights, inaugurations have all been ritualized through television's special passages into extraordinary spaces. Moreover, successful politicians carefully plan ceremonial events to draw viewers into other "sacred" spaces. In the distant past some people were allowed audiences with kings and religious leaders. Today press conferences and "photo opportunities" are, among other things, ways of opening up spaces normally shared by very few people. In our television-saturated society, we "enter" press conferences or "join" dignitaries through "photo opportunities." Thus the camera work of politics, like that of sports, can draw hundreds of thousands into the sacrosanct precincts of a president.

Ronald Reagan's television persona became legendary, so powerful that many critics now fault the press for the subservient, uncritical role it assumed.[7] From the beginning of his presidency to the last public appearances, he and his aides controlled the ritual spaces of television, filling them with dramatic, heroic action and stunning portraits. One may recall the ceremony at the White House, early in the Reagan era, that celebrated the return of the men and women who had been held hostage during the Carter years. Later, he was the chief celebrant when the torchlight of the Statue of Liberty, the nation's most revered symbol, was rekindled. And in one of the nation's darkest hours, he officiated as priest and pastor in commemorative ceremonies at NASA headquarters in Houston, Texas, for the men and women who had been killed in the Challenger disaster. Concerned people all over the nation could thus collectively express their grief and mourn the loss of these heroes. Only with the Iran-Contra scandal and Reagan's increasing ineptness in unrehearsed situations like press conferences, did the some of the public begin to suspect that their Commander-in-Chief had mastered the symbolism, but not the substance of leadership. Still the "Gipper" left office with the highest popular rating of any previous president.

To sum up: The ritualistic qualities of professional sports and politics are highlighted through the medium of television. It has re-emphasized in a secular society the importance of special times and places set apart from our day-to-day spatial and temporal experiences. It is important to underscore, however, that the use of ritual as an analogue does not obscure the differences between secular and sacred rituals. These too must also be explored. While this task is beyond the scope of this essay, we may nevertheless frame a few questions. What is the nature of the "sacred" present in the these secular events? Are there salvific dimensions to these cultural activities? Or do they just momentarily organize a sense of community? Where is the community? In the stands? At the conventions? Or among the millions of viewers? What is the nature of the self-transcendence attributed to TV "participation?"

3. Myth as Analogue

Scholars in religious studies differ in interpretations of the nature and function of myth, as well as of the significance and role of ritual.

---

7. See Mark Hertsgaard, *On Bended Knee: The Press and the Reagan Presidency* (New York: Farrar, Strauss, and Giroux, 1988).

Some see myth and ritual as autonomous symbolic expressions and contend that myth may be objectified in literary or visual forms. Others insist that myth and ritual are fundamentally correlative: ritual is the form that myth takes when it is lived. Myths of creation and redemption are enacted in the rites themselves, and communicants, through their participation in ritual time and space, actually live in the events. Thus during certain rituals of the Australian aborigines the great rainbow serpent of the plains, Bolong, creates all life anew. Ritual experience or "dreamtime" explains both how things are and how they came to be. Moreover, it is the continuing drama of creation that must be ritually enacted in order for life to go on. For Catholics the celebration of the Eucharist is an entry into the mystery and reality of grace. Through repeated participation our lives are continually recreated and transformed. In both instances myth and ritual are in a symbiotic relationship. More experiential than cognitive, ritual action is a confirmation of one's being and one's world, rather than an assent to dogma or belief.

A number of television critics and interpreters have also used the term "myth" in analyzing the medium. Several have adapted its broader sociological and anthropological signification. British critic Roger Silverstone, for example, sees myth as an identification of shared meanings and a setting of limits to what is socially acceptable. Even secular societies, he argues, need stories that are readily identifiable, that offer reassurance and establish boundaries. They provide "something of the elementary, the primary, the fundamental and stable." In this sense they answer a fundamental need for meaning, for individual and social identity. Sitcoms, dramas, and commercials sort out for us the truths and falsehoods, the values and disvaluations of a society. For Silverstone the mythic worlds of television operate as well in a conservative and restraining way—politically, socially, and economically.[8] In the narratives of popular TV mythology the conflicts and resolutions tend to reinforce existing institutions. If, however, in earlier times myths and rituals were also vehicles for change, can the same be said today?

4. TV Mythology

Clearly, comparing the myths of television with those enacted in traditional religions, strains the limits of analogy. At the same time, the tales of the good life that constantly flow across the TV screen do resemble religious myths that provided heroic models and dramatized virtues and vices for ordinary people. "The Cosby Show" similarly framed heroic images of contemporary life and the American Way. Some criticized the show for its unreality and misleading pictures of black family life, argu-

---

8. Roger Silverstone, "Mass Communication Relies on Narrative and Myth," *Media Development* 34/2 (1987):2.

ing that the plots are artificial and offer false hopes to millions of under-classed blacks. Bill Cosby, however, defended his show and its mythology: "To say that they are not black enough is a denial of the American Dream and the American way of life. My point is that this is an American family—an *American* family—and if you want to live like they do, and you're willing to work, the opportunity is there."[9]

Here Cosby is standing by one of the basic tenets of American public religion—that "liberty provides the framework for individual and collective development."[10]

In our fantasies and in reality the great American dream holds out the promise of individual growth and development and the chance of a better life. In this sense "The Cosby Show" is mythological, and many blacks and whites support its sentiments; furthermore, they see the characters as long overdue counterimages for previous negative stereotypes.

Television critics writing from a religious perspective worry that the mythology of the American dream has focused much too narrowly on an excessive individualism and consumerism. Moreover they point to the ways in which particular viewers are targeted, especially the youth culture. Music Television, for example, is said to be one of the most carefully researched and well planned business ventures in the industry. MTV was aimed specifically at the teen-age market. MTV provides a continuous flow of mini-mythologies that are superbly designed and filmed. Taken together they provide a musical, visual, and verbal iconography that tends to homogenize values. What to *be* is totally synchronized with what to wear and how to behave.

Whether or not we watch television, or even own a set, we are nonetheless wired into a symbolic circuitry that affects us all. When the vast majority of Americans get their news from this medium, a common worldview is transmitted. And while we do not know in detail how this affects the psyche of individuals, we do know that politicians, military leaders, and corporate executives well understand the need to control the images that can sway millions of people. While we may pay no attention to commercials, game shows, sports, soap operas, or sitcoms, these programs, taken collectively, combine to form a huge panoply of images that visualize the American Way.

There are many pressing questions about our TV mythologies: Has the ideology of individualism been countered in any way by a concern for community? Have commercials and half-hour sitcoms so saturated our minds with relatively quick, simple solutions that we are no longer capable of understanding complexity? Or perceive the lack of resolution that

---

9. Richard Zoglin, reported by Scott Brown, Dan Goodgame, and Jeannie Ralston, "Cosby, Inc.," *Time* (September 28, 1987), p. 60.

10. John F. Wilson, *Public Religion in American Culture* (Philadelphia: Temple University Press, 1979), p. 96.

often characterizes human situations? Are we sufficiently aware of ways in which even news programs generally follow a pattern set by a national socio-economic-political agenda? Are we conscious of popular culture's powerful force in communicating and sustaining ideology?

Persons interested in secular myths and rituals may profit by a second reading of George Orwell and Jacques Ellul. Both men clearly understood the power of an environment of symbols created by news and entertainment. Orwell's chief character in *1984,* Winston, worked in communications at the Ministry of Truth. This government agency was responsible for news, entertainment, education, and the fine arts. It supplied the citizens of Oceania with "newspapers, films, textbooks, telescreen programs, plays, novels—with every conceivable kind of information, instruction, or entertainments, from a statue to a slogan, from a lyric poem to a biological treatise, and from a child's spelling book to a Newspeak dictionary." Since the proletariat makes up about 85% of the population, special departments serve this group, creating culture "at a lower level." Newspapers for them contain "almost nothing except sport, crime and astrology." A specific literature, music, drama and general entertainment is designed for them: "sensational five-cent novelettes, films oozing with sex, and sentimental songs." Primary commodities for this group are "films, football, and beer.[11]

In his book, *Propaganda,* Ellul draws attention to what he calls a horizontal and rational propaganda that comes from within the society itself, particularly information. Modern information mechanisms, he says, "induce a sort of hypnosis in the individual, who cannot get out of the field that has been laid out for him by the information."[12] Ellul could have been describing the early weeks of the war with Iraq, when information, carefully controlled by the Bush administration, became a technological gnosticism, substituting high-tech images for the brutality of war with high-tech images. Not until pictures of burned bodies of civilians, removed from a bombed bunker in a Baghdad suburb, were seen on TV was war's fundamental fact—death—shown. Up to that time there were only occasional images of oil-soaked birds, caught in the blackened waters of the Persian Gulf.

It is not surprising that many artists see themselves in revolt against the forms, messages, and philosophies of popular culture. They frequently view themselves as free, critical spirits, less bound to the establishments of a materialistic society than their popular-culture counterparts. Moreover, unlike the painters or sculptors of earlier times, they are usually

---

11. George Orwell, *1984* (New York: Harcourt Brace Jovanovich, Inc., 1949), pp. 39, 61.

12. Jacques Ellul, *Propaganda: The Formation of Men's Attitudes* (New York: Random House, 1973), p. 87.

solitary seekers with no commitments to the ideologies of either church or state.

II. High Art

The high arts have a different symbolic function. They are more concerned with the engagement between an isolated viewer in the museum and particular works. Directors, quick to point out that their museums are increasingly popular, quote statistics showing that as many people go to museums as to sports arenas. Painting and sculpture, indeed all the so-called high arts, play a sacramental role in today's world. Yet the sacrality of the museum is quite different from that of the Red Sox stadium. Late in the twentieth century, the artist has assumed a shamanistic or priestly position; and a work of art is often accorded the reverence once given to a saint's bones.

After the arts were removed from the churches by radical Protestant reformers, painters, sculptors, glass workers—artisans in all media—sought new settings and patrons for their work and consequently new symbols appropriate to the changing functions of images. Religiously sensitive artists began to turn inward in search of symbols appropriate for their experience of spirituality. In the nineteenth century, Vincent Van Gogh, for example, commented that traditional religious subjects had lost their vitality. The few paintings he made with biblical subjects were copies of other artists' works. For van Gogh all of the physical world was spirit filled; thus a still life, an interior scene, or landscape could communicate a religious vision. A number of American painters held similar views. George Inness, deeply enmeshed in the writings of Swedenborg, produced landscapes that seem to reveal an animating spirit that moves through all the natural world.

In the early twentieth century two painters and theorists, Wassily Kandinsky and Piet Mondrian, as they searched for universal religious symbols, moved from landscapes—indeed from all representational images—to non-objective painting. Viewing art as a protest against their culture's materialism, they were convinced that art could be a source of spiritual reform. Both believed that abstract forms, lines, and colors communicated a common religious language, transcending national values and orientations. The business of the artist is to explore the soul, and the works produced can reveal metaphysical reality, leading others as well to venture into a spiritual realm.

In the existentialist mood of the late 1940s and 1950s critics and interpreters shifted the focus from universal symbols to the immediacy of the artist's spiritual experience. Many intellectuals of the time became involved in interpreting the visual arts and the role of the artist. The philosopher Suzanne Langer and the theologian Paul Tillich helped significantly to reinforce the idea of the artist as a solitary seeker—one who searches within in order to express the inexpressible emotions. To Tillich the artist was a religious hero who in the creation of a work expressed a fundamental human "courage to be." During the fifties—and continuing into the late twentieth century—the making of art became for many religiously inclined artists a meditative or ritualistic activity. For viewers, museums feature these symbols of the spirit. No need to worry about those graven images in churches—and in fact, no need to go there for religious symbols. And for artists no need to try to work with an iconography which seemed to have lost all meaning or significance for the world in which they lived. During the twentieth century artists have increasingly been viewed as seers and mystics who select and render visible symbols that express individual spiritual odysseys.

Susan Sontag observed that each era has to re-invent the project of spirituality for itself. In modern times, she noted, one of the most active metaphors for the spiritual project is "Art." We may ask: Why has this happened? Why has art making and art viewing become so sacrosanct in our world? There is no shortage of theories. Let us, however, quickly sketch some ideas, returning again to traditional modes of religious communication as analogues.

If we begin from the artist's point of view, the creative process becomes analogous to ritual experience. In both there is a similar pattern of withdrawal, transformation, and return.

1. Ritual as Metaphor for Art Making

When painters, sculptors, photographers embark on a project, there are important times when a deliberate effort has to be made to withdraw, to focus totally on the canvas, the stone, the negative. The discipline of shutting everything out of one's mind takes over. Consciousness becomes creative action. At this moment there is no assurance of a successful completion and sometimes not even an idea of where one is really going to end up. The preparation for this dislocation in time and space—gathering materials, setting up the developers or washes, priming the canvas—is a time of separating from everyday chores in order to give oneself fully to bringing into being something that does not currently exist.

Victor Turner used ritual as an analogue for understanding the inner dynamics of the performing arts, especially drama. He described the transformative stage of religious ritual as "liminal," which involved the supernatural. To describe comparable transfigurative experiences of secular rituals in modern dance or theater, the anthropologist invented the term "liminoid." Turner's concept is equally useful in understanding some aspects of creativity in the visual arts. Like a performer—a dancer, musician, or athlete—the visual artist may experience a period of heightened sensibilities in which the mind is consumed by colors, textures, lines, and shapes that engage and absorb one's total consciousness. For the visual artist the forms may seem almost out of control or even chaotic. Visual sensations are unreal, surreal, and fantastic. But this is not by any means only a cerebral experience. There is a physical stuff to paints, brushes, wood, chisels, canvas, spilled ink, the smell of turpentine, the feeling of hunger because you could not take time out to eat lunch.

In tension with the exuberance of materials that often seems inchoate is a passion for order and wholeness that moves first in one direction, then another, and another, and another, almost endlessly until things begin to fall into place. When order seems to gain a slight edge over disorder, other emotions or feelings surface. There is less apprehension now about the final outcome, even though one may have to start the whole thing over tomorrow. At such moments a sense of play may take over. As colors or lines are orchestrated, the creative sorting and assembling becomes almost like dancing. And while there's always the ever-present danger that like the dancer, one may "fall"—the water color may become blotchy or the chisel cut too deep and spoil the whole thing—nevertheless, at a certain stage, the playfulness and improvisation seem to work in harmony with the drive for an ordered, completed whole.

The theologian Etienne Gilson speculated on the religious dimensions of the creative process. He concluded that the exhilarating feeling some artists experience may come from the discovery that they are in contact with "the closest analogue there is, in human experience, to the creative power from which all the beauties of art as well as nature ultimately proceed." Its name, he said, "is Being."[13] Parallel sentiments were expressed by the early modern painter Paul Klee when he wrote in his diary: "Art is like Creation: it holds good on the last day as on the first." ". . . I place myself," he continued, "at a starting point of creation, whence I state a priori formulas for men, beasts, plants, stones, and the elements and for all the whirling forces. A thousand questions subside as if they had been solved. Neither orthodoxies nor heresies exist here."[14]

When they disengage themselves from the creative process and return to the everyday world, artists may feel renewed and better able to cope with the vicissitudes of ordinary routines. At the same time, the objects or images produced are in themselves an expression of that inner experience. The painted surface or textured marks become a testament to the raw emotions of the artist and the internal processes. While the artist may experience a sense of personal transformation, the images themselves represent a re-visioning of the world that may evoke in viewers a new perception of reality.

---

13. Etienne Gilson, *Painting and Reality* (New York; Meridian Books, 1961) p. 275.

14. Paul Klee, *The Diaries of Paul Klee: 1898-1918*, ed. by Felix Klee (Berkeley and Los Angeles: University of California Press, 1968), p. 345.

2. Meditation in the Museum

Walking through art galleries today you will find a mood of reverence, people speaking in muted voices, some sitting on benches concentrating on particular works for long periods of time. In the contemporary wing of the National Gallery in Washington, there is a room, almost chapel-like in its design, in which Barnett Newman's series of paintings, *Stations of the Cross,* are exhibited. There you will see persons making their way slowly, almost meditatively, as they process along the way that has been cordoned off for viewers. There is no way of knowing, of course, what attitudes individuals bring to these works. But there is a general air of piety, as though paying homage to the nearest thing we have to the holy in a secular society. Tom Wolfe has referred to art as the "religion of the educated classes." They "look upon traditional religious ties— Catholic, Episcopal, Presbyterian, Methodist, Baptist, Jewish—as matters of social pedigree. It is only art they look upon religiously." Wolfe further noted that he was not using religion as a synonym for "enthusiasm" but was specifically referring to Max Weber's objective functions of a religion: "the abnegation or rejection of the world and the legitimation of wealth."[15]

Very near the Newman *Stations of the Cross* is a gallery of similar size which also seems to serve as a meditative space. Both Mark Rothko and Newman are among the mid-twentieth-century painters most often viewed as artists with religious concerns. In this room Rothko's large luminous paintings by their scale and intensity almost engulf the viewer with reflected color. The mind is absorbed in radiating, vibrating colors. This is an aesthetic of emptiness, not unlike that of aniconic religious traditions, such as the Cistercian. The burden of a more precise religious interpretation becomes the responsibility of the viewer or critic. In another instance, the Interdenominational Chapel in Houston, Rothko's abstract paintings fuse with particular religious symbols when specific liturgies— Jewish, Protestant, Catholic, Buddhist—are enacted in that space.

Questions related to the sacramental impulse manifested in high art are quite different from those of popular culture. First there is the question of interpretation. In the 19th and 20th centuries the icon generally emerges from the imagination of the artist, reflecting his or her own spiritual odyssey. The subject may be anything—landscape, still life, non-objective painting or sculpture. This selection shifts to the individual beholder the burden of religious communication which in traditional icons is usually borne by the symbol itself. Can we expect viewers today to share the religious sensibilities of the artist?

---

15. Tom Wolfe, "The Worship of Art: Notes on the New God," in *Harper's* (October, 1984), pp. 61, 62.

Other issues may be related to the context in which a work appears. Does the placement of a painting give it an overtone of meaning? What difference does the museum atmosphere make? Would the same painting be conducive to meditation if it were placed in a bank? Does the placement in a commercial establishment change it from "religious" to "decorative?" What if we placed our meditative piece in a subway or bus station or a hotel lobby? Traditional icons were generally set in sacred spaces for both private and corporate worship. What kind of community is formed around the icons of museums? Does the experience of the artist in the process of creation become a form of private ritual or meditation? Where is there concern for corporate ritual or the formation of a community?

In this chapter I have contrasted the directions that the sacramental impulse has taken in popular and high culture. There is, however, a common ideology prevailing in both spheres. In both one can detect a governing ideology of individualism or personal self-fulfillment. This ideology is, of course, central to American public religion. In different ways both high and popular culture celebrate this faith.

For painter or sculptor, art-making continues to satisfy the need to make sense out of reality, to discover oneself, or to explore one's psyche or spirit. When successful, the artist becomes a rich celebrity, and the works of art produced sometimes take on an astronomical monetary value, providing investment possibilities for wealthy individuals or corporations. The same principles of individual success and self-fulfilment are disseminated throughout popular culture. Ads, sitcoms, MTV, sports, soaps, even news, reinforce the fundamental goals of our American Way of life liberty and material success. Yet, even as we package freedom and individualism for poor and middle-class consumers, critics voice concern about the informational entertainment monopolies which threaten genuine democratic principles.[16]

The significant difference between the two spheres of culture may lie in the audience or followers, not in the essential ideology. Popular culture inundates the entire population with symbols of a public religion—the American Way, understood as the pursuit of success, individuality, personal freedom. By contrast, high art has a large appeal to the educated and wealthy and enhances their visions of individuality, success, liberty and happiness. Rarely seen in either cultural sphere are prophetic images bold enough to criticize both the symbols and substance of each. Popular secular sacraments, from print and electronic media to theme parks, are in danger of producing a symbolic environment, without cultural self-examination or criticism. At the same time, as Tom Wolfe has pointed out, "high art" constantly runs the risk of being simply entertainment or high-priced investment commodities for those who can afford them.

---

16. See Ben Bagdikian, *The Media Monopoly* (Boston: Beacon Press, 1983).

III. Reclaiming the Sacramental Impulse

From what I have said one might surmise that in traditional religious institutions the sacramental impulse has somehow been lost and that now we have to go out and retrieve it. This is not what I am saying. The strength of churches, temples, and synagogues is that their symbols of self-transcendence, community values, and corporate worship are grounded in the experience of a divine Being. While concepts of a radical Other may vary, the history of sacraments begins with our attempts to communicate with a divine being and to share faith and values with others. Yet many theologians and artists believe that some of the traditional symbols have lost their meaning and are no longer adequate for the embodiment of faith in the present pluralistic world. They struggle to find appropriate forms through which traditional beliefs and practices take on new life in the complex, multi-leveled, materialistic world in which we live. Thus the challenges to contemporary religious institutions are both theological and formal. What kind of faith is meaningful for our time? And how can this be communicated? How do we give material expression to invisible values while all around us secular institutions are doing so much better at just that? What myths or rituals do religious groups offer in the United States, for example, that are more attractive and compelling than those associated with the American Way?

Stating the problem and actually trying to do something about it are obviously two different things. As a designer working with a variety of religious faiths, the first thing I try to do is to determine just where a church locates itself in relation to its tradition. Before anything can be proposed or even vaguely sketched it seems essential that minister or priest and congregation collectively examine their faith and liturgy. The artist should, if possible, take part in these reflections or at least try to get a clear understanding of the intangible faith which enlivens the church. Following that, the responsibility of the artist is to try to make visible these invisible convictions.

Many churches today may have very mixed congregations, rather than clearly defined denominational constituencies. Thus there is an even greater need for members to reflect seriously upon what symbols of faith are most important to them. Every individual church group in this nation would probably present a unique set of concerns or needs that would have to be addressed on a case-by-case basis. Nevertheless, let me broadly sketch some starting points. First we must recognize that there are historically two types of aesthetic associated with liturgical spaces the aniconic and the iconic.

Many congregations, especially in the Protestant tradition, adhere very strongly to an imageless aesthetic. But do not forget that even here —maybe especially here—the total symbolic space has to take careful account of the visual elements that frame liturgy and all of its various components. Whether intentional or not, the Cistercians and the Shakers created worship spaces of extraordinary beauty using the visual elements and principles of light, pure geometric shapes, and proportionality. Although there is no representational imagery in these traditions, the design, elements, and colors which shape the worship area may be very expressive forms. Implicit in the aniconic aesthetic is a certain empathy for the *via negativa*. Yet, as we know from St. Bernard and others, this kind of space may be filled with poetry, psalms, liturgy, sermon and scripture. To Bernard this aesthetic was absolutely essential for the monks' environment.

Later the reformers of the 16th century, John Calvin and Ulrich Zwingli, were to adopt an imageless aesthetic for all worshipers, not simply the monastic community. Many American churches have roots in this tradition. For such congregations the challenge is to re-examine their own beliefs, rituals, and symbols and to look critically at the current spaces that exist. The key question: Does a particular space bring vitality to the living liturgy? If there is no vital liturgical life in the congregation, then we should not wonder why rushing home to watch a televised football game becomes so attractive to parishioners.

Other religious groups have practiced an iconic aesthetic. In general, this aesthetic can be related to a more positive attitude toward material culture, especially representational imagery. These groups have followed the path of the *via affirmativa*. On the whole, this tradition has been more open to a variety of forms, including the depiction of myths, stories, legends within the liturgical space. Although the style and function differ considerably, both Roman Catholic and Eastern Orthodox churches have over centuries used images. Some of these have been integrated with architecture, while others are freestanding. Moreover there are opportunities for vestments and liturgical objects, and in large cathedrals there may be smaller chapels within the larger worship space.

One of the most articulate exponents of this tradition was Suger, the Abbot of St. Denis and a contemporary of St. Bernard. In contrast to Bernard who grudgingly accepted the use of images to instruct the unlearned laity, Suger's basic argument for beautiful objects in the church was not simply didactic. The Abbot believed that material beauty—in objects and images—sets us on a path of self-transcendence. To appreciate this today we would have to try to recover the connection between truth and beauty, spirit and form found in both classical and medieval philosophy.

Another challenge to churches in the iconic tradition would be to look critically at the symbols that may abound in the sanctuary. Do the representations there mean anything to the congregation or have they become more like a broken piece of furniture which one walks around rather than mend? Do members of the congregation know anything about the symbols that appear on the walls, vestments, or baptistry? Do they have to get outside of the church into the open air of secular society to find a symbolic environment in which they feel more at home?

The greatest challenge to churches in both the iconic and aniconic tradition is to understand the pervasive symbol system in which we all exist. Few people understand how in their day-to-day lives they are being sustained in an environment of symbols. Particular religious symbols are frequently lost—or worse, seem totally insignificant—in a great sea of competing icons, myths, and rituals that celebrate the American Way. The public is saturated with images of mythic, informational, and political authority. It is not at all clear, however, how much religious groups want to critique their own symbols in light of these larger cultural ones. This raises a serious question that goes far beyond the scope of this chapter the relationship between power, political and economic, and the production of an encompassing world of symbols. Crucial to the exploration of this issue is the role of a prophetic iconoclasm that constantly monitors and critiques the images of popular culture and the ideologies they support.

Can churches themselves get into the business of mass communication through the electronic media and thus compete with existing communications institutions? This is problematic. TV productions, for example, require massive amounts of money, and except for public broadcasting, the communications industries are big businesses which, like other large corporations, must show profits and answer to stockholders. Moreover, the forms and techniques of the electronic preachers illustrate what can happen when religious groups begin to mimic some of the techniques and substance of popular culture. On the other hand, independent producers, public radio and television organizations, and specially funded artists have shown that important alternative visions and voices may arise in a democratic society. We saw an example of this in the documentary film, *Roses in December,* which told the story of the four women murdered in Salvador. Churches and other institutions interested in mass communication might collectively support film or TV work of young artists who have a prophetic vision.

Ironically a fundamental problem for religious institutions is embedded in a pervasive sentiment present in both popular and high culture that religion has become a personal, highly individual matter—"so personal," Ernest Becker noted, "that faith itself seems neurotic, like a private fantasy." Becker pointed out that a human's lonely leap into faith has to be supported in some way. People need "pageants, crowds, panoplies, special days marked off on a calendar . . . something to give form and body to internal fantasy, something external to yield oneself to."[17] Thus the challenge to the creators of both high and popular images is to create meaningful images of faith that are palpable and shared.

---

17. Ernest Becker, *The Denial of Death* (New York: Free Press, 1973). P. 200.

Twentieth-century artists working in all media—paint, stone, mosaic, prints, photos, film, and television—have understood this basically human sacramental impulse. What is less clear is how they would move from the symbolization of an "I" to a "We." How could they take us beyond a solitary spiritual odyssey or an ideology of individualism and success into a commonly held faith? Still more basic is the question What is the nature of the faith that artists—both high and popular—are seeking to embody?

5

The Church as Communion and Communication

Klaus Kienzler

In its consideration of the nature of the Church of God, Vatican II articulated its deepest insights concerning the meaning of the communicative event between God and humanity in general and the understanding of the Church in particular. *The Constitution on the Church, Lumen gentium*, and subsequent documents refer to the Church above all as *communio* (communion). The Church is, in all its dimensions, the *communio* willed by God: with God, among all humans, and for the world. It is quite astonishing that Vatican II gave theology here a truly comprehensive "communication model" of the communion that is the Church and may not have really intended to. The 1971 postconciliar instruction, *Communio et progressio*, further developed this model of the Church and gave us a new understanding of Christian communication.

The 1985 Synod of Bishops reconfirmed the clear meaning of this fundamental concept of the Church, by making the following observation.

> The ecclesiology of communion is the central and fundamental idea of the Council's documents. *Koinonia*/communion, founded on Sacred Scripture, has been held in great honor in the early Church and in the Eastern churches to this day. Thus, much was done by the Second Vatican Council so that the Church as communion might be more clearly understood and concretely incorporated into life.

Having established the position of this concept within ecclesiology, the Synod went on to explain it more fully.

> What does the complex word *communion* mean? Fundamentally, it is a matter of communion with God through Jesus Christ in the sacraments. Baptism is the door and the foundation of communion in the Church. The Eucharist is the source and the culmination of the whole Christian life (cf. *Lumen gentium* 11). The communion of the eucharistic Body of Christ signifies and produces, that is, builds up,

the intimate communion of all the faithful in the Body of Christ which is the Church (1 Cor 10:16).[1]

According to this document, *communio* is first and foremost a theological expression. Is that all it is? We next read:

> For this reason, the ecclesiology of communion cannot be reduced to purely organizational questions or to problems that simply relate to powers. Still, the ecclesiology of communion is also the foundation for order in the Church and especially for a correct relationship between unity and pluriformity in the Church.[2]

Let us restate the question. To what category does the term *communio* belong? The Synod document clearly affirms its theological reality. Does it also concern Church order? The Synod does not give an absolutely clear reply. The answer seems to be yes, no, and but. Yet clearly Vatican II was also thinking about the order of the life of the Church when it spoke of an ecclesiology based on communion. So what meaning does this concept have for Church order?

Klaus Hemmerle, the Bishop of Aachen, expressed the implications of communion as follows:

> Since the ecclesiology of communion was first announced as a theme, it must not ever be reduced to silence. At the opening of Vatican II, this approach to ecclesiology definitively abolished the earlier "pyramid ecclesiology," which viewed the Church as a structure going from the apex of the hierarchy in a series of steps all the way down to the lowest level, that of the laity. To be sure, the differences have not been resolved, but now they are interpreted in a new way. The Extraordinary Synod of 1985 clarified the meaning of the communion theology of the Council, and the 1987 Synod of Bishops in Rome set it in a broader context. This beginning can only be seen as history-making.[3]

Hemmerle notes that *communio* does not merely suggest but actually gives a specific idea regarding the constitution of the Church. The constitution of the Church must be interpreted entirely according to the standard of *communio*. What does this mean? The implications are considerable. Every community—whether national, political, social, or private—gives itself a particular constitution. This is more or less what the idea of *com-*

---

1. *Extraordinary Synod of Bishops, Rome, 1985: A Message to the People of God and The Final Report* (Washington: NCCB, 1986), II,C,1, p. 17. Also see W. Kasper, *Zukunft der Kirche aus der Kraft des Konzils. Die ausserordentliche Bischofssynode '85. Die Dokumente mit einem Kommentar von W. Kasper* (Freiburg, 1986), pp. 89-97.

2. *Extraordinary Synod*, II,C,1, p. 18.

3. K. Hemmerle, "Im Austausch Gestalt gewinnen. Nach-Denkenswertes zur Bischofssynode 1987 über 'Die Berufung und Sendung der Laien in Kirche und Welt'," in J. Müller, E.J. Birkenbeil, eds., *Miteinander Kirche sein. Idee und Praxis* (Munich, 1990), p. 12.

munio has to add to the concept of the Church as the People of God, a concept that played a profound and leading role at Vatican II.

The concept of the People of God, however, failed to address the Church's constitutional form. After Vatican II, various interpretations surfaced. Some gave priority to the concept of the People of God and interpreted the constitution of the Church quite liberally. Others, emphasized the "People" part of the concept and demanded quite radical democratic or revolutionary forms of Church order. None of this is implied in the understanding of *communio* as the form of the Church's constitution.

In the next section I shall begin to elucidate the meaning of *communio*, since its meaning is not immediately obvious. I will do this in five parts: first, the meaning of communion in the world and in the Church; second, the formation of the concept of communion; third, the theological context of communion; fourth, a presentation of communion as the specific constitution of the Church in the same way democracy is, more or less, the constitutional form of the Federal Republic of Germany in the post-war period; and fifth, some observations on the 1971 document from the Vatican, *Communio et progressio*.

I. Communion in the World and the Church

1. Communion in the World

Human beings are community-oriented. Thus, Aristotle referred to them as "*zōon politikon*"—social animals whose physical and rational qualities are directed entirely toward others and who discover their humanity in the social community of the *polis*. This view of humanity has become most necessary in the world of today. As a result of the media and the advances of technology, humanity has grown closer than ever before. Yet modern mass society also produces loneliness and individualism in quantities previously unknown. However, since modern mass societies are primarily vast groupings of separate individuals, they do not form an organic whole. Individualism and collectivism are both prominent in contemporary society. Both of these extremes, however, fail to address the nature of the human person as a "*zōon politikon*."

Thus, we need not be surprised if young people have expressed the desire for a new society ever since the collapse of the bourgeois world following World War I. Even today, new attempts at communal life are widespread: small groups and initiatives, new form of families, base communities, and the demand for solidarity and dialogue on a large scale. At the same time, all major institutions are suffering from a substantial lack of credibility. This applies equally to churches as institutions.

2. The Church as Communion

Parallel to these changes in the way the modern world is experienced, similar changes and aspirations have also manifested themselves in the Church. During the first major youth movement after World War I, noted priests and theologians managed to tap into the new desire for community among young people and to use it to renew an awareness of the Church. They succeeded in portraying the Church as a community of faith and sacraments and as an answer to issues prevalent in contemporary society. Let us, for example, remember the exhortation of Romano Guardini: "A religious event of unfathomable consequences has begun: the Church has awakened in the souls of its members."[4]

This awakening of the Church soon led to a renewal in biblical, liturgical, pastoral, and patristic thought. It developed into one of the essential historical prerequisites for Vatican II, especially with respect to the Council's understanding of the Church. The concept of *communio* became one of the principal ideas of the ecclesiology of Vatican II. The Council thus selected one of the most profound issues not only for the Church but also for today's world. It also attempted to consider it in the light of the Gospel and to propose it as a solution.

II. The Development of the Concept of Communio

The commentaries on *Lumen gentium* indicate in several ways the primacy of the concept of the Church as communio.[5] The biblical[6] and early Christian[7] concept of the Church as *koinonia* clearly inspired a large number of the Fathers of the Council and shaped their reflections on the Church of God. They arrived at a decisive insight in the conciliar discus-

---

4. R. Guardini, *Vom Sinn der Kirche* (1922), (Reprint Mainz, 1955), p. 19.

5. See A. Grillmeier, "Commentary on the Dogmatic Constitution on the Church," in H. Vorgrimler, *Commentary on the Documents of Vatican II* (New York: Herder and Herder, 1967), I: 138-185, 218-225; J. Ratzinger, *Das neue Volk Gottes. Entwürfe zur Ekklesiologie*, 2nd ed. (Düsseldorf, 1970); G. Philips, *L'Eglise et son mystère au IIe concile du Vatican* (Paris, 1966), I: 7, 59, II: 24 ff, 54, 159; and idem, *Lexikon für Theologie und Kirche* I: 139 ff.

6. Cf. H. Seesemann, *Der Begriff koinonia im Neuen Testament* (Giessen, 1933); F. Hauck, *Koinos* in *Theological Dictionary of the New Testament*, III: 789-809; K. Kertelge, *Koinonia* in *Okumenische Rundschau* 27 (1978): 445 ff.; and M. Gielen, "*Communio* in biblischer Sicht," in J. Müller, *Miteinander Kirche sein*, pp. 19-44.

7. For the patristic theology of *communio* see Cyprian, *De oratione dominica*, 23, *Patrologia latina* 4: 553; Philips, *L'Eglise et son mystère*, I: 91-93; and H. de Lubac, *The Motherhood of the Church followed by Particular Churches in the Universal Church* (San Francisco, 1982).

sion.[8] Thus Aloys Grillmeier made the following comments on *Lumen gentium* and communion.

> Here we have one of the dominant themes of the Constitution. The Church is a unity of communion in the Holy Eucharist, in the Holy Spirit, in the (visible) hierarchical government, and in the various forms of service. It is an animated bodily unity in the variety of its members and their functions. And the hierarchical order is a self-communication of the Spirit just as are charismatic endowments. Thus the Spirit is embodied in the Church, where he produces "a mystical person from many persons."[9]

The historical development of this form of *communio* in the early Christian Church has been described by the now Cardinal Ratzinger in the following summary of his views. Every individual local community of the early Church perceived itself as a representation of the one Church of God by celebrating the mystery of the Eucharist in the presence of the presiding bishop and the presbyters. The unity among these individual local churches, which saw themselves as representatives of the entire Church, was not primarily administrative but consisted in the fact that the individual churches "communicated" with each other They agreed mutually to permit members of other congregations to receive Communion with them. Heretics were primarily those who communicated only among themselves but not with the whole Church. How, then, was it possible to distinguish congregations truly in communion with each other from those which were not? Christians obtained from their bishop a letter of communion which certified that they belonged to the community. Rome was the ultimate norm that determined that a community was in communion. The basic rule was: Whoever communicates with Rome communicates with the true Church, and whoever does not communicate with Rome does not belong to the correct *communio*. The unity of the Church, therefore, was not based primarily on its central government but on the fact that it lived from the one Lord's Supper, the eucharist[10] Thus, the communion-community in the early Church understood itself as a living organism of a Church of unity and diversity, practicing active mutual exchanges within the unity and the individual institutional responsibilities of the local churches.

---

8. For the development of this idea prior to Vatican II see Y. Congar, *Chrétiens désunis* (Paris, 1937); H. de Lubac, *Catholicism: A Study of Dogma in Relation to the Corporate Destiny of Mankind* (New York, 1950); M, J. Le Guillou, *Mission et unité* (Paris, 1960); and J. Hammer, *The Church is a Communion* (New York, 1964).

9. Grillmeier, "Commentary," I: 142.

10. Ratzinger, *Das neue Volk Gottes,* pp 87 ff.

III. The Theological Reality of Communion

The first source for the concept of *communio* is *The Constitution on the Church, Lumen gentium,* where the Church is largely understood from the perspective of *communio*. It must be noted, however, that in addition to the newly rediscovered ecclesiology of communion in Vatican II, substantial ecclesiological elements from Vatican I and earlier times were also incorporated into *Lumen gentium*. We often find both ecclesiologies directly juxtaposed in the text of Vatican II.[11] Let us take a brief look at a few essential dimensions of *communio* which can be found in the documents and where there is broad theological consensus.

1. Communio: Community with God[12]

Lumen gentium begins, as is well known, by reflecting on the nature of the Church. The nature of the Church is seen as a "mystery." Hence, the first chapter of *Lumen gentium* bears the heading, "The mystery of the Church." Walter Kasper links mystery to communion.

> . . . according to the Council, the mystery of the Church means that in the Spirit we have access through Christ to the Father, so that in this way we may share in the divine nature. The communion of the Church is prefigured, made possible, and sustained by the communion of the Trinity. Ultimately, as the Council says, echoing Cyprian, the martyr bishop, it is participation in the trinitarian communion itself (*Lumen gentium* 4; *Unitatis redintegratio* 2). The Church is, as it were, the icon of the trinitarian fellowship of Father, Son, and Holy Spirit.[13]

2. Communio: Eucharistic Community[14]

A further dimension of *communio* is, in the view of Vatican II, the community which is formed by the word and the sacraments and above all by the Eucharist. Kasper's words are appropriate.

> It may therefore be said that, just as the trinitarian confession of the Creed is the summing up and the identifying mark of the whole Chris-

---

11. Cf. A. Acerbi, *Due ecclesiologie: ecclesiologia giuridica ed ecclesiologia di communione nella "Lumen gentium"* (Bologna, 1975), and H. J. Pottmeyer, "Kontinuität und Innovation in der Ekklesiologie des II. Vatikanums," in G. Alberigo et al., eds., *Kirche im Wandel. Eine kritische Zwischenbilanz nach dem 2. Vatikanum* (Düsseldorf, 1982), pp. 89 ff.

12. On this point see W. Kasper, "The Church as Communion," in *Theology and Church* (New York, 1989), pp. 148-65; H. de Lubac, *The Motherhood of the Church*; and B. Forte, *La chiesa: icona della Trinità* (Brescia, 1984).

13. Kasper, *Theology and Church*, p. 152.

14. Ibid., pp. 153-156. Also see W. Elert, *Eucharist and Church Fellowship in the First Four Centuries* (St. Louis, 1966); A. Gerken, *Theologie der Eucharistie* (Munich, 1973), pp. 111 ff; and W. Kasper, "Einheit und Vielheit der Aspekte der Eucharistie," *IKZ* 14 (1985): 215.

tian faith, so the eucharist is the sacramental and symbolic actualization of the whole mystery of salvation. As eucharistic communion, the Church is not merely the reflection of the trinitarian communion; it also makes that communion present. It is not merely the sign and means of salvation, but also its fruit. As eucharistic communion, it is the all-surpassing response to the fundamental hum an cry for fellowship.[15]

3. Communio: The Unity of the Church[16]

The *communio* with God and the life of the Church based on eucharistic *communio* becomes visible through the structure and order of the Church. This is evident inasmuch as it is brought into being in the local churches which are based on the eucharist. This means that the concept of *communio* in the conciliar texts is of the greatest significance within the Catholic Church. Basically, the Council stated that in and from the local churches the Catholic Church comes into being (*Lumen gentium* 23).

This dimension of ecclesial communion was also the background of one of the most discussed and contested doctrines at the Council: the doctrine of the collegiality of the episcopacy and the relationship of the Roman Pontiff to the local churches. This aspect of *communio* touches most deeply on questions of the structure and shape of the universal Church and not only those affecting the Pope and the bishops. In any event, Vatican II dealt primarily with the doctrine concerning bishops.

The Church as *communio* also provides provides us with an important ecumenical principle concerning the unity of the Church and its relations with other churches. Kasper writes about communion ecclesiology:

> This formula, more than any other, shows how much the revival of the ancient church's concept of *communio* represents a turning point of the first order in the history of theology and the Church. For a return to the *communio* ecclesiology of the first ten centuries means departing from the one-sided "unity" ecclesiology of the second millennium of the Church, which was, and still is, one of the essential reasons for the separation of the Eastern churches from the Latin church of the West. The interpretation of the Church's unity as a unity in communion again leaves room for a legitimate variety of local churches within the greater unity in the one faith, the same sacraments, and the same

---

15. Kasper, *Theology and Church*, p. 155.
16. Ibid., pp. 156-61. Also see L. Hertling, *Communio: Church and Papacy in Early Christianity* (Chicago, 1972); Elert, *Eucharist and Church Fellowship*; Y. Congar, "De la communion des Eglises à une ecclésiologie de l'Eglise universelle," in Y. Congar and B.-D. Dupuy, eds., *L'épiscopat et l'Eglise universelle* (Paris, 1962); and Congar, *Ministères et communion ecclésiale* (Paris, 1971).

ministries. This points the way forward, as the Church moves into its third millennium.[17]

4. Communio Fidelium[18]

The People of God is the community of communication of the Church. The People of God is the name that the Council gave to the original community of the Church in both its earthly and salvific form. It is also the subject of the second chapter of *Lumen gentium*. This view determines the entire Constitution on the Church. *Lumen gentium* helps us understand the shape and structure of the Church as a whole by enumerating and describing in subsequent chapters the various persons and representatives of the Church of God who figure prominently in this community of communication. It points out the contribution they can make to the building up of the entire *communio* of the Church. The trinitarian mystery of God is the first and ultimate subject of the Church. Whatever the Church does, proceeds ultimately or originally from this source that is described in Chapter One of *Lumen gentium*. The People of God, however, must also be seen as a separate subject in its own right, as the earthly manifestation of the community of *communio* as it is presented in Chapter Two of *Lumen gentium*. Thereafter, *Lumen gentium* discussed in detail the persons who carry on the life of the Church: the Roman Pontiff, the bishops, priests, and deacons (Chapter Three); the laity (Chapter Four); and religious (Chapter Six). They are all mentioned according to their special responsibilities. It may be an open question whether this allocation of services is sufficient for *communio* on its own. At any rate, the basic idea of such comprehensive communication within the Church is impressive. Through it, the Church reveals both its great individuality and its unity as an assembly of individually communicating persons.

5. Communio: Sacrament for the World[19]

The Church does not exist for its own sake, but, by its very nature, it is intended to be the sign of salvation for the world. It follows that the *communio*, which is the Church, must be a type, model, and example of the *communio* among all human beings and nations (see *Ad gentes* 11:23; *Gaudium et spes* 39; *Nostra aetate* 1). According to Irenaeus of Lyons (*Lumen gentium* 2), God intends to renew everything in Christ and thus prepare the definitive Kingdom of God through the *communio* of the Church.

---

17. Kasper, *Theology and Church*, p. 157.

18. Ibid., pp. 161-63. Also see Pottmeyer, "Kontinuität und Innovation," pp. 89-110, and H. Legrand, "Die Entwicklung der Kirche als verantwortliche Subjekte. Eine Anfrage an das II. Vatikanum," in Alberigo, *Kirche im Wandel*, pp. 141-74.

19. Kasper, *Theology and Church*, pp. 163-65.

The Church can and must be a sacrament, a sign and instrument of unity and peace in the world. Therefore, the commitment to justice, peace, and freedom for all human beings and nations and to a civilization based on love is a fundamental perspective for the Church today.

IV. The Ecclesiology of Communion after Vatican II

The period following the Council was characterized by increasing competition between the two ecclesiologies found in *Lumen gentium*. One side combined the ecclesiology of communion with a more adventuresome spirit, while the other side renewed the emphasis on the ecclesiology of Vatican I. Ambitious expectations were unfulfilled and disenchantment set in. As a result, the spirit of the ecclesiology of communion receded noticeably; indeed, it appeared almost forgotten. It hardly ever surfaced in the writings of the Magisterium and of theologians. Only a handful of theologians preserved its memory.[20] This lack of interest was regrettable in light of the decision to begin work on a new Code of Canon Law for the Latin Church which went into effect in 1983. A few major passages in the new Code reveal some hesitation concerning the ecclesiology of communion.[21] Perhaps a return to this kind of ecclesiology began in 1980, when an international congress in Bologna dealt with the ecclesiologies of Vatican II.[22] It concluded that the ecclesiology of communion was a fundamental idea of the Council. Many were surprised when the concept of communion was affirmed at the 1985 Synod of Bishops. Finally, after twenty years, the ecclesiology of communion is once again found often in official Church documents.

The programmatic statements regarding the *communio* of the Church are primarily theological in nature. But at the same time *communio* refers to the concrete form of the life of the Church.[23] This corresponds to the

---

20. Han Urs von Balthasar founded the international journal *Communio* in 1972. The first issue outlined its program. Several theologians wrote on *communio*: H. de Lubac, W. Kasper, W. Breuning, and K. Hemmerle. Also see M. Böhnke and H. P. Heinz, eds., *Im Gespräch mit dem Dreieinen Gott, Festschrift für W. Breuning* (Düsseldorf, 1985), and K. Hemmerle, *Thesen zu einer trinitarischen Ontologie* (Einsiedeln, 1976).

21. H. Müller, "Communio als kirchenrechtliches Prinzip im Codex Juris Canonici von 1983," in *Im Gespräch mit dem Dreieinen Gott*, pp. 481 ff.; K. Walf, "Lakunen," in *Kirche im Wandel*, pp. 195 ff.; O. Saier, *Communio in der Lehre des 2. Vatikanischen Konzils. Eine rechtsgeschichtliche Untersuchung* (Munich, 1973).

22. See Alberigo, *Kirche im Wandel*.

23. See W. Breuning, "Das Verständnis des katholischen Bischofsamtes nach dem II. Vatikanischen Konzil," in W. Sanders, ed., *Bischofsamt: Amt der Einheit* (Munich, 1983), p. 13: "If the Church is *communio*, then the life form of this community does not exist alongside an external structure of order. Such an external order is vital for the organizational tasks of the Church. But as far as its vital dimensions are concerned, it is not decisive in its life. Rather, the form and the formation of the Church must clearly be characterized by the ultimate reality of its *communio*."

original spirit of the Fathers of the Council, when they stated in the *Nota explicativa praevia,* No. 2: "Communion is an idea which was held in high honor by the ancient Church (as it is even today, especially in the East). It is understood, however, not as a certain vague feeling but as an organic reality which demands a juridical form and is simultaneously animated by charity."

This insight has far-reaching consequences for Church order, especially concerning various persons in the Church, such as the Pope, bishops, priests, religious, and laity and their mutual forms of communication. Since the Council had dealt in detail with the relationship between the Pope and the bishops and with the collegiality of bishops, it was only natural that the postconciliar discussions on the life of the Church as communion would be extended to other persons in the Church, such as priests and lay people. In the following sections, I shall concentrate on some of these postconciliar touchstones: first, the 1983 Code of Canon Law and second, priests and laity in the community of communication which is the Church

1. The Code of Canon Law and Communio

I have already alluded to the widespread disappearance of the theology of communion during a certain period after Vatican II. In any case, it must be said that the drafters of the Code were really only partially aware of this conciliar concept. Hence, there are varying views as to how far the ecclesiology of communion may have entered into the new Code or may even have shaped it as a guiding principle.[24]

W. Aymans, a canonist from Munich, gives the following account of the principal idea of the new Code:

> To a great extent, the basic socio-philosophical concept of the perfect society (*societas perfecta*) became normative for the legal description of the Church in the Code of 1917. . . . In the newly promulgated 1983 Code it is quite clear that there has been an effort to abandon a principle drawn from social philosophy and to move to a theologically based principle. The basic concept, expressed by *communio,* can be expressed in three ways: the Church is the *communio fidelium* (the communion of believers), a *communio hierarchica* (the hierarchically ordered communion), and a *communio ecclesiarum* (the communion of local churches).[25]

Thus, the new Code of Canon Law represents a fundamental advance in the legal consciousness of the Church, at least in regard to its

24. Cf. H. Müller, "Communio als kirchenrechtliches Prinzip," pp. 481 ff.; W. Aymans, *Einführung in das neue Gesetzbuch der lateinischen Kirche,* (DBK-Arbeitshilfen 31), (Bonn, 1983); and Walf, "Lakunen," in *Kirche im Wandel,* pp. 195 ff.; and Saier, *Communio in der Lehre.*
25. Aymans, *Einführung,* p. 17.

basic theological idea in the ecclesiology of communion. Others, however, are hesitant to describe this advance as profound. H. Müller, a canonist from Bonn, finds in the Code two competing models of the Church: the one focusing on *societas perfecta* and the other one based on the conciliar idea of *communio*. The two models are not defined with respect to each other nor are they reconciled with each other.[26] Müller concludes:

> In the principles proposed for the new Code, we find juxtaposed both models of the establishment of law in the Church: the theological model and the model derived from social philosophy. Hence, it is no surprise that there are also consequences that each of these theoretical, canonical positions have on the new Code of Canon Law for the Latin Church.[27]

Müller then points out some of these consequences. According to him, the sections on the *communio hierarchica* offer a more unified picture, whereas significant gaps are noticeable in the understanding of the *communio fidelium*. The ecumenical sections regarding the *communio ecclesiarum* similarly lag a long way behind the theological statements of Vatican II.

This somewhat divergent vision of the Code of Canon Law with regard to its understanding of the Church seems to reflect the general situation of academic theology and the Magisterium at that time. Nevertheless, one should not underestimate the impact that the permanent, written expression in the Code of such uncertainties had on the future. Müller draws the following conclusion: "The Code of Canon Law presently in force in the Latin Church can be deemed a 'temporary solution'. . . . The task remains of implementing the view of *communio* as introduced by the last Council into all fields and regulations of the ecclesiastical legal order without exception."[28]

2. Priests and Communio: The 1971 and 1990 Synods

The 1971 Synod of Bishops discussed the role of priests and issued a document entitled "The Ministerial Priesthood." This document acknowledged to a suprising degree the ecclesiology of communion with respect to the priesthood. The Synod clearly wanted to respond to the criticism that Vatican II did not give enough time to the discussion of the priesthood, although it was arguably in no position to do so.

The preparations for the 1990 Synod of Bishops, insofar as they are known, have not brought much clarity to this question. It is true that the *Lineamenta* of 1989 reveal a determination to implement the newly discovered ecclesiology of communion and to apply it to the areas of priesthood and priestly formation. Sections 11-14 and 25-28 of that document

---

26. See H. Müller, "Communio als kirchenrechtliches Prinzip," pp. 483-84.
27. Ibid.
28. Ibid., pp. 497-98.

contain the central ideas of a genuine ecclesiology of communion: the mystery of the Church, community (*communio*), and mission (*missio*). However, the presentation of the idea of *communio* for priestly ministry appears to be somewhat restrictive. It hardly corresponds to the original idea as a formal theological principle of the Church. Hence, under the heading "Formation in the Spirit of Communion," number 27 states in passing that "the common life of the seminary leads to a renunciation of one's will and to obedience, which is learned through a permanent relationship to authority and a conscious acceptance of specific rules of life." Such a disciplinary order within an ecclesiology of communion seems almost grotesque.

3. The Laity and Communio: The 1987 Synod

The 1987 Synod of Bishops on the laity is an important milestone in the application of the ecclesiology of communion to Church order.[29] During the preparation for the Synod, there were a few criticisms and warnings. There were, for example, comments on the *Lineamenta* made by the Central Committee of German Catholics or the statement of the German Bishops' Conference on the same issue.

> *Communio* and *missio* are basic attributes of all who are the Church (cf. *Lumen gentium* 10, 32). . . . In order to understand the mission and the vocation of lay people theologically in the sense of *Lumen gentium*, it is not enough to limit oneself merely to Chapter 4 on the laity or simply to select a few statements from that chapter. . . . Chapter 4 and likewise Chapter 3 on office must be interpreted on the basis of Chapter 2 which is on the People of God. . . .
>
> Emphasizing this today is of great significance. Postconciliar developments in Western European countries which threatened to neglect the special character of spiritual ministry and spiritual authority have made it necessary, by way of reaction, to give a precise account of spiritual ministry. Nevertheless, this absolutely legitimate emphasis that the present situation dictates can be reversed if the common foundations are pushed into the background or lost sight of. Some regrettable effects are false polarizations illustrated by such slogans that come in pairs: "Church from above"/"Church from below" or "the official Church"/"the real Church (of the laity)." These are non-ecclesial ways of thinking in terms of competition or competence. They lead ultimately to a loss of mutual trust, to the abandonment of dialogue, and to an inappropriate style of reciprocal interaction.[30]

What was the result of the 1987 Synod with regard to the question of the laity within a Church of *communio*? Let us give a few passages

---

29. John Paul II, *Christifideles laici, Apostolic Exhortation on the Laity* (1988), in *Origins*, February 9, 1989, Vol. 18, no. 35: 561, 563-595. Here sections 18 ff.

30. *DBK-Arbeitshilfen* 45 (1986): 6-8 .

from the Apostolic Exhortation of John Paul II, *Cristifideles laici* (1988). First, the Church's structure as communion is emphasized in accordance with the 1985 Synod and "the participation of the lay faithful in the life of the Church as communion" (Section II). The Pope says: "In a primary position in the Church are the ordained ministers, that is, ministers that come from the sacrament of orders" (II, 22). Then follows a reference to canon law.

> When necessity and expediency in the Church require it, the pastors, according to established norms from universal law, can entrust to the lay faithful certain offices and roles that are connected to their pastoral ministry, but do not require the character of orders. . . . However, the exercise of such tasks does not make pastors of the lay faithful. In fact a person is not a minister simply in performing a task, but through sacramental ordination. . . . It is also necessary that pastors guard against a facile yet abusive recourse to a presumed "situation of emergency" or to "supply by necessity'" where objectively this does not exist or where alternative possibilities could exist through better pastoral planning (II, 23).

Finally, the task of lay people is once again restricted to the classic role of service in the world. Paul VI wrote about the special mission of the laity:

> Their own field of evangelizing activity is the vast and complicated world of politics, society, and economics, but also the world of culture, of the sciences and the arts, of international life, of the mass media. It also includes other realities which are open to evangelization, such as human love, the family, the education of children and adolescents, professional work, suffering.[31]

It should have become clear from these statements that, on the one hand, we ought to welcome the inclusion of the laity as an integral part of the ecclesial *communio*. On the other hand, we must also observe that the results fall far short of the possibilities. Hence, it is all too easy to understand a certain dissatisfaction on the part of public opinion within the Church. This applies to the realization of the Church as *communio* in all areas of Church order. In words that recall the "Open Letter" from Italian theologians in 1989, we can say that the understanding of the Church as a community of *communio* must be realized. This fundamental ecclesiological idea must lead to changes in the institutional balance as it has developed in the second Christian millennium, so that in the unity of the faith and of its "great discipline" the riches of plurality may once again be suitably present.[32]

---

31. Paul VI, *Evangelii nuntiandi* (1975), # 70.
32. *Herder Korrespondenz* 43 (1989): 285.

V. The Pastoral Instruction *Communio et progressio*

One of the most significant results of the decree on communication—*Inter mirifica*—from Vatican II was the introduction of the concept of "social communication" (*"communicatio socialis"*). Criticism of the decree began quickly. A common criticism was that *Inter mirifica*, since it had been deliberated on and ratified early in the Council, was not at the same high level of the later conciliar documents. Its arguments and phraseology were presumed to be preconciliar.[33] Hence, it was hardly a surprise that *Inter mirifica* itself announced a forthcoming postconciliar instruction which appeared several years later in 1971 as *Communio et progressio*.[34]

The development from *Inter mirifica* to *Communio et progressio* is astounding. At the outset, *Communio et progressio* presents a theology of communication (CP 6-18) which had been absent from *Inter mirifica*. It had had apparently grown out of some more important conciliar documents such as *Lumen gentium, Dei Verbum*, and *Gaudium et spes*. Upon closer examination, the message in these documents reveals a kind of theology of communication as it was first formulated at the Council. Thus, communication is recognized as a basic concept present in the essential operations of faith itself. We shall now point out some of the major elements of a theology of communication in the texts of Vatican II and in subsequent documents.

1. The Bases for Communicative Theology

The actual step that *Communio et progressio* takes beyond *Inter mirifica* is indicated by the title, *"communio."* It enlarges our understanding of *communicatio*. *Communio et progressio* expresses the Christian view that "the supreme goal of all communication" is intimate Christian *communio*, the communion that exists among the Persons of the Trinity. It is here that communication has its source. The event and understanding of Christian communication is seen in relation to an intimate point of faith, the *communio* of the Trinity. A genuine understanding of all Christian communication is developed on the basis of this *communio*. Christian communication must be understood above all within the center of Christian *communio* and from the *communicare* of Christian life.

---

33. See H. Wagner, *Einführung und Kommentar zur Pastoralinstruktion "Communio et progressio" über die Instrumente der sozialen Kommunikation. Nachkonziliare Dokumentation* (Trier, 1971) : 11 : 1 ff.

34. Pontifical Commission for Social Communications, *Communio et progressio, Pastoral Instruction on the Means of Social Communications* (1971). English translation in Austin Flannery, ed., *Vatican II: The Post Conciliar Documents* (Northport, N.Y.: Costello Publishing Co., 1975), pp. 293-349.

2. The Bases for Communication

The further development of this comprehensive program in *Communio et progressio* occurs rapidly through brief suggestions. We discover immediately the profound idea that grounds this development. Communication is not an extraneous concept co-opted by theology. Rather, it leads to the very center of fundamental Christian data and beliefs. In other words, the Christian message with its central tenets and contents of faith is itself expressed in terms of communication. As proof of this, we will take a brief look at the most important points in *Communio et progressio*.

2.1 Christian communication is based on divine *communio*. This original and basic idea of *Communio et progressio* deserves to be quoted in full. "In the Christian faith, the unity and brotherhood of man (*communio*) are the chief aims of all communication and these find their source and model in the central mystery of the eternal communion (*societas*) between the Father, Son, and Holy Spirit who live a single divine life" (*Communio et progressio* 8). Communication involves the very center of theology to such an extent that we must always refer to it whenever theology speaks about its central mystery, the life of the triune God.

2.2 The history of salvation must be understood as God's willingness to communicate. In a beautiful and thoroughly phenomenological manner, two dense articles (CP 9 and 10) describe God's will for communication as his major intention in salvation history. The fall of man had, above all, devastating consequences for brotherly communication within humanity. It brought discord and confusion in its wake until, finally, the communication willed by God itself collapsed. Human beings, by dint of their guilt-impaired efforts alone, are unable to restore this communication. As a result, their incapacity leads them to experience a need for salvation and for communication which brings liberation. Yet God's love cannot be rebuffed. At the beginning of the history of salvation, God himself resumed the dialogue. He is himself the promoter and guarantor of successful communication, which, in essence, is the very goal of the history of salvation. God sent his only son in order to renew humanity's once shattered community of communication, to redeem it, and to lead it to new freedom.

2.3 Jesus Christ is the definitive and most powerful communicator (*perfectus communicator* [CP 1]). When the fullness of time had come, Jesus Christ, the son sent by God, reestablished the lost communication. He did so with all his being and nature. He communicated himself and thus refounded in his person the communication between God and humanity. He who shares in the divine *communio* also shares in the human *communio*: "As the only mediator between the Father and mankind, he made peace between God and man and laid the foundations of unity among men themselves. From that moment, communication among men found its highest ideal and supreme example in God" (CP 10). This basic conviction gives us a deeper insight into the Incarnation and the life of Jesus, and it also greatly influences the Christian concept of communication. "Communication is more than the expression of ideas and the indication of emotion, At its most profound level, it is the giving of self in love. Christ's communication was, in fact, spirit and life" (CP 11). This communication occurs in the center of the People of God and comes from them. The will of Christ to communicate is fully realized in the new People of God.

2.4 The will of Christ to communicate is fulfilled by the gift of the Holy Spirit. The coming of Jesus signifies the new beginning for the community of human beings with God and the promise of the perpetual duration of this communication. This promise is fulfilled by the gift of and by the assistance of the Holy Spirit. It is the Holy Spirit who sustains and furthers the community that has begun. Furthermore, his gift is, above all, the gift of life-giving *communio*. "Christ communicated to us his life-giving Spirit, who brings all humanity together in unity" (CP 11).

2.5 The Church is the realization of the community of communication between God and humanity on earth. The Church carries within herself the mystery of the ideal *communio*. She is the Mystical Body of Christ. Moreover, the Church must strive to realize the intimate *communio* which she possesses in its visible form (CP 11).

2.6 The eucharist is the most effective sign of the divinely intended *communio* and *communicatio*. The word and sacrament which are offered by the Church make it possible for us to communicate with the innermost reality of the Body of Christ and to move in the direction of divine *communio*. The eucharist constitutes the fullness of *communio*. "In the institution of the Holy Eucharist, Christ gave us the most perfect, most intimate form of communion between God and man possible in this life, and out of this, the deepest possible unity among men" (CP 11).

2.7 Every human community of communication finds fulfillment in the People of God, The divinely willed community of communication as realized by the People of God does not represent simply a particular Christian form of human *communio*. Rather it is nothing other than the prototype and model of human communication in general, and it is concretized in every form of communication.

> A deeper understanding and a greater sympathy between men, as well as fruitful co-operation in creative work, these are the marvelous benefits that should come from social communication. These are ideals which are completely in tune with the aims of the People of God. Indeed, they are strengthened and reinforced by them. "For the promotion of unity belongs to the innermost nature of the Church," since she is "by her relationship with Christ, both a sacramental sign and an instrument of intimate union with God, and of the unity of all mankind" [*Gaudium et spes* 42, *Lumen gentium* 1] (CP 18).

The enumeration of these communicative themes of theology throughout *Communio et progressio* alerts us to the fact that communication is no stranger to the Christian faith. On the contrary, it leads us to the very center of the faith. The basic themes of the Christian faith are indeed illuminated by the theological concept of communication itself and must be based on it.

3. The Subsequent History of Communio et Progressio

In conclusion, it is appropriate to point out that the programmatic statements in *Communio et progressio* have not been fully incorporated into the official, postconciliar pronouncements of the Church on the subject of communication. The Bishops' Conference of Latin America published a working paper in 1983 entitled, "Towards a Theology of Communication in Latin America."[35] That document linked the theological dimensions of communication with anthropological, cultural, sociological, and pastoral components. Upon closer examination, it is clear that the fundamental theological and communicative statements of faith are taken as the point of departure in order to gain important insights for the Christian practice of communication. Although these broad considerations applied only to Latin America, they nevertheless open up significant horizons for Christian communication. Finally, another Pastoral Instruction on Social Communications issued by the Pastoral Council for Social Communications in 1992, *Aetatis novae* has furthered the discussion on the meaning of communication in the Church and in the world.

---

35. Latin American Bishops' Conference, "Hacia una teología de la comunicación en América Latina" (1983). Text in *Documentación CELAM* 8 (1983): 167-294.

6

Dialogue as a Model for
Communication in the Church

Hermann J. Pottmeyer

I. Dialogue as the Key to the Ecclesiology of Communion

The theological understanding of the Church allows for a wide range of emphases. This is shown in the history of the Church and in ecclesiology. History also reveals a direct connection between the image of the Church that may be predominant at any given time and the forms of communication which the Church favors during that same time. As Klaus Kienzler noted in his chapter, Vatican II continued the tradition of the early Church. It defined the Church as the People of God and as the *communio fidelium* (the communion of believers). This vision of the Church as a community of brothers and sisters included dialogue, which became the guiding principle and the basic model for communication in the Church. The Council affirmed:

> The Church stands forth as a sign of that brotherliness which allows dialogue and invigorates it. Such a mission requires in the first place that we foster within the Church herself mutual esteem, reverence, and harmony, through the full recognition of lawful diversity. Thus all those who compose the one People of God, both pastors and the general faithful, can engage in dialogue with ever-abounding fruitfulness. For the bonds which unite the faithful are mightier than anything that divides them. Hence, let there be unity in what is necessary, freedom in what is doubtful, and charity in everything (*Gaudium et spes* 92).

The word "dialogue" as a description of communication within the Church is new. It is not found in preconciliar ecclesiology whose key words were "jurisdiction" and "obedience." The following priorities characterized preconciliar ecclesiology.

- the priority of the universal Church over the local Church (universalist ecclesiology)
- the priority of the ordained office holder over the congregation and the charisms (clericalism)

- the priority of the monarchical over the collegial structure of office (centralism)
- the priority of unity over plurality (uniformity)
- One-way communication "from above to below" corresponds to the hierarchical system of strict superiority and subordination.

The ecclesiology of communion reveals a different picture. The *communio fidelium* (the communion of believers) is structured as the *communio ecclesiarum* (the communion of churches). The following characteristics distinguish it from preconciliar ecclesiology.

- an organic connection between the universal Church and the local churches
- the cooperation between ordained office holders and lay people
- the theological necessity of both primacy and collegiality
- unity within plurality

The above qualities are necessary for that communication which is characterized as dialogue. Paul A. Soukup rightfully noted: "Those who choose this model of dialogue as defining the communication process usually choose a model of the Church or local community that is small enough to facilitate the face-to-face communication they seek."[1] Dialogue means mutual communication in which the partners—their experience and their judgment—are taken seriously. This does not exclude the official authority of the pastors and the obedience due to them, but it requires the pastors to exercise their authority in dialogic fashion."[2]

II. The Danger of Reverting to One-Way Communication

The transition from a style of authority that was part patriarchal and part authoritarian to a style of authority that is exercised in the form of dialogue creates difficulties for the Church. The new awareness that "we are all the Church" creates fear in some people. This is one of the reasons for the tendency to return to one-way communication. One indication of this is the emphasis in recent Church documents on obedience to the hierarchical teaching authority and on the relationship between hierarchical superiority and subordination.

This development can be briefly outlined as follows. *Dei Filius* of Vatican I (Denzinger-Schönmetzer 3008) and *Dei Verbum* 5 of Vatican II demanded full submission of "intellect and will" as the "obedience of faith" which we owe to God who reveals himself. *Lumen gentium* 25,

---

1. Paul A. Soukup, *Communication and Theology: Introduction and Review of the Literature* (London, 1983), p. 50.
2. See *Lumen gentium* 37.

however, demanded "religious obedience of the will and the intellect" to the teaching of the bishops and the Pope. Although the use of the expression "of the will and intellect" to designate obedience toward the hierarchical teaching authority creates problems, its exclusive application in *Lumen gentium* 25 to non-infallible teaching authority is still not clear. Canons 752 and 753 of the 1983 Code of Canon Law use the expression "religious obedience of the intellect and will," which has become the specific way of describing adherence to non-infallible statements of the hierarchical teaching authority. This creates the unfortunate impression that when the teaching authority of the Church cannot or does not wish to make a definitive statement and in principle leaves open the process of searching for the truth, this process is at once terminated by the demand for obedience.

This same line of thought is continued in the new version of the *Professio fidei* and the Oath of Fidelity of 1989.[3] Although Canon Law had already required it, "religious obedience" must also be promised and sworn to by all theologians and office holders. The "Instruction on the Ecclesial Vocation of the Theologian" issued by the Congregation for the Doctrine of the Faith in 1990, stated that no public discussion of non-infallible doctrinal statements is permitted within the Church. Although Pius XII had already said as much in 1950, Vatican II did not adopt that declaration.[4] According to Canon 1371.1 of the Code of Canon Law, any "pertinacious rejection" of non-infallible doctrines is punishable, even if the rejection is based on justifiable doubt.[5]

This development concerns many Catholics. It makes dialogue in the Church more difficult, and it can hardly be reconciled with the following recommendation of Vatican II: "Let there be unity in what is necessary, freedom in what is doubtful, and charity in everything" (*Gaudium et spes* 92). Nor does it correspond to the actual position of the majority of the faithful today. Their fidelity to the faith and their acceptance of the truths of the faith are based less on obedience to their pastors than on understanding and conviction. Such an approach also corresponds to what Vatican II called the "dignity of human person and their social nature." Even in the area of religion, men and women attain to the truth through "right and true judgments of conscience" which are formed as a result of "free inquiry, carried on with the aid of teaching or instruction, communication, and dialogue" (*Dignitatis humanae* 3).

---

3. See Catholic Theological Society of America, *Report from the Committee on the Profession of Faith and the Oath of Fidelity* (Washington, 1990), and Gustave Thils and Theodor Schneider, *Glaubensbekenntnis und Treueid* (Mainz, 1990).

4. See Giuseppe Alberigo and Franca Magistretti, eds., *Constitutionis dogmaticae Lumen gentium synopsis historica* (Bologna, 1975), pp. 296 ff.

5. See Bernard Häring, "Erzwingung von Verstandesgehorsam gegenüber nicht-unfehlbaren Lehren?," *Theologie der Gegenwart* 22 (1986): 213-19.

III. Reception within the Process of Dialogic Communication

In order to prevent Church communication based on dialogue from becoming abstract or merely turning into a moral appeal, it will be worthwhile to take a close look at a specific aspect of the process of communication—reception in the early Church. Structurally, the early Church was a communion of local churches (*communio ecclesiarum*). Each individual local Church considered itself to be a communion of believers (*communio fidelium*). Even though the Church of Rome acquired particular respect because of its association with the apostles Peter and Paul and eventually became the point of reference for the whole Church, the relationship among the local churches and with Rome was not understood in the sense of jurisdictional superiority or subordination. Commmunication among the churches was achieved by mutual exchange of information concerning their respective traditions of faith and ecclesial customs and by mutual reception. In this way—whether through normal communal relations or at synods and councils—a consensus developed. It took place first among local churches and ultimately within the entire Church.

We must pay particular attention to the process of reception in the early Church. There are good reasons why the concepts of reception and dialogue have not played a role in modern ecclesiology prior to Vatican II. In fact, within a system of jurisdictional superiority and subordination, reception has no separate or legally relevant significance. In such a system, it is presumed that official decisions will be received without hesitation and out of a spirit of obedience. This differs from the practice within a Church that perceives itself as being a communion of sister churches. The manner of reception in the early Church was part of a process of communication based on dialogue.

As a result of his investigations, Yves Congar defines reception in the early Church as follows: "By 'reception,' I mean the process by means of which a Church body truly takes over as its own a resolution that it did not originate in regard to itself, and acknowledges the measure it promulgates as a rule applicable to its own life."[6] This definition is purposely couched in general terms in order to cover the many processes of reception. What is received is not only doctrinal truths but also disciplinary matters, ecclesiastical laws and customs, as well as persons. The recipients may include not only local churches but also institutions of the universal Church or synods of the local Church. The processes of reception can go from the level of the universal Church to that of the local churches or vice versa.

Yves Congar characterized the special character of reception at the time of the early Church as follows:

---

6. Yves Congar, "Reception as an Ecclesiological Reality," in *Concilium* (English edition), no. 77 (New York: Herder and Herder, 1972), p. 45.

Reception includes something more than what the Scholastics called "obedience." For the Scholastics it is the act by which a subordinate submits his will and conduct to the legitimate precepts of a superior, out of respect for the latter's authority. Reception is not a mere realization of the relation "*secundum sub et supra*": it includes a degree of consent, and possibly of judgment in which the life of a body is expressed which brings into play its own, original spiritual resources.[7]

According to Congar,[8] the method of reception practiced by the early Church was "dangerous" to preconciliar ecclesiology, since in the early Church the adoption of papal and conciliar decisions by the local churches or individual believers was not simply the fruit of obedience but rather that of the recipient's own judgment regarding the truth or expediency of such decisions. This does not exclude due consideration being given in this judgment to the authority of a pope or a council. However, it is important that the ratification of a decision through ecclesial consensus gives it considerable weight. According to current terminology, reception by consensus does not per se validate a decision. Rather it confirms the decision and its intrinsic authority and thus contributes to its respect. Moreover, this makes it easier for any additional reception to take place. Indeed, the consensus of the universal Church regarding doctrinal decisions was, from the outset, the most important criterion in determining whether a doctrinal statement was to belong to the Church's binding tradition of faith. This is linked to the idea that the Church is a community in which all the members have joint responsibility. This is why canon law adopted the secular Roman legal maxim: "*Quod omnes tangit ab omnibus tractari et approbari debet*" ("What concerns all must be discussed and approved by all").[9] This idea is also the basic premise of communication that is based on dialogue.

Vatican II emphasized the active and creative role played by the faithful during the process of tradition and reception. "There is a growth in the understanding of the realities and the words which have been handed down. This happens through the contemplation and study made by believers, who treasure these things in their hearts" and also through the "intimate understanding of spiritual things they experience" (*Dei Verbum* 8). At the same time, the People of God are guided by their sense of the faith. Their faith "penetrates" the Word of God "more deeply by accurate insights and applies it more thoroughly to life" (*Lumen gentium* 12).

---

7. Ibid.

8. Ibid., p. 43.

9. See Gaines Post, "A Romano-Canonical Maxim 'Quod omnes tangit,'" in Bracton," *Traditio* 4 (1946): 197-251. Also see Yves Congar, "Quod omnes tangit ab omnibus tractari et approbari debet," *Revue historique de droit français et étranger* 36 (1958): 210-259.

IV. The Exercise of Ecclesial Authority in Dialogue

The above discussion leads us to posit three demands for the exercise of authority in dialogue. First, bishops should consider to whom their decisions are addressed as serious conversation partners and take their insights and judgments into account. This is best accomplished by prior consultation. Second, the manner in which bishops seek the truth and arrive at decisions should lend credibility to their decisions; their decisions should have a convincing ring to them and thus make reception easier. Third, the new experiences acquired in the process of reception by the faithful should be taken into consideration and, if necessary, lead to the improvement or correction of the decisions.

The United States Bishops' Conference in its pastoral letters on peace (1983) and the economy (1986) are good examples of the exercise of authority in dialogue. In both instances, the bishops first released a draft of the pastoral and invited members of the faithful to comment on it. The bishops carefully screened the responses, and, if they were useful, they took them into account as they prepared the next draft. That draft was in turn also submitted for discussion. Finally, relying on their authority, the bishops ratified the final version of the text. As a result, those pastoral letters received great attention, in contrast to many other Church documents. In 1990, the Austrian Bishops' Conference followed the same procedure in preparing its pastoral letter on social matters.

What is remarkable in this process is the linking of consultation and creative reception which leads to consensus. This was done without questioning the higher responsibility of the bishops. During the reception of the various drafts, the faithful were invited to reflect on the issues under discussion and to form their own opinions. By asking the faithful to share the results of their deliberations, the bishops consulted the faithful with a view to the subsequent draft of the document and, ultimately, the final version. We should add that at issue were matters which many members of the faithful had already reached a reasoned judgment on the basis of their own experience and insights. Obviously, modern communication media are extremely important in this kind of consultative process.

An objection has been raised concerning the process used by the American bishops' conference. Some say that it distorted the divinely founded distinction between the teaching Church and the listening Church. Behind this accusation stands a preconciliar ecclesiology, although one must acknowledge that the distinction does have some positive value. It means that not everyone in the Church has the right to speak for the Church and to claim that such teaching is binding. However, in the search for truth, the distinction between the teaching Church and the listening Church does not apply. The bishops must also be listeners and, like all the members of the faithful, must seek guidance in Holy Scripture and in the tradition of the faith of the People of God.

The pastoral letters we have mentioned dealt with contemporary social questions. They showed, however, that the transmission of the faith involves not only the imparting of dogmatic truths but also the living witness of the Gospel in the modern world. Responding to the challenge of "the signs of the times" (*Gaudium et spes* 4), the Gospel must be continually reinterpreted and witness must be given to its healing and liberating power in life. The contribution made by the faithful is indispensable if "the signs of the times" are to be recognized and a living witness is to be given to the Gospel in the Church and in the world. Bishops, therefore, must take into account the judgment of the faithful. All we have said adds greater weight to the necessity of exercising authority in dialogue.

Although we have limited ourselves in this chapter to the discussion of dialogue within the Church, we must not forget that Vatican II also used the term "dialogue" to refer to communication with separated Christians,[10] with non-Christians and atheists,[11] with the entire human family, and with the world.[12] This aspect deserves our attention even more than the use of the dialogue model for exchanges within the Church.

Of course, dialogue may have its own special conditions according to the various partners involved. Yet the latter should be recognized as such and be taken seriously. The ghetto mentality of preconciliar ecclesiology is thereby abandoned. However, in order for the Church to show itself "the sign of that brotherliness which allows honest dialogue" among all human beings, it will be necessary "to foster within the Church itself . . . dialogue with ever abounding fruitfulness" (*Gaudium et spes* 92). The important goal of global dialogue on which the future of humanity depends will not be served by a relapse into preconciliar one-way communication.

---

10. See *Unitatis redintegratio* 9, 14, 18, 19, 21.
11. See *Gaudium et spes* 21, 92.
12. See *Gaudium et spes* 3, 40.

7

Ecumenism as Communication

Francis A. Sullivan, S.J.

Ecumenism is the theory and practice of the effort to restore full communion among the presently divided Christian churches. Communication has been described as "the procedure by which communion is achieved and maintained."[1] The thesis of this paper is that while good practices of communication were instrumental in achieving and maintaining communion among the Christian churches of the early centuries, a gradual breakdown of communications was largely responsible for the schism that divides the Eastern from the Western churches, and the rebuilding of good communications is an indispensable first step toward the restoration of communion which ecumenism seeks to achieve.

I. Practices of Communication Among the Early Churches

In this section I am relying mainly on the study which Ludwig Hertling has made of communion among the churches during the patristic period."[2] By the middle of the second century, the Church in each locality was under the leadership of a single bishop. Hertling describes ecclesial communion as "the bond that united the bishops and the faithful, the bishops among themselves, and the faithful among themselves, a bond that was both effected and at the same time made manifest by eucharistic communion."[3] *Communio* was not the only word the Latin Christians used to translate the Greek *koinonia*; they also used *communicatio*, as well as synonyms like "peace" and "love." Thus, for instance, the words *in pace* found so frequently on Christian tombs of that period, refer to the fact

---

1. Avery Dulles, "The Church is Communications," *IDOC International* (North American Edition), 27 (June 12, 1971): 69.

2. Ludwig Hertling, S.J., *Communio: Church and Papacy in Early Christianity*, translated with an introduction by Jared Wicks, S.J. (Chicago: Loyola University Press, 1972).

3. Ibid., p. 116.

that the person had lived and died "in the peace of the Church," that is, in Christian communion.

For our purpose, the most important part of Hertling's study is the section which he devotes to the way in which bishops achieved and maintained communion among themselves, and thus among their churches, through the letters which they sent to one another. He tells us that in the early centuries, when a Christian set out on a journey, he would first obtain from his bishop a letter addressed to the bishops of the churches he would be visiting on the way. Such letters were called "letters of communion" or "letters of peace"; a bishop would address them only to other bishops with whom he was in full communion. They served to assure the recipient that the travelling Christian was in communion with his own bishop, and thus worthy of hospitality from bishops in communion with him. Such letters also served to keep bishops informed about the election of new bishops, and also about the exclusion from communion of bishops who might have fallen into heresy or schism. The frequency of travel during the centuries of the *pax romana* meant that bishops could easily keep up a regular correspondence with their fellow bishops through the letters of communion they sent with travelling members of their flock.

Besides these letters carried by travellers, newly-ordained bishops sent out official "letters of communion" by which they informed one another of their election to the episcopate, and assured the recipients of their orthodoxy by including their profession of faith. The replies which they received were a confirmation of their communion with the bishops to whom they had written. These official "letters of communion" served both to manifest and to strengthen the bonds of unity among the bishops and hence among their churches. St. Augustine, referring to St. Cyprian, could say: "He had no need to fear having a great number of enemies, because he knew he was linked by letters of communion both with the Roman church, and with the other lands from which the gospel had come to Africa."[4] Augustine's reference to communion with the Roman church suggests the importance that came to be attached to receiving letters of communion from the bishop of Rome, as the criterion of being in the genuine "catholic" communion. This was recognized even by the pagan emperor Aurelian (270-273), who solved the dispute as to the rightful tenant of the bishop's residence in Antioch by decreeing that it was to be handed over to the one who received letters from the bishop of Rome.[5]

Other communications which served to strengthen the bond of communion among the early churches were the circular letters which were sent to inform the other churches of the decisions taken in regional synods. Prior to the first "ecumenical" council, that of Nicea in 325, there

---

4. St. Augustine, *Epist.* 43: 2, 7, *Patrologia latina* 33: 163.
5. Eusebius, *Ecclesiastical History*, 7: 30, *Patrologia latina* 20: 720.

had already been a regular and frequent practice of bishops meeting in regional synods. We are well informed by both Cyprian and Augustine about the annual synods of the bishops of North Africa during the third and fourth centuries. The decisions taken at these synods were sent not only to Rome but to the other great churches of the empire; the responses indicating the reception of such decisions by other bishops strengthened communion by manifesting or bringing about a common solution to problems of faith or practice that had arisen in various regions of the Church.

As the numbers of local churches multiplied, and became structured into ecclesiastical provinces, it was seen as sufficient to send letters of communion to the leading bishop of each province, the "metropolitan," who would keep the other bishops of his province informed. Eventually, as the provinces became structured into the five patriarchates, the most important letters of communion were the "synodal" letters by which a new patriarch, when enthroned in his see, would inform the other four of his election and send them his profession of faith. When the others were satisfied with the regularity of his election and with his orthodoxy, their reply would assure him of their communion with him and thus with his church.

In the major churches, lists were kept of the names of the bishops with whom the local metropolitan or patriarch was in communion. These names were inscribed in special tablets called diptychs, which were kept at the altar, so that prayer could be offered during the liturgy for all those named on them. Prayer for those listed on the diptychs was an effective way of expressing the reality of communion among bishops and their respective churches. The exchange of letters of communion, and the diptychs which were the fruit of this regular communication among bishops, were among the most important instruments for maintaining the bond of communion by which the many particular churches were in reality one universal or "catholic" Church.

II. The Breakdown of Communications Between East and West

In this section I am relying principally on the treatment of this question by Yves Congar in his book: *After Nine Hundred Years: The Background of the Schism Between the Eastern and Western Churches.*[6] He describes this schism as "the acceptance of a situation by which each part of Christendom lives, behaves and judges without taking notice one of the other. We may call it geographical remoteness, provincialism, lack of contact, a 'state of reciprocal ignorance,' alienation, or by the German word

---

6. Yves Congar, *After Nine Hundred Years: The Background of the Schism between the Eastern and Western Churches* (New York: Fordham University Press, 1959).

'*Entfremdung*'. The English word 'estrangement' expresses all this quite admirably. The Oriental schism came about by a progressive estrangement: this is the conclusion to which the following analysis seems to lead us."[7]

While Congar does not use the term: "breakdown of communications," it seems obvious that this is another way of describing the "progressive estrangement" by which the lasting schism came about. Congar distinguishes three kinds of factors that contributed to the estrangement: political, cultural, and ecclesiological. Our intention is to suggest how each of these factors contributed to the breakdown of communications between the Eastern churches and those of the West. In the course of the first millennium, such communications became more and more concentrated in the letters of communion exchanged between the Bishop of Rome, sole patriarch of the West, and the Bishop of Constantinople, first in rank among the patriarchs of the East. Hence we can use a short formula, and speak of the factors that led to the breakdown of communications between Rome and Constantinople. Following Congar's lead, I shall also describe them as political, cultural and ecclesiological factors, keeping in mind, however, that they are closely related one to another.

1. Political Factors

The first step toward the eventual schism between Eastern and Western Christianity can be seen in the decision of the first Christian emperor, Constantine, to move the imperial capital from Rome to Constantinople. This would probably not have had such an effect on the life of the Church had not the Christian emperors seen themselves as sovereign in affairs of the Church as well as of the state. This was the result of the establishment of Christianity as the religion of the empire, with the consequence that the unity of the Church was seen as essential for maintaining the unity of the empire. When doctrinal disputes threatened the unity of the Church, the Christian emperors took it upon themselves to summon the bishops to an ecumenical council, and it was imperial authority that turned the conciliar decrees into civil law, with penalties for bishops who refused to accept them.

The rise of the Bishop of Constantinople to the highest rank among the patriarchs of the East was due simply to the fact that he was bishop of the imperial city. The attitude of the patriarchs of Constantinople, and generally of the Eastern bishops, was to accept the role of the Christian emperor as sovereign in ecclesiastical affairs, and as primarily responsible for the visible unity of the Church. Accepting such a role on the part of imperial authority, they saw no need to develop social and juridical structures of the Church itself in order to maintain its unity.

---

7. Ibid., p. 5.

The Christian West, on the contrary, saw the universal Church as united under the Bishop of Rome, who derived his supreme authority not from the civil rank of his city, but from his being the successor of Saint Peter. Western Christians saw the universal Church as being held in unity not by the oneness of the empire under the sovereignty of the emperor, but by the supreme authority of the Roman Pontiff. For the bishops of the East it was unthinkable that Christendom should be divided into two empires, with two emperors; in their eyes it was not only civil treason, but the dismemberment of the Church, when Pope Leo III in the year 800 crowned Charlemagne Emperor of the Romans. Western Christians could accept the presence of two emperors, because the unity of the Church depended not on there being one emperor, but on there being one Supreme Pontiff. It is not difficult to understand how such a fundamental difference between the East and West concerning the respective roles of emperor and pope in the life of the Church would lead to conflicts between Rome and Constantinople, and contribute to their gradual estrangement.

The schism between East and West is usually dated from the year 1054, but in fact, during the first millennium there were at least five periods during which ecclesial communion was broken off between the popes and the patriarchs of Constantinople. In most of these instances, the break was due to the fact that the patriarchs acquiesced in an imperial intervention in the life of the Church which the popes found unacceptable. These several temporary states of schism came to an end and communion between the bishops of Rome and Constantinople was restored only when a new emperor withdrew the offending decree.

Another political factor that contributed to the estrangement between East and West was the conquest by Islam in the seventh century of much of the Christian East and North Africa. Thus the Mediterranean, which had been a unifying agent between the two parts of the Christian world, became a Moslem domain, seriously diminishing commerce and communication between Rome and Byzantium. Thus, for instance, Philip Hughes, describing the series of events that led up to the Photian schism in the ninth century, says: "Misunderstandings were inevitable in an age when means of communication had all but disppeared, and Rome might wait twelve months before it received replies from Constantinople."[8] Hughes refers also to E. Amann who remarks, in his history of the same period, that the slowness of communication between Rome and Constantinople explains much of what happened at that time to bring about a state of schism.[9]

---

8. Philip Hughes, *The Church in Crisis: A History of the General Councils 325-1870* (Garden City, N.Y.: Hanover House, 1961), p. 166.

9. E. Amann, *L'Epoque Carolingienne*, Vol. 6, Fliche-Martin, *Historie de l'Eglise*, (Paris: Bloud & Gay, 1947), p. 475, n.4.

2. Cultural Factors

Along with Congar, Aidan Nichols also stresses the importance of cultural factors in the gradual process of alienation between the Latin West and the Byzantine East. He points out the fact that "differences in culture are not always an enrichment for the Church. They can also be a problem, a handicap. When different local Churches are habituated to markedly different ideas, images, and institutions in the embodying of faith, this may threaten their communion one with another. As we know from our experience of human relationships at the ordinary level, difficulties in communication generate misunderstandings, misunderstandings produce hostility, hostility leads to the total breakdown of communications. This is a perfectly possible analysis of what transpired in the relations between the Roman church and the churches of the Byzantine-Slav East."[10]

Both Congar and Nichols stress the importance of the difference of language between East and West as a fertile source of misunderstanding and eventually of estrangement. Nichols' account of this development is as follows:

> The first and most obvious difference between Rome and Byzantium was *language*. In the first two centuries of the Christian era, educated people in the cities of the West could understand and write Greek. Similarly, in the East, officials and soldiers knew Latin. But the diffusion of the two languages followed very different patterns. Latin was essentially the language of the imperial administration, on the one hand, and of the Western cities on the other. Greek, on the other hand, was the language of culture throughout the Mediterranean world. . . . Users of Byzantine Greek came to identify their speech with civilised standards of discourse at large, and to hold in contempt those who could neither read nor speak it. When in the West the knowledge of Greek failed, not only did this impede communication, it also made eastern snobbery a compulsive habit. . . . At the same time, it was becoming harder for the Greeks to grasp Latin. . . . As a result, little Latin Christian literature was turned into Greek. Hardly any Augustine was translated until the fourteenth century. . . . When Westeners went East, the possibilities of communication were limited. . . . The lack of adequate communication, both popular and technical, underlay the parting of the ways between Latin and Greek theological method, which preceded by centuries the notion of a schism between the Latin and Greek churches.[11]

Congar likewise stressed the role of language in causing the estrangement between East and West, as in the following passage.

---

10. Aidan Nichols, O.P., *Rome and the Eastern Churches: A Study in Schism* (Collegeville, Minn.: Liturgical Press, 1992), p. 112.
11. Ibid., pp. 112-13.

Unfortunately it is a fact that the Christian world split in two according to a line that practically corresponded to the linguistic boundary. The Greek Fathers were amazingly lacking in curiosity regarding the Latin Fathers, and the latter were scarcely better informed as to the Greeks. Such a situation was an obstacle to the true unity that lives by the exchange of ideas and by the awareness thus acquired of the existence of ways other than one's own for approaching, and feeling, and conceiving intellectually the Holy Mysteries, and also other ways, equally legitimate, of expressing one's faith in worship and of organizing the life of the church. The toll exacted by linguistic provincialism was bound to be, sooner or later, a certain provincialism in thought, perpective and judgment, a certain narrow separatism in the theological and canonical tradition. In short, it was bound to bring about a serious lessening of the spirit of communion and of the likelihood, if not of the very possibility, of communion.[12]

Besides the problem of language, other cultural differences between East and West contributed to the gradual estrangement between the churches during the first millennium. The Latins considered the Greeks inordinately subtle; they often complained about the Greeks' quibbling and accused them of having invented all the heresies. The Greeks, on their part, contemned the Latins as barbarians, totally lacking culture. While in the West after the barbarian invasions few but monks and clergy could read and write, there always remained in Byzantium a cultivated laity.

Because the Greek language survived as both a liturgical language and the language of ordinary life, the Byzantine liturgy remained intelligible to laity and clergy alike, whereas in the West, the gap between the classical Christian Latin of the liturgy and the language of the common people became so great that the laity were reduced to passivity and relative silence. This meant that in the West, matters of faith and practice were handled exclusively by the clergy; in the East, on the other hand, a liturgically instructed and highly conservative laity played an important role in Church affairs. There was a tendency among them to identify liturgical rite with the faith itself, with the consequence that differences of rite between Eastern and Western Christianity came to be seen as differences in faith. For instance, the use of unleavened bread for the eucharist in the Latin West was judged heretical by Eastern Christians who were accustomed to the use of leavened bread.

3. Ecclesiological Factors

Although the understanding of the mystery of the Church was fundamentally the same in both East and West, two different canonical traditions developed independently and inevitably clashed with one another, especially since they took on dogmatic value. This was particularly true of

---

12. Congar, *After Nine Hundred Years*, pp. 29-30.

the Western tradition regarding the primacy of the Bishop of Rome, based on his being the successor of St. Peter, which became the focal point of Western ecclesiology. While the East certainly recognized Rome as first in rank among the apostolic churches, and there were many appeals made to Rome by the bishops of the East when they were divided on doctrinal or practical issues, still we do not find in the writings of the Greek Fathers the kind of recognition of the universal primacy of Rome by divine right such as we find in the Latin Fathers. While both East and West attributed a primacy to the Bishop of Rome, there was a profound difference in the way this term was being understood, leading inevitably to conflict about its consequences for the life of the Church.

One of the clearest indications of this difference of understanding regarding the meaning of Roman primacy is found in the history of the three ecumenical councils which decided the major christological disputes during the first millennium. These were the councils of Ephesus (431), Chalcedon (451), and Constantinople III (680-81), which, with variations of detail, followed a common pattern. In each case, appeal was made to Rome for help in settling a doctrinal dispute that was dividing the Eastern churches. The popes, after consultation with a Roman synod, issued a doctrinal decision, which they considered definitive. However, the Byzantine Emperor summoned the bishops of the East to a council, to which the popes sent their legates with instructions to insist on the council's acceptance of the papal decision. The Eastern bishops listened politely to the papal legates, but insisted on a full conciliar discussion of the issue, on the grounds that only the council could give the ultimate decision that would represent the mind of the universal Church. In each case the councils decided the matter in agreement with the papal teaching, condemning those whom the pope had condemned. However, there remained a deep difference regarding the definitiveness of the papal intervention. In the view of Rome, the papal decision ought to have been accepted without further discussion and simply ratified by the council; in the view of the Eastern bishops, who made up the vast majority at all these councils, the council itself had the right to test the papal teaching in the light of Scripture and tradition, and only after a full discussion of the issue, come to its decision, which, in its view, would be the really definitive one. Two quite different ecclesiologies were at work here, which made it practically impossible for the two sides fully to grasp and appreciate the other's point of view. It is obvious how a failure to reach a common understanding on the question of Roman primacy would lead inevitably to the conflict that resulted in schism.

III. Rebuilding Communications, the First Step Toward the Restoration of Communion

The modern ecumenical movement seeks the restoration of full communion among all the presently divided Christian churches. Since in this paper I have been describing the breakdown of communications that led to the schism between the Roman Catholic and the Orthodox Churches, I shall focus primarily on the effort that has been made during the past few decades to rebuild communications between these churches, as a first step toward the hoped-for restoration of communion between them. Fortunately, this effort has been thoroughly documented: first, in a volume entitled *Tomos Agapis*, published jointly by authority of Pope Paul VI and Patriarch Athenagoras of Constantinople, and more recently, in the volume: *Towards the Healing of Schism: The Sees of Rome and Constantinople.*[13]

In order to put this recent effort into its context, it would seem useful to recall the almost total lack of communication between Rome and Constantinople in the aftermath of the failure of the Council of Ferrara-Florence to bring about the reconciliation which that council seemed for a brief time to have achieved.[14] The decree of reunion solemnly promulgated in 1439 was formally repudiated by the Greeks in 1484. There followed a period of over four hundred years without any direct communication between the Bishop of Rome and the Patriarch of Constantinople.

An instructive example of how not to rebuild communication is provided by the letter of 1868 which Pope Pius IX addressed to "all the Bishops of the Eastern Rite not in communion with the Apostolic See" on the occasion of the First Vatican Council. After strongly asserting papal prerogatives, he exhorted those bishops to come to the "General Synod, as your ancestors came to the Councils of Lyons and Florence. . . ." However, the papal letter appeared in the press before the Patriarch of Constantinople received it. When Rome's emissary presented it to him, he commented that he already knew its contents from the newspapers; furthermore, it should have been given to each of the several patriarchs, who should have been consulted as to the conditions under which they would

---

13. *Tomos Agapis* (Volume of Charity), Istanbul and Vatican City, 1971. *Towards the Healing of Schism: The Sees of Rome and Constantinople.* Public Statements and Correspondence between the Holy See and the Ecumenical Patriarchate, 1958-1984. Edited and translated by E. J. Stormon, S.J. (New York : Paulist Press, 1987).

14. On July 6, 1439, the papal bull *Laetentur coeli,* proclaiming reunion between the Roman and the Greek Churches, was signed by the pope and the emperor, along with 133 Latin and 33 Greek bishops. However, much of the readiness of the Greeks to restore communion with Rome was due to their hope for Western military help to prevent the fall of Constantinople to the Turks. When, for lack of such help from the West, Constantinople fell to the Turks in 1453, the alienation of the Orthodox from Rome became more profound than it had been before.

agree to the holding of a general synod. With these remarks, the Patriarch returned the letter to the papal representative unopened.[15] One can see from this fiasco how much Rome had to learn about the art of communication, and how wide a breach had to be overcome.

The first friendly contacts between a Pope and an Orthodox Patriarch in almost five hundred years took place between John XXIII and Athenagoras of Constantinople in 1959. The previous careers of these two men had prepared them for this breakthrough. Prior to his election as Pope, Angelo Roncalli had served for nine years as Apostolic Visitor to Bulgaria, and then for twelve years as Apostolic Delegate to Turkey. In both of these countries he had established good relations with the Orthodox hierarchy. In 1948 Athenagoras was elected Patriarch of Constantinople, after having resided for eighteen years in the United States as Archbishop of the Greek Orthodox Church in America. During this time he had friendly contacts with Cardinal Cushing, Archbishop of Boston, and other Catholic prelates.

The first signs of a thawing of the long chill between Rome and Constantinople are the press releases in which Patriarch Athenagoras expressed his grief at the news of the grave illness of Pope Pius XII, his sympathy on the occasion of the Pope's death, and then his congratulations and prayers for John XXIII when he was elected, October 28, 1958.

When Pope John, on January 25, 1959, announced his intention of convoking the Second Vatican Council, he made it clear that one of the aims of this council was to promote the reunion of the separated Christian churches. Athenagoras took the initiative of requesting an audience for his personal representative, to obtain direct word from the Pope about his intentions in this regard. Shortly thereafter, John XXIII instructed the papal delegate to Turkey to visit Athenagoras, to brief him more fully about the Pope's hopes and intentions for the council.

On June 5, 1960, Pope John XXIII established the Secretariate for Promoting Christian Unity, one of whose purposes was to act as host to the non-Catholic observers at the council, and to facilitate their following of its work. Cardinal Bea, appointed President of the SPCU, became the Pope's liaison officer with the Patriarch, and Monsignor Willebrands, its secretary, became the travelling envoy to negotiate the invitation to the Orthodox Churches to send observers to the council. On two occasions, prior to the first session of the council, Msgr. Willebrands visited the Patriarch, to explain the intentions of the Holy See in inviting observers from the other Christian churches. Subsequently an official invitation was sent by Cardinal Bea in the name of Pope John; in his reply the Patriarch expressed his best wishes for the success of the council, but said that the sending of Orthodox observers was not feasible. At the close of the first

15. Stormon, *Towards the Healing of Schism*, pp. 2-3.

session, Fr. Pierre Duprey was sent to give the Patriarch a personal briefing on the work done at the council.

When John XXIII died in June, 1963, a very warm message of condolence was sent by Athenagoras to Rome. Upon the election of Paul VI, the Church of Rome restored an ancient custom, long abandoned: it announced the election directly to the Patriarch and the other heads of the Orthodox Churches. Three months later, just before the second Pan-Orthodox Conference was to convene, Paul VI sent a handwritten letter to Athenagoras. This was the first direct correspondence between a Pope and a Patriarch since 1584, when Gregory XIII wrote to Jeremiah II about the reform of the calendar. The patriarchate published the papal letter in its bulletin, under the title: "The Two Sister Churches" (the first modern use of an ancient expression). Athenagoras sent a very cordial reply to the Pope's letter, and sent his personal representative to the second session of Vatican II. At the close of this session Pope Paul decided to make a pilgrimage to Jerusalem, and sent Fr. Duprey to sound out the Patriarch about the possibility of a meeting between him and the Pope in the Holy City. The historic embrace and kiss of peace which took place on the Mount of Olives on January 5, 1964 were evident signs that a "dialogue of charity" had begun between the two "sister churches" that had for so long been estranged from one another.

"Dialogue of charity" was the term that Paul VI used in his address of welcome to the delegation sent by Athenagoras to communicate the decision taken at the Third Pan-Orthodox Conference to promote brotherly relations with Rome with a view to preparing for an eventual theological dialogue. The Pope explained the intention of this "dialogue of charity" by saying: "We must, by means of more numerous and fraternal contacts, restore step by step what the time of isolation has undone, and create anew, at all levels of the life of our Churches, an atmosphere which will allow us, when the time comes, to set about a theological discussion likely to yield good results.[16] In fact, "fraternal contacts" did become more and more numerous; Orthodox observers attended the third and fourth sessions of Vatican II, at the close of which there took place the symbolic act of "removing from memory and from the midst of the Church" the mutual excommunications which had been pronounced in 1054 between the papal legate Cardinal Humbert and the Patriarch Michael Cerularius. It was made clear that this act did not suffice by itself to restore communion between Rome and Constantinople, but it was undertaken on both sides as a public act of repentance for past wrongs, for the healing of memories that had for so long blocked communication between East and West.

---

16. Ibid., p. 88.

Two years later Paul VI took the unprecedented step of visiting Athenagoras at the Phanar, the seat of the Patriarchate in Istanbul. On that occasion he said: "For centuries we lived the life of 'sister Churches,' . . . and now, after a long period of division and mutual misunderstanding, the Lord is enabling us to discover ourselves as 'sister Churches' once more."[17] Several months later, Athenagoras returned the Pope's visit; in his speech in St. Peter's Basilica he stressed the need to continue and intensify the dialogue of charity, as a preparation for the theological dialogue to follow.[18] In his reply, Pope Paul said: "We must courageously follow up and develop this effort on both sides, being as far as possible in contact with each other as we do so, and cooperating in ways that should be discovered by joint effort."[19]

The sincere intention on both sides to be "as far as possible in contact with each other" is amply proven by the publication, in 1971, of the *Tomos Agapis*, containing no fewer than 284 documents exchanged between Rome and Constantinople between 1958 and 1970. This number is all the more striking, when one remembers that it was preceded by almost four hundred years of silence. After the death in 1972 of Patriarch Athenagoras, the "dialogue of charity" continued under his successor, Dimitrios I. In 1975, ten years after the lifting of the 1054 excommunications, the official announcement was made of a decision to establish a joint commission to prepare for a theological dialogue between Rome and the Orthodox Churches. At a ceremony in the Sistine Chapel in which this announcement was made, Pope Paul VI knelt and kissed the feet of the leader of the Orthodox delegation, Metropolitan Meliton: a symbolic action which was surely a more effective mode of communication than any speech would have been.

During the ensuing four-year period while negotiations were underway to prepare for the theological dialogue, it is evident that both Pope and Patriarch were very much aware of how crucial good communications between the two Churches were for establishing a favorable atmosphere for the success of the theological dialogue. Thus Paul VI said: "Over these last years the happy understanding between our Churches has become deeper and more frequently expressed, with the result that we now have twice a year an exchange of delegations which enables us to impart useful information to one another, something which is quite necessary if we are to harmonize our endeavors while advancing toward renewed communion."[20] Patriarch Dimitrios expressed similar sentiments: "We are convinced that both these regular 'face to face' discussions and our exchanges

---

17. Ibid., p. 162.
18. Ibid., p. 173.
19. Ibid., p. 176.
20. Ibid., pp. 310-11.

through 'pen and ink' (3 Jn 13-14), over and above the reaching out of our hearts in fellowship of feeling, form as it were so many stones in the construction of the edifice of reconciliation and union in Christ of our Churches."[21]

Pope John Paul II has continued the "dialogue of charity" begun by Paul VI, and has also expressed his sense of the importance of this rebuilding of communications between Rome and Constantinople. Little more than a year after his election, John Paul II took the initiative of visiting the Patriarch Dimitrios at the Phanar. On this occasion he said: "With realism and wisdom . . . it had been decided to renew relations and contacts between the Catholic Church and the Orthodox Churches which would enable them to recognize one another and create the atmosphere required for a fruitful theological dialogue. It was necessary to create the context again before trying together to rewrite the texts. . . . A great deal has been done, but this effort must be continued."[22]

Dimitrios stressed the same point in the letter which he wrote to John Paul II on the occasion of the Feast of Sts. Peter and Paul in 1982: "Holy Brother, not only the tradition of communicating with each other for feast-days, but in a more general way, the development and continual cultivation of brotherly relations, and the mutual sharing in each other's sorrow and joy—these things, in so far as they are the fruit of love, have clearly proved to be the really sound Christian way leading to the sacred goal envisaged, which is unity not only in love but in truth and faith."[23]

The long-awaited theological dialogue which began in May, 1980, on the Island of Patmos, has thus far produced three agreed statements: the "Munich Statement" of 1982: "The Mystery of the Church and of the Eucharist in the Light of the Mystery of the Holy Trinity," the "Bari Statement" of 1987: "Faith, Sacraments and the Unity of the Church," and the "Valamo Document" of 1988: "The role of the ordained ministry in the sacramental structure of the Church."

Despite the fact that the subjects treated so far have been among those on which Catholic and Orthodox traditions are not far apart, the dialogue has had its difficult moments. It is significant that the problems have arisen more as a result of failures of communication than for theological reasons. Thus, the preparation of the Bari Statement was troubled by a controversy surrounding the display in the Vatican of Macedonian icons: an exhibition thought by some Orthodox to constitute papal support for unwelcome claims of independence that were being made by the Orthodox Church of Macedonia. More recently progress has been interrupted by the suspicion created among the Russian Orthodox by the decision of

---

21. Ibid., p. 316.
22. Ibid., pp. 361-62.
23. Ibid., p. 438.

the Holy See to name bishops for the Eastern Catholics living in the former Soviet Union. Rome has been criticized for not having prepared for this move by first communicating to the Orthodox hierarchy a satisfactory explanation of its intentions in this regard. Whatever the justification of this criticism may be, the suspicions that have been raised, and the chill they have cast on the dialogue, provide another indication of how essential good communications are to the cause of ecumenism.

8

Christian Catechesis as Communication

Henri Bourgeois

Your neighbor helps to catechize a group of children. Is she a communicator? If you told her that she was, she would probably be surprised. She has no interest in the term "communication." It is just that she loves children and wants to share with them those things that make her live her faith.

One of your friends is attending a series of talks on the Christian faith today, because the subject interests him. Does he feel that he communicates with the speaker? Perhaps, but not necessarily. In any case, he would probably find such a point of view somewhat irrelevant. Communicating? Yes, of course. But what does it add to what he knows?

Today people often talk about communication in Christianity and about catechesis. But is catechesis only a language game that makes little difference to the facts? I invite you to consider this question with me. I shall make eleven observations on the relationship between Christian catechesis and communication.

1. *Catechesis sometimes enters into communication through a gate that is too narrow.*

Etymologically, the term "catechesis" comes from the Greek and refers to phenomena of resonance or vibration. The Word of God seeks and finds an echo in human experience and is articulated. This etymology, however, does not say much about how the catechetical process can be understood in terms of communication. We must take a look at practice. Even then the matter does not become immediately clear, because catechetical practices differ according to place, custom, and community. As I start my reflections, I hope that you will continue to keep in mind your own experience in this area.

People are often content to integrate communication and catechesis as simply as possible and according to a very limited perspective. They insist, for example, on incorporating audio-visual elements—slides, videos, music—into the techniques of catechetics.

My first observation is that some consider technology the hallmark of communication. Of course it does have a role to play. Students of media culture have told us often enough in recent years that technology is of major importance. But this view is overly narrow, for people tend to incorporate audio-visual methods into an unchanged approach to catechesis. They satisfy their desire to find better ways of transmitting a message, but they do not reflect on whether communication in the catechetical situation gains something from such technological developments.

My second observation is that people who work as catechists often make use of the venerable but linear model of H. D. Lasswell. In that model there is a sender and an audience, or in other terms, a transmitter and a receiver. It presumes a code, a reality, to which it bears witness (a referent), and a context in which it is to be interpreted. This model finds considerable favor among catechists who find it useful. It allows them to have a picture of what apparently takes place when they enter into a relation with children or adults to whom they proclaim the Word of God. The situation, however, is more complicated than that. Communication is not simply the transmission of a message more or less adapted to the needs of an audience and a cultural context. Communication is a *form of society,* a grouping of connections that intersect in various ways. It needs a broader cultural viewpoint than one that simply relates a transmitter to a receiver. Catechesis takes place in a much wider communicational field than itself which constitutes its ground.

My third observation is that concentrating on the *effects* produced by a message is an over-restrictive way of understanding communication in catechesis. This view may have some positive aspects. In principle, catechesis produces effects that we can sometimes observe in the catechized: growth in religious knowledge, a developed sensitivity to the Bible, fidelity to prayer. But this perspective is also too narrow. It does not take into account the social environment in which the effects take place. Moreover, it often considers the effects only in a one-sided way—as produced by catechists in the catechized. It is as if no effects occurred in the opposite direction or were produced by the catechized in the catechists: such as disappointments, wonderment, or confirmation in faith. We must, therefore, adopt a broader view of catechesis, moving beyond immediate experience.

2. *Catechesis is a practice that takes place in a social and ecclesial context.*

If we try to broaden our point of view too much, we run the risk of falling victim to muddled or woolly thinking. Yet the whole question is simpler than it might at first appear. The catechists and the catechized are not solely what their names signify; they also have other roles, other positions, other aspects. Both of them are also adult citizens or school children, male or female, consumers, people of the late twentieth century etc. These multiple *partial* identities contribute to defining them as persons; each one personally appropriates these features. Such identities are social. They correspond to images or models that circulate in a social group. Human beings personalize themselves in relation to their social environment.

These partial multifold identities are also linked to one another, both in social life and in the psychology and spirituality of the persons. When one of these factors is involved, the others may come into play in varying degrees. Potential elements that are in reserve can, if necessary, manifest themselves. When catechetical identity is more fully realized, the other features are not far away and can possibly appear.

How can we organize this field of socio-personal identities? In order to avoid abstract generalizations, the best way is to constitute it each time anew, in each situation, and in connection with each catechesis. It is helpful to organize the field in two distinct ways: from a social viewpoint and from an ecclesial viewpoint.

Let us first consider the *social* viewpoint. I assume I am in a catechetical situation. I know that certain of my identities are probably clearer than others, because they tend to be brought out more strongly when catechesis takes place. I think particularly of age and sex, family situation, and the kinds of sensitivity—affective or aesthetic—that characterize each person. For adults there is the work situation (a job or no employment) and the status persons believe they have in the social body. These elements are found both in the catechized and in the catechists. The catechetical relationship is affected, to some extent, by the elements of complicity or divergence that become visible in a situation. The manner in which this whole complex of elements will come together in different contexts of life depends on a complicated combination of factors. We cannot predict precisely what shape will appear.

Second, let us deal with the *ecclesial* viewpoint of the catechetical situation. We can make analogous observations. Catechists and the catechized are to varying degrees affected by the situation in the Church at the time, the images people have of it, and the events which influence it. First, there is a particular way Christians understand themselves, see society, and express among themselves the fraternal or reconciled relations to which their faith calls them. Second, in its own way society relates to the Church, opposes it or approves it, disregards it or uses it.

All of these factors affect the catechetical process more than we sometimes imagine. Catechesis is not only the statement and transmission of a message. It is also an action that deals with the social and ecclesial elements that we carry within us. In more classical theological language, catechesis is one of the places where the relationship between the Church and the world occurs. It is one of the places where people define themselves, thanks to, and sometimes in spite of, multiple meanings that are in circulation.

3. *In the public sphere of communication where catechesis exists and where multiple interactions take place, we must discover the image that catechesis gives itself.*

Curiously, not much attention is paid to the fact that catechesis is not only an operation but also an image, a symbol system. The most authoritative recent texts on catechetics—the Apostolic Exhortation of John Paul II, *Catechesi tradendae* (1979) and the document from the International Catholic Council for Catechesis, *On the Catechesis of Adults in the Christian Community* (1990)—insist that the catechetical act has goals, methods, and means. However, this is very general and in practice catechesis is manifested differently by both catechists and the catechized. Sometimes catechesis is seen as very structured, anxious to provide precise reference points. It seeks to bring the catechized eventually into the Christian order, an order that catechists are, to a greater or lesser extent, the witnesses of and responsible for. Some accuse catechesis as being at fault because of its generalized fussiness and sentimental verbiage. Some say it wastes time and gives up when it faces the values of the present age.

I do not want to enter into this debate. It is largely ideological and probably of little interest. It is, however, true that the reputation of catechesis affects its credibility and its effectiveness. It is as if official words about catechetical activity were in practice less important than the image people have of this Christian work—an image that is often clouded by emotion and polemics. Catechesis today is not only a classical and traditional practice; it is also a test of evangelical and ecclesial sensitivity. Something vital is at stake here. Christian groups confront one another on this point, because they are aware of its consequences for the future.

Even so, the picture I have sketched does not give a full idea of what shapes the reputation of catechesis in public opinion. Another factor should be mentioned, a factor that is connected with the combination of different forms of catechesis in a given place.

The catechetical situation varies depending on whether the catechized are children or adults. *Catechesi tradendae* quite rightly stresses that fact. The catechesis of adults, however, often has a minor place in comparison to the personnel and investment devoted to the catechesis of children. That is also true in other aspects of the Christian life, particularly baptism which is too often seen as being more or less reserved for infants. This child-oriented image, which so often predominates, rules out forms of catechesis offered to others than children. For most Christians, any reference to catechesis makes them think of childhood. After that it is either too late, or it is no longer "the right time." Christian communities should change this unilateral image. The eyes of public opinion—both Christian and non-Christian—must be opened to the variety of proposals offered by the Church in this regard.

One of the difficulties is that Christian leaders themselves often have too narrow a view of what is involved in the catechesis of adults. Although Church documents address this question well (*Catechesi tradendae*, 43-44), the practice lags behind. Poor communication exists between higher authorities and experts and the working catechists. The results are: a) we confuse the catechesis of adults with the training of Christians for a specific task; b) we generally limit catechesis to people who have the intellectual and cultural means of engaging in fairly learned discussion, and c) we ignore people who are beginning to believe or who are beginning again, if they have already been baptized. This is a serious defect. This puts catechesis at risk from a communication perspective, because it gives it an image that is *a priori* limited and does not correspond to what is being called for today.

Christian catechesis has a blurred image today, either because it is criticized or because it is not practiced enough. The best intentions can do nothing unless this image is changed. This image generally reflects the state of the Catholic Church that suffers from conflicts in sensitivity or that still lives as if the evangelization of children is a sufficient fulfillment of the Christian mission.

4. *Catechesis has been renewed to a great extent over the last fifty years, but still it needs to move forward confidently, if it is to make an impact in this age of communication.*

Catechetical methods, styles, and means have been rejuvenated since the days of teaching the catechism by memorization and the question and answer approach. As this century draws to a close, however, we are still left with formulae that are inadequate.

Many catechists use a contemporary "vulgate" in the catechesis of children and adults. Catechists are aware that they have to be attentive to their dialogue partners, to their expectations and experience. They realize that the catechized are not passive, and that they are subjects who play a joint role in the search. Catechists know that teaching is important, but it is not the only thing. Knowledge must go hand-in-hand with sensitivity, affectivity, and with practice and action. This approach is due not only to meditation on the Gospel but also to the transformation of educational and teaching methods. The "new catechesis" is the result of communication with contemporary culture. Once catechesis entered the world of communications, that world forced it to keep moving forward.

Mere talk about reciprocity and interaction is not enough. We must explain how actions can be put into practice. If we are in agreement with the socio-cultural view that I described above, then we can see that the complexity of catechesis goes well beyond teaching methods or group techniques. It is a question of developing catechetics according to the wide horizon that we call the world and the Church. In concrete terms, this perspective calls for three practical steps: to clarify the conditions for the possibility of the catechetical operation; to confront present-day unbelief and indifference and to make the voice of the catechized, even if discordant, ring out in the Church. I shall briefly discuss each of these three tasks.

First, the act of catechesis presumes that both the catechists and the catechized have a kind of *pact of trust,* something that cannot be taken for granted. Placing ourselves in the hands of another person in what concerns the most intimate and decisive area of our life calls for remarkable trust. Perhaps it is now that catechesis, which has suffered many crises, has the almost unexpected opportunity of realizing what an exceptional relationship it represents in both human and spiritual terms. Even so catechesis can develop only if one has time. This may come as a surprise to many people who have too much to do or who tire easily. So once again, catechesis intersects contemporary culture and must explain itself to it. Communication cannot be established between the catechists and the catechized, unless both clarify their reaction to the lack of time, the lack of trust, and the excess of distrust which affects us today.

Second, contemporary catechesis cannot confront the collective dimension of existence, unless it is attentive to what we currently refer to as unbelief and indifference. The word "unbelief," although it is becoming a little worn, refers to a spiritual situation which certainly does not mean a complete absence of belief (one can believe in man) but refers to an alienation from religious attitudes and meanings. In this sense, unbelief indicates the gap between the Christian message and the very different interests of many of our contemporaries. Indifference, on the other hand, expresses a more or less generalized disinterest in broad, global perspectives or long-term projects, especially those dealing with religious and political matters. Unbelief points to the gap between Christianity and culture which grows with indifference.

Why talk about unbelief and indifference which are common in our society, when the catechized themselves are positively oriented toward Christianity? Catechesis is taking place, and, at least in principle, there is a certain interest in the religious sphere and in the Gospel. But many of the catechized in our times, including children, are more affected by unbelief and indifference than we may think. They feel some sympathy with those attitudes, because of those around them, because of their personal relations, and because of the age in which they feel they belong. Catechesis must deal with this point of reference or this form of identification. It cannot do so without broadening its horizon. It must see that what takes place here and now is manifested there and there.

Third, the task of Christian catechesis also involves communication. The catechized must have an impact within the Church. Their experience, their difficulties, their way of expressing the faith, and their way of living must be recognized within Christian groups in order to stimulate them. It may sometimes shake them, but it often renews them. This approach is a rare one. Many texts from Rome and from the dioceses say that catechesis should have a communitarian dimension and involve the participation of the community. That may be so, but we must take a closer look at what it really means. The documents do not say that the Church receives a spirit of youthfulness from the catechized and probably also from the catechists because of their relationship with the catechized.

5. *From the perspective of communication, catechesis is not only a relation between persons but equally an intersection among orders of value and meaning.*

In order to explain this new proposition, I shall begin by giving what is commonly held. Accordingly, catechesis, which is interactive, is carried out by catechists and the catechized in a reciprocal relation. It should be noted that it is not totally reciprocal, because the catechists bear a word of which they are only witnesses, the Divine Word. This Word comes to humans who cannot produce it on their own. Since catechesis announces a message to be received in the hearing of the faith, it follows that there is an unequal relation between the catechist and the catechized. Not that one group is more valuable or meritorious than the other. The equality between them is, in principle, total, but their roles are not on the same level.

This is an acceptable interpretation. It is verified in practice, even if always in an imperfect way. Nevertheless, one can make it more precise according to the perspective I have proposed. What happens between the catechists and the catechized transcends the persons themselves. In them God and the world meet. That is founded on the social and ecclesial dimension of the process of catechesis. The catechetical relationship opens up worlds of meaning by which both the catechist and the catechized are able to communicate with one another.

How does this two-way communication operate? I see it in both cases as an *intersection*—an expression I borrow from the German specialist in hermeneutics, H. G. Gadamer. Understanding is an act that brings two spheres closer together, at least partially. The two spheres may be a text that one seeks to interpret and the person who is the reader-interpreter because of history and skill. Understanding lies in the superimposition of two groups of meaning, although they can never be confused with one another. Understanding links what is the same and what is different. I would suggest that this hermeneutical view, which is reflected today in numerous theories of reading and reception, can throw light on what is called communication.

There are four forms of intersection. First, in catechesis there comes to both the catechized and the catechist an intervention between themselves and the world of faith that is established by the Word of God. A second intersection is also present, because both the catechist and the catechized are equally in relation to the cultural, ethical, and social world. A third intersection brings together and distinguishes the Gospel universe and the cultural universe from the perspectives of each individual conscience and of different groups. Being a Christian means confessing that the revealed gift is linked to creation where daily life takes place—close enough for the revealed gift not to be extrinsic to creation, but not too close for there to be confusion or fusion.

People have their own way of bringing about these three intersections. Even if the terms of a question are the same for all, the solution adopted or the actions performed differ from person to person, from moment to moment, and from group to group.

A fourth or new form of intersection between the catechist and the catechized must be noted. Neither party is confused with the other. Their previous knowledge, their experience, and their role in catechesis is not identical. Both communicate with one another according to the way they each communicate with the divine message and with the world in which they life and according to the way they each articulate these two spheres. Catechesis is the bringing into play of four simultaneous and linked intersections: between the persons and the message of faith, between persons and culture, between the world of faith and the world of culture, and, lastly, between the persons themselves. We can say that the "game" of catechesis is played with four "hands": the catechists, the catechized, the universe of faith in the divine Word, and the universe of living in the world.

Catechetical work gradually sets up relations between these four elements. Catechists do not have a monopoly on initiative. The catechized also contribute their views. The catechists, however, have the skill and the mission that authorize them to teach, but not with the intention that the catechized should copy or mimic the catechists' own experience. The catechized are all the better catechized and all the more active in catechesis, the more they respond in their own distinctive manner, bringing to bear their own experience as new or renewed Christians.

6. *Catechesis, as a process of communication and intersection, uses symbol systems.*

Catechesis has a number of components. It transmits knowledge, but it also has aspects of celebration, sensitivity, and aesthetics. There are also practical elements relating to behavior and decisions to be taken. The problem is that these components are often juxtaposed, and sometimes they barely communicate with one another. Moreover, catechetical discourse today is often polemical as it tries to develop features of sensitivity or, on the contrary, as it pleads for an expression that will very likely be misunderstood.

One perspective of communication that affects our world in the areas of politics and advertising can help us integrate these various components. That unifying viewpoint is symbolism. By this I mean a form of experience in which imagination and the relation to another person enter into action simultaneously. Symbolism is a cognitive and relational formation in which the image has a predominant role which greatly influences the other alternative elements—argumentative knowledge, sensitivity, ethics, celebration. This is true of the symbols used in the search for truth and unity, or the symbols we have of ourselves and of society. Images, as these examples show, are organized into clusters around a mother cell which corresponds to a vital interest of an individual or a group.

Communication operates in practice with symbol systems. The world of meanings that I mentioned earlier are in fact groups of symbol systems linked to the Gospel or culture. We must add to these the image of catechesis which also has value as a symbol.

How are we to understand symbol systems, granting that they involve, in the final analysis, several intersections? We can specify two operations in the use of symbol systems: the making of connections and the process of identification.

The first operation is that of making connections. Catechesis moves from symbol system to symbol system and from image to image, as it seeks to establish connections and correlations. Most often, it feels its way, without being able to state in advance the expected result. Catechesis has plans of a pedagogical nature and relies on traditions which allow it to anticipate more or less what will take place. However, some elements remain unforeseeable. This reality should not be understood from an anthropological point of view: symbol systems are not objects that can be manipulated according to mechanical or physical laws. This has special evangelical and theological importance. Both the catechized and the catechists act within the sphere of mystery.

To describe how the catechetical process "feels its way," we can say that symbol systems are matrices of intelligibility and relation. They emit a kind of harmonics, resonances, or associated vibrations not unlike the alpha waves that the brain emits. These harmonics are both cognitive and affective. Information or knowledge (coherence, prestige) play a part, just as sensitivity and the heart do (enjoyment, fear, satisfaction). Catechesis proceeds in the field of affinities and co-vibrations in a way similar to what literary analysis or research on the unconscious call metaphor and metonymy. In this manner, links are set up between the image of the self as such (the symbolism of the self), the image of the Christ of the Gospel, the image of culture, the image of the Church, and so forth.

Symbol systems have not only cognitive and affective capacities but also meaningful content and a mode of presentation, enunciation, and manifestation. A catechesis on Abraham, for example, gives information about this great figure and brings out harmonics of faith and trust. Yet it also operates in a particular context and employs a certain tone of voice and emotion.

Resonance in catechesis operates on two levels and uses two ranges of possibilities. Experience shows that a connection can sometimes be set up between the image of Abraham and the image of oneself because of the content but not because of the tone or the manifestation. One gives information or is informed, but one remains apart from what one knows. The opposite can also happen.

It is no less frequent for a person to be touched by a sign, a witness, a biblical or contemporary figure without knowledge being brought into play. In both cases, there is obviously something lacking.

Catechesis is not satisfied simply with making connections. It also works with symbol systems that make contact. This role, which may be better known than the previous one, is of major importance. It should be noted that it cannot happen without the co-vibrations or harmonics that I discussed earlier.

The second operation that catechesis uses in conjunction with symbol systems consists in identifying the symbol systems that are involved. They are often present without being clearly defined. We must enrich them, explain their harmonics, explore their content, verify their relations, and examine their shortcomings. This operation can be performed at the same time as the task of connection, and it entails both cognitive and affective aspects. The cognitive element usually tends to be large. It consists basically in understanding what is taking place, of providing a rational explanation of the effect produced by the catechetical proclamation, and of intellectually justifying the acceptance or resistance that rises in oneself. In this way, catechesis is made rational and is related to communication. Catechesis seeks to improve its performance of the tasks of intersection that I discussed above. It becomes rational in order to understand better and to be understood.

7. *Catechesis, as part of socio-cultural communication, contributes to raising and sometimes resolving the question of individual identity.*

Identity is a major problem today. Many people have trouble in understanding who they are and what their vocation is. The way in which the great institutions, both political and religious, respond to this problem is not completely relevant. Too often, their reaction is that of over-protectiveness. By whittling away the freedom of thought or action, they want to think for their members or adherents. At times, social bodies, including churches, feel the need to reinforce or create a new public image of their own collective identity, as if the reaffirmed identity of the institution will necessarily contribute to the identity of the individual members.

The perspective of communication leads to a different view. The identity of individuals is not a private matter linked to introspection. Even if we tried to look at it this way, facts would soon change our view. It is communication that constructs the identity of individuals. Not that individuals are simply the epiphenomena of communication systems, somewhat like the blinking warning lights signaling a moving vehicle. Nevertheless, individuals can exist only insofar as they are constituted through what surrounds them, passes through them, and makes demands upon them. Individuals can gain access to themselves only through their environment.

In practice, personal identity is born when persons identify the influences that affect them. Each of us is taken up into a network of interactions that are made and unmade without us, but of which we are in part the result. Do we have to sacrifice ourselves to a kind of fatalism, as if the individual were simply a product of society? I do not think so. In the media culture, we now see clearly that spectators and listeners are less conditioned by the messages they receive than we would have thought. Individuals at least have the possibility of constructing the meaning of what they receive.

If we apply this process of active reception of the media to the catechetical context, we can analyze in similar fashion the establishment of individual identity through communicative action. There are three important elements in this process.

First, there is the conviction that individuals count, and that they have the possibility of being informed and of stating their opinions. Catechesis is a space for words. Daring to speak out is part of the process, and it offers this opportunity to both the catechists and the catechized.

Second, a minimum of trust must be put in the other person. This attitude is not automatic in the present world, where distrust often rules human relations. In catechesis, however, the two sides decide to trust one another. They may not be in agreement, but they do not suspect one another. If they do, they should stop and start over in a different way.

Third, catechesis provides the means for naming the worlds of meaning or symbol systems which operate in the world in which we live, whether it be the world of culture or the world of the Gospel. Instead of simply accepting rumors and ambiguous hearsay, individuals should take time to discern the context of their lives. If this is done, a certain clarification of the situation results. People feel the birth of the desire to situate themselves. If we identify the influences to which we are subject in society and the influences we submit to more freely in the religious tradition, we are able to identify ourselves.

This search for personal identification presumes that we work on the image we gain of ourselves. The image may be confused, its strength sapped by the imaginary or crushed by rules. Catechesis invites us to enrich the definition of this image. It also provides the means of enrichment by calling us to listen and to speak, inviting us to find a place related to culture and the Gospel, and asking us to give up naive approaches that overvalue individual autonomy or minimize the need for relations with others.

It is in this perspective that we can understand what is called conversion. Catechesis does not as such aim at converting the catechized. The latter are either already sensitized to the Gospel and the presence of Christ, or they are hesitant and uncertain about giving an assent that would make them disciples of Christ. In either case, the decision for conversion is not, properly speaking, up to catechesis. It is linked to the mystery of each person and to circumstances. Catechesis, however, contributes to conversion, either by explaining it or by making it credible and possible. Being converted means experiencing the symbol system of the Gospel on the same wave-length as that of my personal self. The Gospel displaces the image of self, stripping it of its pretensions and giving it a mysterious center of gravity other than that to which individual experience spontaneously tends.

8. *Catechesis, which is related to an individual's identity, can be seen either as the exercise and maintenance of an already acquired christian identity or as the initial establishment of a christian identity that is to be acquired.*

The solution to the problem of Christian identity in relation to catechesis involves clarification of the reality of conversion. There are non-catechized converts who will in some cases never be catechized. There are also non-converted catechized people in whom the catechetical experience does not give rise to the experience of a stable and sound faith that would make them disciples of Christ. We must, therefore, be careful not to confuse conversion and catechesis, however clear the links between them may be.

The question of Christian identity leads to another point that is very important today: the relation between catechesis and initiation. Not all catechesis is initiating, but it is indispensable that it be available for uninitiated people, whether children or adults. Catechesis, however, should be distinguished from both conversion and initiation.

What is meant by initiation? This term, which was not widely used in early Christian times nor in the Middle Ages in the West, has now taken root in the language of Catholicism. Vatican II spoke about the sacraments of Christian initiation, and postconciliar theology often uses this expression applying to it characteristics from ethnology or cultural anthropology. Initiation is the responsibility that society exercises in regard to its young members. The process of initiation links transmission of knowledge, the affective experience of a powerful and special moment, the learning of behavior suited to the shared life of society, and, lastly, the identification of each person within a common, shared identity. Several of these features are akin to some of the hallmarks of Christian catechesis. The unique feature of initiation is that it involves a distancing from everyday life. The initiation process consists of several distinct steps and tests as a part of each step.

Such a program of initiation is a feature of catechesis when the catechized are at the start of their Christian experience. In principle, we are talking about children and also about adults who are either just discovering Christianity (catechumens) or who are baptized but have fallen away to the point of forgetting nearly everything. They are now starting to believe again and are following the path of the Gospel and the Church. Initiation seeks to establish the foundations of Christian identity. It does so according to a proved method made up of a series of steps and tests that allow individuals to develop a Christian personality within themselves. Initiation places the person in a position to communicate with other Christians. Through initiation, catechesis leads people to follow a path along which they learn, in Gospel terms, who they are.

Initiating catechesis is proving to be indispensable today, especially in a world of communications. In order to be able to take part in these multiple connections that make up the fabric of life without "losing one's soul," it is valuable to have a clear identity. We cannot give ourselves an identity by dint of our own efforts, but it can be acquired in the course of a process specifically designed for that purpose. Initiation presumes that the person is receptive to the plan. Regrettably, a willingness to spend time and an openness of spirit are often lacking. To benefit from initiating catechesis, a person must voluntarily attend the meetings and must freely consent to participate in a recognized program. Not all children in catechesis are in this situation, nor are all the young people or adults who are "interested" in Christianity ready to invest time and effort and to risk their personal identity. For initiation to be successful, those in charge must take responsibility and present a heritage that they value. Even in churches, some persons, including leaders, often lack the will to initiate.

The likelihood of initiation is uncertain. But let no one say that we no longer live in a society capable of initiating their members. I do not believe it. Media culture shows, on the contrary, that initiation is sought by many people, even if they do not always find it easy to attain.

Yet not all catechesis is necessarily initiating or, to use the language of *Catechesi tradendae*, catechumenal. There is a place for non-initiating forms of catechesis, for example, when the catechized are already sufficiently initiated or when they have finished the program and still enjoy the benefits. In such a case, we can speak of a catechesis of maintenance or deepening. It has a certain relation to initiation, but it presumes the latter and therefore uses another tone and style.

If I stress initiation, it is because one aspect of communication demands it. If catechesis contributes to personal identity because of communicational exchanges, we must recognize the predominant form of communication today—mass communications—tends to discredit and marginalize initiating procedures. For mass communications we can either communicate immediately without initiation or we can initiate ourselves in a sort of high-speed self-initiation. This is an illusion. Our contemporaries who are plunged in the vortex of the media are certainly kept abreast of events and "massed" by the media in affective terms. The media brings them closer socially. But they lack the opportunity to be guided so they can realize their potential and make their own identities effective.

9. *Catechesis as communication bears witness to the truth.*

The question of truth arises, when we consider communication. First of all, people rightly fear that truth is being defined by the law of the majority. In this perspective public opinion is the form that truth takes at any given moment. Second, people are concerned that the truth in communication is corrupted or at least threatened by affectivity, seduction, and manipulation, which to some extent affect social relations.

Such is the context in which catechesis is situated today. Catechesis is traditionally accustomed to relating to the truth that is found in revelation. The truth of revelation depends on its source: God who communicates himself to humanity. Catechesis has the role of transmitting the divine message to societies and individuals who live in history and make history. That is correct, but it is unilateral. Actually, the question of the truth in catechesis is much more complex. It is not defined solely in terms of the revelatory source. It is also opened up by its relation to the actors involved in the catechetical process. These actors are the catechists and the catechized, both of whom play an active part in catechesis.

It is necessary to formulate precisely the question of how catechesis produces the truth. We could use the classic schema of communication in which the "addresser" is God and the "addressees" are human beings. The addressees are both the catechists and the catechized. Catechists are also listeners and recipients of the Word that they announce.

It would be better to approach this question in operative terms. Two factors that are connected must be considered: a) How do catechists and the catechized related to the source which is the Divine Word? b) How do both catechists and the catechized enter into a relation with the Word? Do the catechized do so thanks to the catechists and the catechists thanks to the catechized? The two actions are simultaneous and not successive. But it is preferable to make a distinction between them for the sake of clarity. How, then, does catechesis relate to its source?

In the first place, it appears that the catechists and the catechized are put together by an initiative from God. What they express depends on a prior divine intervention which authorizes their words. Before they speak, they are spoken to. What they speak is articulated in a field already opened up by the primordial Word, and it echoes the Word. The act of God connects people and gathers them together. Not only is the work of the catechists and the catechized preceded by the divine Word, but, because of the initiative of the Word, they enter into a relation, and they talk to one another. Catechesis flows from this preliminary stage. In the final analysis, the catechists and the catechized have no other reason for entering into a relationship than the call received by both to perform the work of faith together.

In the second place, the relation of catechesis to its source brings out an inevitable gulf between God who speaks and humans to whom he speaks. Nobody can honestly claim to be a full and exhaustive witness to the mystery of God. Of course, we can presume that catechists try to be as faithful and as objective as they can. We can likewise say that the catechized may receive more than they realize or dare to tell. And all this certainly counts. There is, however, always a gap between human words and the divine Word. It is for this very reason that the Bible is an essential element in catechesis. The Bible gives us the beginnings. The present reality of faith, which is necessarily partial, must constantly measure itself against "those times," so that it does not make an idol of itself.

How do catechists and the catechized pass on their hearing of the Word, and how do they express it? This action should benefit both parties, because of their relationship and their reciprocal communication. For a long time, much thought has been given to the mission of the catechists. The Church empowers and sends them on a mission. This authorizes the action of the catechists and calls upon them not to remain prisoners of their own subjectivity. Since catechists have to "speak the Gospel," they are encouraged to receive the Word more completely and more objectively. Thanks to the catechized, the catechists are, in principle, given the opportunity to become more evangelical.

Ordinary catechesis too often forgets a complementary factor: the catechized bring to catechists more than an invitation to receive the Gospel better. The catechized bring out certain aspects of the Word of God, which they may be in a better position to experience. They are "newcomers" in the field of the Gospel, without habits or accustomed routine. The clumsiness or unexpected reactions of the catechized, like their enthusiasm and their wonderment, are signs of a living Gospel which the cate-chists receive in part from them.

The catechists and the catechized become all the more evangelizers for one another when third parties enter into their relationship. The latter is not some exclusive and closed encounter. The relationship passes through figures of biblical witness (Abraham, Moses, Jesus) and also through contemporary figures (members of the Church and members of society). The relationship to these "third parties" is not quite the same for catechists and the catechized. This helps maintain the difference between them and to make this difference an opportunity for both parties.

What about the fears expressed earlier concerning truth in communi-cation? Catechesis never totally avoids the dangers expressed above. Catechesis, to a greater or lesser extent, is sensitive to public opinion—such as slogans of the day or the image of catechesis in a given group. The catechetical situation is so structured that it can avoid the most seri-ous deviations. This is because catechesis refers to the Word which is al-ways other than the catechists and the catechized. It brings "third parties" into play and thus prevents dangerous short-circuits. It is legitimate to say that catechesis "makes the truth" in the evangelical sense of the world, that is, by receiving it.

10. *Catechesis, in terms of communication, involves a "code of conduct" without which it cannot properly fulfill its mission.*

The specification of such a code would require many details and ex-planations that would take us beyond the framework of this study. What follows are some of the most important elements in catechesis today.

a) Catechesis is an undertaking of human communication that rests on a particular strategy of communication: the relationship of God with human beings. Catechesis would not exist without the covenant and without the Gospel proclamation. Without giving up its socio-cultural and psycho-cul-tural responsibilities, catechesis is aware of being a channel of divine en-ergy. God is at work when the task of catechesis begins its task. The Word that catechesis listens to relies on the mysterious presence of the Holy Spirit in the hearts of the catechized and the catechists.

b) It is not wise to overestimate catechesis, but it is equally mistaken not to establish it wherever possible. The churches have a catechetical respon-sibility that is part of their mission to the world.

It would be an overestimation, if we thought that catechesis alone satisfied the requirement that the Gospel be proclaimed, the memory of Christ be secured, and the Christian faith be alive. Other communication networks are indispensable for those tasks. I have in mind the information media (newspapers, newsletters, radio, television) which provide informa-tion and programs that go beyond the picturesque or the merely anecdotal.

I also think of what is called formation, which is more technical than catechesis inasmuch as it provides greater depth and prepares people for a role in the Church.

To avoid any possible overestimation of catechesis, it is necessary to have "contracts" that clearly define objectives and means for the interested parties: the catechists, the catechized, and the ecclesial institutions. Catechesis must, as far as possible, define what it wants to achieve and what can be expected of it. People should not enter into catechesis without realizing what is involved. Otherwise, it would mean confusion and would very quickly lead to disappointment. It is vital for adults and children to draw up a clear statement of the most important "rules of the game," such as regular attendance, interaction, etc.

The catechetical contract, however, should not be too demanding. If it errs on that side, it runs the risk of not encouraging effective communication. I see two disturbing practices.

The first questionable practice is to hold that catechesis presupposes faith, as *Catechesi tradendae* 19, says. In my view, that demand is unwarranted, at least at the beginning of the process. It is possible that some of our contemporaries sincerely wish to begin the path of catechesis, without being able to say at the outset that they truly believe. We could say that they fit into the category of "precatechesis." But the distinction between catechesis and precatechesis is merely formal and difficult to apply in practice. I do not see what it contributes to the discussion. The whole point is whether one has agreed to listen to and to speak the Word which Christians say is divine and which one feels can have some vital results in our common existence.

The second questionable practice is to consider catechesis according to the norm of "all or nothing." In this view, some say that the catechized must necessarily become regular Sunday church-goers. If this is not the case, they regret that a catechetical program that began well has ended prematurely; they judge too hastily that the time invested has been wasted. Such a demand, in my opinion, is excessive. In Christian experience there is, of course, an evangelical line of reasoning that leads to the duty and even the desire for the Sunday assembly. A catechetical contract assumes in principle that the parties will follow to the end what is stipulated. Persistency is not accepted by everyone today. Even so, a lack of understanding does not mean that the catechetical world is useless or a waste of time.

The churches have to offer catechesis, especially when it would not automatically be expected. An operation of this kind needs to be performed according to what people want. Sometimes we must even go out of our way to meet demands that are not yet properly articulated. I have in mind particularly the catechesis of adults, especially the initiation catechesis of beginners or re-beginners.

c) A third element in the code of good conduct for communicational catechesis is the attention given to the quality of exchanges. Each communication is unique in catechesis. Communication presupposes a relation in which the roles are not identical; we have the catechists and the catechized. These communication exchanges require a work contract, since they should not be rambling conversations. The experience and formulation of faith are truly sought in receiving a Word that no one has invented.

For the uniqueness of catechesis to be respected and honored, certain practices are necessary. I will not give a long list. There is a risk of increasing the number of practical aids or directions, while forgetting that the essential point is the spirit, the tone of the proclamation, and the unpredictable harmonics of the message in circulation. We can, however, at least mention certain important concerns.

Catechetical communication, for example, assumes that both sides will show the patience needed for reformulation or for twofold formulation. Reformulating the message from the dialogue partner allows one to ask for a confirmation of it and to explain to oneself what has been received. As regards twofold formulation, the concern here is simple. It is a question of making an effort to express what one means in at least two different ways. First, this approach makes it possible to enter more easily into the sense of what is being said. Second, it lays the groundwork for the multiple formulations that are called for by life beyond catechesis.

Two other observations deserve mention. However much catechesis tries to be affirmative, it cannot ignore the difficulties entailed by unbelief and indifference today. However hard a catechesis may try to avoid a systematic approach because it may frighten people, it must realize that is is sometimes necessary for catechists and the catechized to take stock of things and to gather together what is happening in a relationship or in a group.

11. *In conclusion, I hope that Christian catechesis will become more communicational.*

People still say that catechesis seeks to communicate faith. That is a clumsy formula for two reasons. First, it is God alone who can enable a person to believe. Second, catechesis is more a communication *in* faith than a communication *of* faith. Catechesis is an operation that fits into many communication networks of social and political life. My hope is, therefore, that catechesis will dare to recognize the real context in which it takes place, instead of secluding itself in some artificial hothouse.

My second hope concerns ecumenism. At the present, catechesis is generally done according to confessional lines. Although ecumenism can be one of its subjects, it rarely is. Would it not be a good idea for the practice of catechesis to be pluriconfessional whenever that is possible, because that is the situation of Christians in the world today?

My third hope is that people should not consider only how communication—understood in the global sense—can encourage, illuminate, and even promote catechesis. Those functions are, of course essential, as I have tried to explain. I believe, however, that we must be able to go further and to have the courage to consider how the unique character of catechesis can help us to understand something of social communication as a whole. Normal reciprocity is operative here. If catechesis borrows from communication, is it not legitimate that, in return and without making any claims, catechesis should bring to communications something of what it experiences? Could not catechesis share, for example, the reference to a founding word or the understanding of initiation?

9

Christian Witness as Communication

Ricardo Antoncich, S.J.

Communication has changed radically because of mass distribution techniques and the predominance of the visual. These changes profoundly influence the communication of the Gospel, the essential mission of the Church and what constitutes the very source of its existence. Christianity began to exist, indeed, because the community accepted the fact that "the Word became flesh," and that God had initiated a special kind of communication with humanity in the person of Jesus and the witness of his life. The Church was created by an act of communication, by revelation.

The Church in turn exists to communicate the good news of our salvation to the world and thus to perpetuate the communication of God in Christ throughout time. Both the origin and the growth of the Church are linked to communication. Because of that, the subject of communication is of intense interest to it in the exercise of its mission.

The Church encountered many barriers to the communication of its message in the different cultures. It met with the challenge of Greek culture, with Roman imperial power, with the conversion of the barbarian peoples, and with the evangelization of the peoples in America, both North and South. It had to adapt itself in order to be understood, and it also had to seek information and to question in order to be a communication of God.[1] The two thousand years of this labor of communication have demonstrated the Church's creativity in meeting the challenges of each period and in finding satisfactory solutions for them. Despite inevitable historical mistakes, the Church has been able to adapt its message to the incredible variety of languages and cultures.

However, adaptation to various cultures now involves a vast store of modern knowledge in anthropology, sociology, and history. In addition there has been, beginning with Vatican Council II, a greater openness on the part of the Church, one which in Karl Rahner's opinion involved a

---

1. On these two aspects of adaptation and cultural questioning see Alan Figueroa Deck, *The Second Wave. Hispanic Ministry and the Evangelization of Cultures* (New York: Paulist Press, 1989), pp. 92-119.

transition as important as the one made by the so-called Council of Jerusalem. There was in the first council a transition from the Judaeo-Christian community to the community in the Graeco-Roman world and in Vatican II a transition from a European Church to a truly worldwide Church.[2]

In this universalization of the Church, the communications media present a challenge. The Church has sought to "inculturate" the Gospel, to transmit it and to embody it in the culture. Now that the Church feels itself to be truly universal, it is also encountering a universal culture, one that is controlled by the communications media. In contrast to the former processes of inculturation, the new challenges do not come from geographical frontiers or definite cultural traditions. The new challenge is that of a culture which is universal, unified and strongly molded by the modern communications media. We are experiencing a transition toward a new way of getting information, of communicating with one another, and consequently of being and existing as human persons. Communication now is not simply a vehicle for the transmission of a culture that already exists, but it is becoming one of the elements that controls a new culture.[3] The inculturation of the Gospel in this new cultural process that is influenced by the media demands a deep awareness of the implications both of the instruments or means and of the way in which the message is communicated, and all this means significant changes in the very life of the Church.[4]

The importance of this problem derives from the characteristics of the modern world, from its complexities and its seekings, from its potentialities and its sense of technical progress, and above all from the need for evangelization as the fundamental mission of the Church. The problem is complex, and in this article we are limiting our study to analyzing the characteristics of communication that demand a new sensibility in ecclesial communication. Our study is an attempt to point out the importance of "witness" as an appropriate means of communication, given the importance of the visual in modern techniques. However, beginning from this necessary adaptation to the requirements of the media, we will enter upon a deeper theological consideration. In a way, the media challenge us to regain the fundamental importance of witness as Christian communication.

---

2. See Karl Rahner, "Basic Theological Interpretation of the Second Vatican Council," *Theological Investigations* (New York: Crossroad, 1981), XX: 77-89.

3. See Joshua Mevrowitz, *No Sense of Place: The Impact of Electronic Media on Social Behavior* (New York: Oxford University Press, 1985).

4. The new world of media culture is not, however, present in ecclesial consciousness to a great degree. See Robert A. White, "Mass Media and Culture in Contemporary Catholicism. The Significance of Vatican II," in René Latourelle, ed., *Vatican II: Assessment and Perspectives. Twenty Five Years After—1962-1987* (New York: Paulist Press, 1989), III: 580-611.

The communication challenge can awaken a better understanding of evangelization itself. It is not a matter of a mere strategic accommodation or of a pastoral use of certain instruments; it is a matter of rethinking theologically the paths of a communication of the Gospel values. Christian witness is not just an appropriate response on the level of the challenge of the media, but also a recovery of the importance of witness in a communication of the Gospel centered on the orthopraxis of the faith.

I. Innovations in Communication and their Challenges

It is not our intention to discuss innovations in communication in detail, but rather to emphasize certain fundamental aspects concerned with education (and hence of education in the faith) and with human relations, with our way of living.

Communication, above all in the visual media, is changing our way of understanding reality and of understanding our very selves.[5] Communication is the fundamental path of the "socialization" of people in social groups, in the family, society, and nation. Children and young people enter into the adult world through the path of a communication of "learning." For centuries this communication was verbal, in words, whether oral or written. Today one has to ask what proportion of learning the children of this generation owe to formal education, the traditional mode of communication, and how much to informal education through the frequent use of the communications media, above all of television. An attempt to incorporate informal methods into formal education is not sufficient for educational purposes; it is necessary rather to recognize the other source of knowledge, one that is not controllable in specific school programs but which is nevertheless a genuine path to learning.[6]

Modern communications affect not only the way we learn but also the way we live. We live in accordance with what we have learned. In that sense the content of what was communicated is important. However, in contrast with other kinds of communication, where the important element was the content of what was presented, with the media something new has come into being. For the media offer not just the possibility of

---

5. Communication must be studied as part of the whole culture. It is not simply a matter of content. It is the vehicle of communication itself. See Paul A. Soukup, "Communication, Cultural Form, and Theology," *The Way* (*Supplement*) 57 (1986): 77-89. Also see the articles quoted by Soukup: Raymond Williams, George Gerbner, and Kathleen Connolly.

6. Not just children but some 80 percent of adults as well live a television life rather than a real life, according to William F. Fore, *Television and Religion* (Minneapolis, MN: Ausburg Publishing House, 1987). See also Robert P. Waznak, "The Church's Response to the Media: Twenty Five Years after *Inter Mirifica*," *America* 160 (1989): 36-40.

giving content, but in addition they constitute intrinsically a new method of communication and hence a new way of perceiving human reality, of making it known, and therefore of shaping this reality. In the final analysis, it is a different way of living and of being persons.

Within this new situation there are evident ambiguities. Visual communication can have negative influences on people's reflexes, on their capacity for abstraction and for perception of the whole; they are a fleeting, transitory communication that is subject to the influence of other visual impressions. Who among us has not experienced a disagreeable feeling when, in the midst of a very serious subject, a "commercial" that interrupts the program sends us back to very banal aspects of life; or when following a program that impresses us and demands deep consideration, another one comes along that dissipates and erases the impact of the previous program. Communication pulls us toward a level of passing fashions, of superficial attitudes, of conventional cliches. The bombardment of a consumer society designs our attitudes and distorts our needs; we are programmed "to need what is produced," instead of orienting the economy "to produce what is needed." Again, because of the very nature of the communications media, messages that cannot be expressed through these channels, but which may be important for the development of the person, get filtered out. Modern communication if not used critically, can involve a loss of values and of potential for human development.

It would nevertheless be very superficial to remain on the level of criticism of the risks and dangers and to fail to see the marvelous opportunities that the communications media offer. Perhaps the most basic one of all may be that of creating in the whole of humanity a feeling of collective belonging. To achieve that, a good many barriers will have to be broken down. The removal of the Berlin wall was a symbol of a process of unification, not just of one people but of a world divided by ideologies.

The communications media contribute to the breaking down of barriers. In the first place the geographical ones. In ancient times only those who could travel could enter into the riches of other cultures, of other traditions and values. Today we contemplate landscapes, see monuments, and are well acquainted with great cities, the smallest towns, and the quite different faces of the different racial groups.

Language difficulty itself seems to be overcome by access to symbols that are universal. A little sketch of a passenger with his suitcase in front of a customs official says more in airports than the words *Douane, Customs, Alfandega, Aduana.* . . . The media give us a knowledge of foreign languages; a video brings into every house an experienced professor who repeats the lesson as many times as may be necessary to ensure correct pronunciation.

Geographical and language barriers had a great deal of importance in feeding exaggerated nationalism, regionalism, and clashes of interests among neighboring peoples. The European Community is not a phenomenon totally uninfluenced by the progress of the communications media. The economic fact of local interests that are coordinated for a more global interest and the political fact of a supranational parliament and government demand as well the cultural fact of participating in the same shows, news, and cultural events. In Europe, any citizen can see the television programs of neighboring countries in his own house and "coexist" for a few moments in a culture different from the local one.

Perhaps the deepest impact of the media is the overcoming of ideological barriers. To critically evaluate the influence of the communications media on the changes in the socialist countries of Eastern Europe would be the subject of an interesting study. It is beyond doubt that access to the opulence of a consumer society ended with a questioning of the limitations of a planned market economy by the average citizen. The revolution in his expectations brought about the revolution of structural changes, and all this is linked to the social communications media.

This process of the unification of humanity presents a great challenge to the evangelizing mission of the Church, which wants to call all men and women into the universality of the family of the children of God. Possibilities never imagined in the service of the evangelizing message of the Church are present in the media.

A little more careful analysis of several characteristics of communication leads us to see the urgency of accommodating particular subject matters and ecclesial means of communications to the new circumstances. We shall indicate three characteristics that are especially challenging.

1.1 Modern Communication is Instantaneous

The speed of communication permits any fact in any part of the world to be known in all nations, not just at the end of long years of laborious transmission but in seconds. Human events have "historical substance" to the extent that they are observed, shared in, and taken part in by various persons, those immediately involved and other witnesses. The real importance of a historical event is mediated by the judgment that the witnesses of this event make about the relevance of the happening. Deeds that are objectively important may pass unnoticed because of the subjective indifference of the spectators; and vice versa, events that are objectively of little importance may assume great significance through attribution to them of a meaning witnesses give them. This essential and internal makeup of historical meaning is undergoing a profound change. In the past a historical event was witnessed by few people within the limits of space and time. For the rest of humanity, the important event was transmitted through oral or written testimony.

Today the revolution in the media is changing the perception of historical events. The "surrounding world" of witnesses may be all humanity. John Paul II points out the growth of a moral consciousness of solidarity: "The fact that men and women in many parts of the world feel as though they were their own injustices and violations of human rights committed in far-away countries that they will possibly never visit, is one more sign that this reality is transformed into conscience, that it thus acquires a moral connotation."[7] This moral conscience that allows a personal and collective growth in humanity presupposes the communications media; without them these men and women from other parts of the world would never have heard "as though they were their own" of the injustices, nor— on the other hand—of the sharing of other peoples in their hopes and joys. We could again cite the case of the Berlin wall, with universal application, and not just with regard to German reunification.

Now, then, faced with a humanity that is getting used to knowing in an immediate way the important facts that happen in the world, what meaning can the communications of a Church that is attentive to "eternal truths" have? How can it be present with an instantaneous application of meaning to significant historical events? May its message not perhaps arrive too late, when an event has already been put aside, when nobody is any longer interested in it? Can the Church reveal the decisive character of particular events for the history of salvation in a provisional yet immediate way? The response to these questions depends to a great extent on the Church's ability to communicate in today's world. If it has no word to say in these temporal circumstances, it will be left "speechless" in this new world of communication, where governments, scientists, experts, and authoritative commentators are furnishing their versions of events.

1.2 Modern Communication is Universal.

For centuries the Church had control over its listeners. Medieval Christianity was the exactly right medium for efficient ecclesial communications. It has been said that the Church in the Middle Ages offered a genuine system of communications. The orders and instructions of the Pope reached down to the most humble Christians through a structured system of communication and of religious preaching.

The impossibility of controlling listeners was at the root of the wars of religion. There appeared other "heterodox" communicators and listeners who were not very well disposed. It became necessary to ensure the opportunity for the communication of the faith through recourse to political authority and to enter into delicate processes of alliance and of a balancing of respective interests. The history of European Christianity and of its

---

7. John Paul II, *Sollicitudo rei socialis*, 38.

colonies in the rest of the world was darkened by this significant aspect of communication.

Today expectations of any control over listeners are minimal. We come together in a world religiously pluralist and humanly secularized, that is, where there are no confessional monopolies with regard either to persons or to states, and where human beings are intensely concerned with giving meaning to their secular activities, that is, to this world and its current history. A televised Church event is submitted to the indifference, the interest, the criticism, the approval, or the admiration of all those who wish to observe this event.

The Church must get used to being heard among other voices. It must accept the challenge of its message making an impression not because there is an initial silence, but because that silence gets created to the extent that the message is understood, to the extent that hearers begin to understand that what the Church is communicating is so important that it is worthwhile to lower the volume on all other communications in order to pay attention to it alone.

For the rest, the Church must get used to beginning from what is immediate in the secular world in order to be able to speak of the transcendent meaning that also affects this world and gives it its ultimate and definitive meaning.

In a pluralist and secular world, religion can no longer be the bond of national unity or the evident field for a universal communication. However, precisely these "limitations" that the culture imposes oblige the Church to be truly universal, without getting bogged down in local interests that ideologize its message, and to be radical in questioning humanity from the heart of what is human. The dogma of the Incarnation has never had so great a possibility of being communicated.

1.3 Modern Communication is Visual.

If the instantaneousness of communication and the universality of its audience challenge the Church with its message of eternal verities and their religious character, another characteristic, that of visual communication, makes it necessary to transfer the center of interest in communication of the faith from orthodoxy toward orthopraxis.

The mass character of communication implies secularity, but in addition—and because of the mass nature of communication—the preferred genre is narrative communication, including the "news" of television journalism.[8] This mass character of communication is, however, even more reinforced today by the visual character of mass communication.

When we say that orthopraxis is vital today, we are not trying to minimize the importance of orthodoxy. We wish rather, to point out that

---

8. See White, "Mass Media and Culture," pp. 584-585.

the faith as traditionally taught was concerned more with a totality of truths which asked for the assent of our intelligence and not so much with the vital experience of the witness of a life that demanded total conversion in intelligence, love, and commitment. There was an emphasis on a doctrine that had to be "heard," and hence announced verbally, in order to be believed. The visual media, with their particular language that is different from the audible, demand that the faith be "seen." And dogmatic content is not susceptible of being looked at, even though it can be doctrinally formulated through the oral or written word.

The media pose a root problem: the faith touches the totality of the human person and not just his intelligence. The faith directly relates to Christian conduct and to the witness of one's life. The truth in our intelligence cannot dissociate itself from the love in our hearts and the actions of our being. What we believe gives direction to what we do: what is at the base of our convictions must have its "epiphany" in our conduct. The communications media demand by their very nature this change in emphasis from orthodoxy to orthopraxis; from the faith thought and believed to consistent acts which, in the preaching of Jesus, are for the most part the path of the praise of the Father. The modern media challenge us to make the faith more wholly lived.

II. The Responses of Ecclesial Communication

If modern communication presents new challenges, it is the responsibility of the Church to analyze them and to respond to them. It must do this because of the very nature of its presence and its mission in the world.

The Church is in fact the community of those whom the self-communication of God in Jesus Christ has brought together to be the sign and sacrament of God's salvation in history. The Church is the response to God's communication effected in revelation. The Church, fruit and effect of communication, is also communication in its essence. It has no finality in itself, except that of being "witness" to the salvific deeds that brought it to be created, to live, and to project itself toward the world.

By its very vocation the Church must communicate, not, however, a "doctrine" in the style of the ancient gnosis, the knowledge of which involved salvation, but about certain events, certain deeds, that save the totality of humanity out of the special character of what happened at a particular time and place in a little country, Palestine, and about the beginnings of what ever since then has been called the "Christian era."

There is nothing more connatural with its message of salvation than this reference to historical facts. It is from these that the Church nourishes its dogmatic and doctrinal content. The Resurrection is not a theory, it is an event; the coming of the Holy Spirit is not the conclusion of a trinitarian syllogism, but the experience of a believing community. The "Acts of the Apostles" narrate for us the actions of the first evangelizers, who gave an account of the "acts" of which they had been witnesses.

The three challenges that we mentioned earlier ought to find the Church prepared to respond to them. If the message to be communicated were an abstraction from a philosophical system, if its meaning were linked to a particular thought structure peculiar to a culture, if its doctrine were exclusively addressed to reason, perhaps it would be difficult to respond to the challenges of the modern media. However, the Church is linked precisely to history, to facts and events; it lives out of these, out of the memory of, and the liturgical celebration of, events that happened. It knows, furthermore, that these facts mean the salvation of all, that history must be the process of a "recapitulation" of all things in Christ, and that, hence, nothing is alien to the Church's being no language, no people, no culture. And finally, it knows that the faith is in some way linked to what "we saw and touched" as a prolongation of the incarnation of the Word in history. For that reason it honors the saints, because they are visible and exemplary manifestations of Christ's redemption. The "visibility" of Christian witness is part of the sense of the faith, which is united to the liturgy, to the sacraments. The visible in Christian faith participates in the greatness and the holiness of the invisible. All these elements lead us to develop theological responses to the challenge of the communications media.

2.1. The Challenge of Interpreting the Signs of the Times in Light of Instantaneousness.

The instantaneous character of modern communication demands great rapidity on the Church's part in interpreting the signs of the times. Evangelization cannot be reduced to presenting the salvific deeds of the past, but must rather be applied also to seeing the salvific character of current events. It is certainly a difficult task to discern in sufficient depth the salvific value of a contemporary event, but the teaching of Pope John Paul II gives us an orientation. In his encyclical *Solicitudo rei socialis,* Chapter V is entirely devoted to the "theological reading of modern problems." It presents as a complementary element of social doctrine not only the explication of abstract concepts of justice, of development and of underdevelopment, but also a concrete denunciation of sin, which is met in the oppressive mechanisms of imperialism or the abuse of powerful countries vis-à-vis weak ones (SRS 36). It announces—another important aspect of prophetic doctrine—the presence of the saving grace that is encountered in the signs of solidarity with the poor and the oppressed (SRS 40). What the Pope is doing here, in this theological reading or interpretation of historical phenomena, is what it is necessary to do when faced with the instantaneous character of the communication of events.

It is true that prudence requires certain assurances in order to prevent the superficiality of a precipitate and premature judgment. It is also true that humility in ecclesial statements demands that it be said that, given the circumstances, it is not a question of definitive judgments, and that if more complete information were available, the judgments could be changed. With these qualifications, it is necessary that the Church give its opinion; otherwise its opinion would arrive too late, when other interpretations have been presented and "public opinion," perhaps distorted, has already been formed.

To be able to cast light in concrete situations on what are manifestations of grace or a denial of it because of sin is a task that is a responsibility of the Church, one that must be exercised with precise criteria and limits. It is obvious that the Church cannot judge the interior state of consciences, but it is able to cast light on situations that are "objectively" revelations of sin and of grace. Nor is it a question of an ongoing interpretation of all matters, which would make the Church's opinion a banal everyday affair. It should be rather, a reading of significant matters. To retain sufficient moral authority for this interpretation, the Church must show itself to be faithful to evangelical values in its own actions and in the witness of its life, avoiding any temptation toward complicity with the powerful, who may try to distort the truth of events or of ecclesial pronouncements on them. Short-term goals that involve the sacrifice of moral integrity render future communications irrelevant.

2.2. The Affirmation of a Christian Humanism in Light of the Universality of Communication

The secular and pluralist context which is in part fostered by the media presents the Church with a need for a positive understanding of secularity and pluralism as aspects of its own message concerning the Incarnation. Christian faith in fact asserts with certainty that the Incarnation of the Word is the entry of the Son of God into human history. "God has entered into humanity and as man has made himself one of his subjects, one of millions and millions and at the same time unique. Through the Incarnation God has given to human life a dimension that he wanted to give man from the beginning and he has given it in a definitive way. . . ."[9]

The Incarnation does not imply solely the hypostatic union of the divine nature with an individual human nature, but in some manner, and through this, of solidarity with the whole of human nature, generically understood. For this reason the Church can give a religious message through its human concern, because the presence of the divine in the human, in

---

9. John Paul II, *Redemptor hominis,* 1.

Jesus Christ, and in all those in whom his Spirit resides, is essential to its faith.

We have an example of this religious message that comes from concern for human beings in the encyclical *Laborem exercens* of John Paul II. An essential sociability is part of the nature of human beings, but so also is the essential bond it has with the universe that surrounds it, which is the source of its material subsistence. In order for nature to serve the person and human society, work is required. The theology of work in *Laborem exercens* gives importance to the way in which human beings, through their work, participate in the mystery of creation, of redemption, and of their own sanctification and that of the world. However, this religious content can only be understood by the nonbeliever by beginning with respect for the secularity of work, that is, the human, natural, nonreligious, professional dimension of work. This secularity is deeply respected when Christian work enters into a collective effort to transform nature and society. Although this work has a "signification" which comes to it from Christian intentionality, which is given by those who work and live their faith, it also has a strictly secular dimension that is the foundation for believers and nonbelievers living together. The theoretical and practical problems of science and technology are the same for both and constitute the area of a mutual collaboration. The Church need not fear the secularity of the world and of history, the autonomy of temporal values, if it knows itself to be nourished by faith in the mystery of the Incarnation.

The certainty of possessing an area where it can be heard in a pluralist world is part of the conviction with which this faith is lived. Paul knew how to begin from polytheistic pluralism to demonstrate the unique character of his message, although he also had to demonstrate its absolute newness with evidence, even where that was in contrast with the cultural traditions of his audience.

In a pluralist and secular world, the Church can get attention to the extent that it announces a Christian humanism. Not simply a "humanism" in competition with others, but still a humanism that arouses the interest of those who respond to what is human. Christian humanism must not reject this, but rather demonstrate it with greater depth. And it must do this, moreover, in the mystery of the cross (a scandal and foolishness for Gentiles and Jews). Pope John Paul II insistently affirms the Christian origin of humanism, and in a particular way in relation to human suffering, a painful extreme experience for the person, but also a moment of openness toward the transcendental. For that reason particular situations (the disastrous effects of violence, the extreme poverty of peoples, the cries of the oppressed) are important moments for the message of Christian humanism, for appealing to all mankind and for showing that development is either for the whole human being and for all human beings or it does not exist.

We can consider the social teaching of the Church a form of this Christian humanism. In addition to the arguments that spring from the faith, the magisterium appeals to human intelligence and to an ethical clarification of human rights. The struggle for these rights—which are violated in respect to the poor, those who are marginalized, and those who are segregated for any reason of sex, religion, or political convictions—is an example of Christian humanism.[10]

The foundation of the faith, which underlies the humanism that the Church presents, does not weaken humanist feeling but rather gives it originality and meaning. However, a pluralist and secular world can only reach this content of faith by first passing through common action with Christians in the demands of a secular commitment and in the humility of a message that is imposed by a deep conviction and not by the powers of this world.

A pluralist and secularized world may hear an abstract doctrinal message with scepticism, but it will be very attentive to concrete witness. The Church must speak on the level of the universality of its message through the profound humanism of its faith. Moreover, some theologians, like Karl Rahner and Robert McAfee Brown, speak of "anonymous" Christians and of those who are God's "pseudonymous" people with regard to the attitudes of nonbelievers who are led by an elevated ethical sense in their actions and who are able to grasp the presence of the transcendental in true justice, truth, fraternity, honesty, and sincerity. For John Ferris Smith, active dedication to human rights and to campaigns against war also becomes a religious experience which he shares, as a university chaplain, with his students.[11]

2.3 The Visual Character of Communications and the Challenge of Witness.

This third challenge requires fuller consideration and is the subject of our next section. The Greek word for witness, *martyrion*, is related to the sending of the disciples by Christ to evangelize the world (Cf. Mt 28:19). Evangelization is rich in shades of meaning and signifies not just communicating something but also teaching others how to be disciples of

---

10. See David Hollenbach, *Justice, Peace, and Human Rights: American Catholic Social Ethics in a Pluralistic World* (New York: Crossroad, 1988), and John Langan, "Human Rights in Roman Catholicism," in C. E. Curran and R. A. McCormick, eds., *Readings in Moral Theology, No. 5, Official Catholic Social Teaching* (New York: Paulist, 1986), pp. 110-29.

11. John Ferris Smith, *The Bush Still Burns: How God Speaks to Us Today* (Mission, KS: Sheed Andrews and McMeel).

Christ.[12] However, while only one person is Lord and Master, the task of making disciples is realized through making oneself a co-disciple and hence by walking with others along the same path of the faith.

The nature of the media has shifted the emphasis from orthodoxy to orthopraxis. However, this shift is not just demanded by communication but also by a correct understanding of the faith and of the nature of ecclesial communication.

III. Witness and Ecclesial Communication in Light of Modern Media

By "witness" we mean here the presence of a person or a community that lives the message of the Gospel profoundly and through this life communicates the good news to others. It is a matter of communication through life. Furthermore, there is particular emphasis on the ecclesial community as the area in which these values grow, even though they are manifested by individuals. Both aspects, the individual one of personal integrity and the community one as the area where these values develop and grow strong, are important for ecclesial communication, which is no mere school of exemplary persons but a living community established around a totality of relations.

We shall try to show in the first place that witness is the privileged manner of God's communication with humanity throughout the history of salvation. There is something intrinsically theological about witness as communication and no mere sociological and cultural need demanded by the communications media (3.1). Subsequently, we shall indicate several necessary conditions for this witness to be really Christian, when it is provided by the social media of communications (3.2).

3.1 Theological Need for Witness as a Form of Communication.

God's communication to humanity came through the personal and collective witness of prophets and a chosen people. Isolated words without the context of actions would be insufficient, because many of the words that reveal God are precisely interpretations of salvation events. God placed persons and living communities as an incarnation of his message, of his plans, of his will, communicating himself precisely through the way that these persons and communities were transformed by faith. The letter to the Hebrews begins by relating: "In times past God spoke in

---

12. The most important English versions offer different nuances. The King James version translates it as "teach all nations"; the American Standard Bible: "make disciples of all nations"; the New English Bible: "Make all nations my disciples'; and the Jerusalem Bible: "make disciples of all the nations."

fragmented and varied ways to our fathers through the prophets; in this, the final age, he has spoken to us through his Son . . ." (Heb 1:1 ff).

Among all the communications in biblical history, that of "the word made flesh" stands out par excellence in human history. In Christ, everything is revelation and communication, and not just his words. And it is communication precisely in the form of "witness."

Christ is a witness by his actions, his miracles, his evangelizing choices. His "witnessing" way of teaching is his way of embodying truths in parables and symbols. It is the "witness" of the father who welcomes his prodigal son and of the shepherd who goes searching for a sheep, which became a way to understand God's fatherhood and his pardon. Jesus is a witness "narrating the testimony" of persons who embody the values that he wants to communicate. It is on this account that the parables are the preferred subject of current studies in biblical theology,[13] and in contemporary theology strong emphasis is given to "narrative theology."[14]

The "witnessing" character of the redemptive death of Jesus is underlined by Paul in Rom 5:5-8. The death of Jesus is a "message" of God's love and of the greatness of this love, which did not hesitate even before the unworthiness of the persons loved. The redemptive death is not the beginning of a condition in which we are worthy of being loved by God, but rather the expression of a love that preceded any condition of worthiness. It is clear that the Pauline interpretation is closely linked to the preaching of Jesus about the forgiveness of sins, to the experience that Jesus had of God's loving fatherliness toward the good and the bad, in virtue of which he can ask all his disciples to love their enemies in order to be sons of the heavenly Father (cf. Mt 5). Paul was the privileged witness of an election to the apostolate in no way merited by an admitted persecutor of the Church. Paul felt the urgency of being a "witness" of this salvation.

Christ wants us to be "witnesses." The command to teach all nations is equivalent to that of being witnesses of Christ and of his message to all peoples. The early community was very conscious of the need for witness. Its simple way of living everyday life was a persuasive force for many gentiles who felt attracted by this witness to the Resurrection. As we have said, the *Acts of the Apostles* are the acts of witnesses to other acts.

What conquered the cruelty of the Roman emperors who persecuted the Church was not the power of a communication that was an "alternative" to Roman communication, nor was it that of Greek philosophy. It was the witness of the martyrs, the presence of the fortress of the faith in

---

13. See Frederick Houk Borsch, *God's Parable* (Philadelphia: Westminster Press, 1976), and Edward J. Leary, *Symbol Interpretation and the Christian Parable* (Hicksville, New York: Exposition Press, 1977).

14. On narrative theology and modern communication, see Soukup, "Communication, Cultural Form, and Theology," p. 85.

the midst of the fragility and weakness of human efforts to protect themselves by themselves and to announce their doctrine. The blood of the martyrs was the seed of Christians, that of a witness united to their words. Words alone did not convince, but rather did the "witnessing" situation in which they were pronounced and the moment when they were spoken.

The circumstances of danger and threats have an enormous power to convince. The "witnessing communication of the martyrs" was the proof that the Kingdom of God could not be conquered by any earthly power.

The saints of the Church, canonized or not, are a demonstration of the value of witness in ecclesial communication.[15] The sculptures and paintings of the grandiose medieval cathedrals do nothing but show forth witnesses to Christian living which were related from generation to generation through family and parochial catechesis. The Middle Ages had their own catechetical method based principally on the witness of the lives of the saints.

The "risen" life of each Christian is the most convincing existential argument that Christ rose. The conviction that love says the final word in history; that hate can win transitory battles but never the whole war of the meaning of human life; all this is "testimony" to the Resurrection of Jesus Christ.

Sacramental theology points in the same direction of communication by witness. The sacraments are visible manifestations of the invisible reality of God's grace. They are a "communication" not just in the sense of "giving" or "producing" a spiritual transformation through grace, but they are also a "communication" in the more proper sense of being signs. They offer grace and they signify grace. Thus, matrimony is a Christian sacrament precisely because the witness of the mutual faithfulness of husband and wife makes visible the eternal and indefectible mutual faithfulness between Christ and the Church. Sacramentality does not end with the seven privileged moments of the work of grace in the life of the Christian, but rather does it saturate the very being of the Church itself and of Christ.

To speak of witness as a form of Christian communication is not just a transitory response to the cultural and technical phenomenon of modern communications but a profound Christian need. The cultural situation does no more than highlight a form of communication that has never been lost, but that must today take a special place in the communication of the faith.

In this sense, just as communication challenges theology, the latter can also contribute to communication, and the fundamental themes of the

---

15. See Waznak, "The Church's Response to the Media," p. 40. He says that a good program on the Christian witness of Oscar Romero, Dorothy Day, or Dag Hammarskjold may communicate more effectively than some specifically religious programs.

Incarnation and of sacramentality will be important aspects of a theology of communication. Witness as a privileged means of communication merges with two current theological themes: that of the following of Christ and that of the Church as a community of disciples.

Latin American theology has emphasized that the following of Christ must become converted into the "method" of theology. Christ and his message are not understood except by entering into the process of "following him" and, hence, of receiving the witness of the community and in turn of giving it to others.[16]

Ecclesiology has in turn framed various "models" for the understanding of itself and its mission in the world.[17] From models that present more its internal structure (the temple, the Body of Christ) to those which present more its historical representation (People of God), there is a range of possibilities. All of them, however, in trying to explain one or another of the aspects of the ecclesial existence and its historical responsibility, must return to the very origins of the activity of Jesus, who raised up a "community of disciples," and hence to the importance of "witness" as ecclesial communication. Relative to models of "sociological Christianity," where membership is ensured by an environment and a tradition never questioned, there is the present challenge of the pluralist world, the variety of opinions, and the distinct and at times contrary positions that the Church takes with regard to the problems of history. All this provokes a crisis of belonging in the Church, and hence creates new experiences that give meaning to whoever wishes to remain in it. It is no exaggeration to say that the greater part of the "reasons" that Christians will find for their faithfulness in times of crisis will be associated with the "witness" of people who are deeply Christian, having faith that has been matured through trials, disappointments, and disillusionment.

What should Christian witness be when it is the subject of social communications media? In other words: How may it be ensured that the media offer a true sign of evangelizing communication?

3.2 Necessary Conditions for Christian Witness in Social Communication.

Without pretending to exhaust the totality of conditions, I wish to indicate four aspects of witness as communication that take their point of departure from the requirements for Christian communication and also from the visual social communications media. How is the integrity of the message to be maintained despite the economic or political control of the

---

16. See Jon Sobrino, *Christology at the Crossroads* (Maryknoll, N.Y.: Orbis Books, 1978). Idem, *Jesus in Latin America* (Maryknoll, N.Y.: Orbis Books, 1987).

17. See the classic study of Avery Dulles, *Models of the Church* (Garden City, N.Y.: Image Books, 1974), and his article, "Vatican II and Communications," in Latourelle, *Vatican II: Assesments and Perspectives,* III: 528-47.

media? What requirement for personal integrity is demanded of a witness in social communication? What importance do extreme situations have on witness? What relationship is there between personal witness and the community?

3.2.1 Integrity of the Message and Control of the Media.

Inculturation of the Gospel is always subject to a double tension: accommodation to the culture in order to be understood by those belonging to it and distancing from the culture because the Gospel is transcultural and in some aspects countercultural.[18]

It seems obvious that given the importance of the media as expression of an already existing culture and as instruments of formation of a culture the existence of which is desired, such media are not always accessible for an evangelical witness that is "transcultural" and "countercultural."

The process of defining the "evangelicity" of content is complex: the tradition of the community exists, but there also exists a "public opinion" generated by the media which already has an image of the Church and its messages. It is going to be hard for many people to detach themselves from the clichés already established has to what the Church is, says, and ought to say. All of this will present limits to Christian witness. The temptation to be more faithful to cultural expectations than to those of the Gospel itself will increase. This dimension of communication hence requires great discernment.

3.2.2 Personal Integrity and the Quality of Witness.

The communications media cannot cover prolonged periods of time. They condense the intensity of a message into a few minutes; editing brings out the important aspects in function of media technology or in the interests of the communication of the content. For the spectator, the witness offered by the medium is at times a question of a few minutes or seconds.

In one direction there may occur the danger of "playing a theatrical role" as Christian witness. Very good actors can convey emotions, feelings, and messages without being in reality vitally concerned with them. The spectator must "feel" the difference between life and fiction. Witness cannot be "fabricated" as though in a theater. The "pretense" of holiness was a danger in the Church which was vigorously combated in the campaigns against the illuminists of all periods. However, such vigilance also ran the risk of pulling up the wheat together with the weeds. Not a few saints were tried out of zeal for combating the pretense of holiness.

---

18. See Deck, *The Second Wave*, p. 99.

This is not a question of an "exterior" instance of power and punishment which can sanction a lack of genuineness in a witness but rather of an "internal" weakness in one's message, when those who convey it do not live it with integrity. Instances are not far distant of preaching in the communications media which served more for the enrichment of the "preachers" than for the announcement of the Gospel.

Although the media in themselves are limited to offering witness just as it is presented, the cultural context becomes a part of the witness when lives are consistent with the message and when the witnesses to evangelical values do not just announce them in visual communication but live them beyond the lights and cameras of broadcasting. Overall context, personal and collective history, ensure the genuineness of the witnessing message.

Accordingly, this is a very serious question. Modern communication faces us with a challenge of "being" in truth what we "communicate that we are." Hence for the protagonist of the testimony a deep spirituality is essential. He must know that he has the charism of witnessing communication as a gift of the Spirit for the good of the community and of all those who see his witness. No other motive can justify witness.

3.2.3 Extreme Situations.

The Gospel announced by Jesus has as its aim acceptance of the unconditional character of the faith even in the face of extreme situations such as the renouncing of affections as fundamental as those of family or even of one's own life. Humanity is sensitive to the witness of personal integrity in difficult situations. It loves very dangerous sports; it acclaims the winners of tense competitions.

The following of Jesus presents occasions for heroism. They are a part of witness. However, we do not have to imagine spectacular heroism. For many Christians extreme situations are very close ones: in family life, in personal crises, when faced with pain or illness.

The media can present these witnesses. There are extreme situations involving a privation of freedom that is suffered out of faithfulness to the convictions of faith, like that experienced by Carlos Alberto Libano Christo (Frei Betto) during his six years of imprisonment that were converted into the life of a monk in meditation and study.[19] In other cases, through an appropriate prison ministry, prison has been a place of encounter with the faith of Christ, as the experience of Paul D. Schoonmaker in his ministry demonstrates.[20]

19. See Carlos Alberto Libanio Christo, *Against Principalities and Powers: Letters from a Brazilian Jail* (Maryknoll, N.Y.: Orbis Books, 1977).
20. See Paul D. Schoonmaker, *The Prison Connection: A Lay Ministry Behind Bars* (Valley Forge, PA: Judson Press, 1978).

Christian witness in personal or family suffering, physical or psychological, helps many to overcome their own crises. It demonstrates the meaning of faith in the meaninglessness of pain. Leslie F. Brandt begins from pain in order to show the path for searching for a mysterious God.[21] Gustavo Gutiérrez has shown in his book, *On Job: God-Talk and the Suffering of the Innocent*,[22] that pain lifts us up to accept the mystery of a God who cannot be contained within our ideas of justice and retribution and enables us to enter into the area of mystery and gratitude, of total trust and abandon. The path of overcoming our "wounded memories" is made easier when we recall the witness of persons who have lived that experience.[23]

Christian witness is also given in the political field, in ideological struggle. To a greater or lesser extent all human beings are involved in political choices and not just those who make politics their professional work.

Witness has special meaning when it is given within specifically religious groups. The transformation of difficult cultural environments has been obtained, for example, through the "Cursillos of Christianity," created in Spain but subsequently spread throughout the whole world. This method has as an important ingredient the communication of witnesses to conversion, above all of adult persons and by adult persons. The same can be said of other ecclesial manifestations, such as the charismatic movement, which give great importance to the public expression of feelings and sentiments.

3.2.4 Personal Witness and Community Witness.

The media can highlight the self-importance of isolated individuals, which would falsify Christian communication. It is not a matter of admiring "stars" of Christian life. Christian witness is by definition not that of isolated individuals but of the community. The relationship of personal witness to the community that nourishes these values is fundamental to perceiving the meaning of Christianity and of the "community of the disciples." Christian life, because it is a participation in the grace of God and because God is the mystery of the interpersonal communion of Father, Son, and Holy Spirit, consists fundamentally in a profound relationship of the personal with the communitarian. It is not mere presence in a group that ensures depth of faith and of conversion, but the latter is in turn ori-

---

21. See Leslie F. Brandt, *Why Did This Happen to Me? God's Answer to Human Suffering* (St. Louis: Concordia Publishing House, 1977).

22. See Gustavo Gutiérrez, *On Job: God-Talk and the Suffering of the Innocent* (Maryknoll, N.Y.: Orbis Books, 1987).

23. See Matthew and Dennis Linn, *Healing Life's Hurts: Healing Memories Through Five Stages of Forgiveness* (Ramsey, N.J.: Paulist Press, 1978).

ented toward the community. The baptism that pardons and purifies the person is at the same time the sign of incorporation into the community. Every sacrament has an ecclesial meaning and dimension.

We need witnessing like that given by Elizabeth O'Connor, who describes the experience of her community in Washington.[24] At other times the witness to Christian community can come from the past, like the missionary experiences among the Guarani[25] or the early Christian communities of the New Testament.

An understanding of important cultural epochs, feasts, and popular devotions and their significance in the communication of the faith has been underlined by Roberto Orsi: priests of Irish or German origin were unable to understand the value of Italian popular religiosity, and the presence of pastors born in Italy was necessary for understanding it.[26] Similar situations have recurred in the more recent migrations of Hispanic origin.

In any event, the essential characteristic of the Church as a community of disciples must be revealed in communitarian experience. LeRoy Eims speaks of the lost art of making disciples.[27] But in Christian terms, because Christ alone is the master, discipleship is learned only through co-discipleship, that is, from a community of faith.

The communitarian sense has developed strongly in the experience of the churches of the Third World. In a meeting of theologians and bishops of various continents to meditate on the significance of Puebla for the universal Church, I heard this testimony of an African bishop: Africa will either grasp the experience of the base communities of Latin America or the Church will cease to be present in Africa, because the Church linked to colonial power is going to disappear.

The base communities in Latin America, established by poor people who are acutely conscious of being members of the Church, are creating new modes of ecclesial communication which are not vertical (authority, community) but horizontal, from one member of the community to another. It is a communication closely related to the daily life of their existence; a communication that is established to lead life in the light of the Gospel; and a communication that opens up to a commitment. These base communities become areas of a life of faith and also of social and political responsibility. In them the witness of one poor man to another concerning the presence of God in their lives is touching. A barrio leader, ex-

---

24. See Elizabeth O'Connor, *The New Community* (New York: Harper & Row, 1976).

25. See Philip Caraman, S.J., *The Lost Paradise: The Jesuit Republic in South America* (New York: Seabury, 1977).

26. See Robert Orsi, *The Madonna of 115th Street: Faith and Community in Italian Harlem, 1880-1950* (New York: Yale University Press, 1985).

27. See LeRoy Eims, *The Lost Art of Disciple Making* (Grand Rapids: Zondervan; Colorado Springs: Navpress, 1978).

tremely struck by the harshness of life, entitled his witness: *"Mesmo as- sim sou feliz"* (Despite everything, I am happy).

Can the witness of the communities help to give another significance to the communications media? Or, on the contrary, will the communications media be the thing that will weaken the Christian meaning of the communities? This dilemma arises from the significance of witness as Christian communication.[28]

While the Gospel challenges our values and is a "counterculture" as we indicated above, the "preferential option for the poor" that the Church speaks of makes us turn toward the witness that the poor give of their faith, to the witness of their community experiences, and to the importance of making them known through the communications media. This little aspect becomes in reality a significant indication of the value we can put on all the thought that has been given to this work. John Paul II says that a just wage is the sign of a just society. We might say analogously that the ability of the media to open themselves up to the witness of the poor demonstrates a flexibility in these media to be the bearers of Gospel values.

There is something fundamental about the experience of the "communities of disciples" of the New Testament: its turning to the poor and its sensibility in sharing all goods. If the communications media can show the witness of this sensibility relative to the outcasts of this world, they will be messengers of hope for the poor, a sign that the Good News is being announced and that the Kingdom of God is present.

---

28. Relative to new aspects of communication in base communities, see several references in Soukup, "Communication, Cultural Forms, and Theology," p. 86.

10

Evangelization as Communication

Angela Ann Zukowski, M.H.S.H.

During the fall of 1965, I began my ministry with the Native American communities in the Four Corners area of the United States.[1] My religious formation offered me a traditional Euro-American theological understanding of missiology. The approach that we were to take in our ministry was called the adaptive way. We did not learn about the concept of evangelization; however, in hindsight it was implied in our training. Courses, workshops, and seminars in communication theory and praxis were not part of our formation. With this background, I courageously approached my first mission with the Native Americans in the Four Corners area.

Upon my arrival in Cortez, Colorado, a Native American woman from a local tribe, who was Catholic, offered to mentor me through the language and customs of her people. Several weeks later I ventured onto the reservation.

The first home I approached I found a Navajo woman sitting before her loom in front of her hogan.[2] I remember being captivated by the delicate swiftness with which she wove the yarn through the warped threads. She paused but a brief moment to acknowledge my presence and continued with her artistic endeavors. I introduced myself and commenced a rapid firing of questions and comments related to my mission. The questions did not seem to have any impact. She simply continued her work with a pleasant expression on her face but with no further visible acknowledgement or spoken words. The long silences between my monologues caused me to be uneasy. After about fifteen minutes, I left.

The next day I met with my Native American mentor. I described my experience. She gazed reflectively at me and asked, "And so, what did you learn?" I was initially puzzled by her question. She continued, "With all your learning, you still do not understand. You are still a novice. You must return to the woman tomorrow and learn to listen through the ab-

---

1. The Four Corners area refers to that area where four states—Colorado, New Mexico, Arizona, and Utah—touch at the same point.
2. A hogan is the earth-covered lodge of the Navajo.

sence of words. You must listen with your heart, mind, and whole being. You must empty yourself. You must allow the silence to create a bonding of sisterhood between you."

In the course of several weeks, I learned to appreciate the contemplative experience of sitting next to my Native American friend. I began to understand the depth of communication required for the nurturing of effective evangelization among peoples of various cultures.

Those who want to be active communicators of the Gospel must be good listeners. A teaching Church that is not, above all, a learning, listening Church, is not on the wave-length of divine communication. The 1971 Pastoral Instruction on Social Communications emphasizes this dimension.[3] Information must not only go out from our evangelization efforts but must flow back in such a way that we, the evangelizers, also learn and are changed.[4]

In reflecting on this idea Bernard Häring believes that the Church can be a prophetic voice if she is willing to listen and to share in the joys and hopes, the anguish and fears of all people.[5] He reminds us that communication in the Church and through the Church is for the sake of community, for the unity among humankind. But communication or evangelization does not automatically bring about community. There is need for dialogue, for conversation, for being with and for each other. The depth of this conversation is what I believe I experienced with my Native American friends.

In this chapter I shall explore the fundamental meaning and relationship of evangelization as a form of communications. It is not my intention to offer a comprehensive review of the topic but only to identify some of the key elements or points which need to be considered in preparing pastoral ministers to interact with contemporary culture. As I indicated in my opening comments, these elements were not present in my formation. I am aware that these elements are only now slowly being incorporated in pastoral formation programs within the Church in the United States. In light of this fact, I shall conclude the chapter with a few recommendations which I feel need our immediate attention in pastoral ministry today if our evangelization efforts are to have an impact in our contemporary world.

---

3. Pontifical Commission for the Instruments of Social Communication, Pastoral Instruction, *Communio et progressio*, 1971.

4. Ibid., #175.

5. Bernard Häring, "Theologie der Kommunikation und theologische Meinungsbildung," in F. J. Eilers, et al., *Kirche und Publizistik. Dreizehn Kommentare zur Pastoralinstruktion Communio et progressio* (Munich: F. Schöningh, 1972), p. 38.

I. The Situation

New and urgent questions face the Church as it seeks to communicate the Gospel in contemporary culture. In one sense each person who engages in evangelization is like a foreign missionary. Today we step onto a new landscape filled with new technologies and mass media attractions, only to find the people speaking a new language or having differing cultural experiences. They may no longer hear voices of religious tradition, or they may simply refuse to even listen. In preparing for the Fifth Centenary of Evangelization in the Americas, the American Bishops stated:

> The evangelizer is faced with the problem of indifference to matters of religion. Relativism makes many wonder why they should hold any truths as sacred. With those forces of our age has come the growth of an extreme form of individualism that sees no need for the faith community or for the necessity of comparing one's own insights with those offered by tradition.[6]

If communication is the heart of the Church's life, then the evangelizer must enter in a decisive way into this new age. The Catholic Church has a long tradition of using media and the arts in its communication and evangelization efforts. It is up to the evangelizer, therefore, to identify the new language and artistic expressions which can stimulate a public dialogue of faith.

Being faithful to the Gospel, we face the challenge of this new culture before us. We are called to explore new ways for opening up dialogue with the people of the culture, presenting the message to them as honestly and authentically as we can, allowing them the absolute right to reject or to accept it. If they accept it, they must be free to understand it and express it in the midst of their culture. And, as evangelizers, we must be sensitive enough to hear what they play back to us, to see if it does not give us an even clearer vision and more refined view of that "naked Gospel."

The Role of Communications

Over twenty years have passed since the closing of the Second Vatican Council and the implementation of The Pastoral Instruction on Social Communion, *Communio et progressio*. When the pastoral instruction appeared, it was received with great enthusiasm. Its broad perspective, both theological and social, was a healthy, fresh, and most welcome change. Without going to the exaggeration of creating a "theology" of social communications media, the instruction offered solid points of theological reflection and clearly established a linkage between the Christian tenets and

---

6. Committee on Evangelization, *Heritage and Hope: Evangelization in the United States* (Washington: NCCB, 1990), p. 32.

the human tasks which are the very fabric of Christian communication. The pastoral called the Church to enter into dialogue with the world. As mentioned earlier, the Church's communication efforts cannot take the form of one-way communication; it must truly listen to others as well. This same process of dialogue also has a place within the Church. If it is to be a community, a communion, then all the members of the Church have a place in its dialogue.[7] If the Church is to effectively evangelize, she must be open to the consequences of transformation which emerges within authentic dialogue. In the perspective of the communications age, we can see that the vocation of the Church is to live out this unlimited communication of God's love, reconciliation, and wholeness to the world. Christ remains the origin and the dynamic power of the Church's communication as it proclaims the Gospel, teaches, heals, and continues the long journey out of the many forms of human enslavement into the reign of God. Since we are to do this through words of hope and through images of God's love, as well as through our own praxis or way of life, communication must then become the heart of the Church community.

Changes in communications media affect the Church's understanding of its own nature and mission. Church structures and theology were radically transformed by the transitions from oral to manuscript culture and from manuscript culture to the age of print. The communications revolution through which we are passing is fully as radical as the invention of printing in the fifteenth century. The electronic media are modeling a new world and perhaps even a new breed of human being.

A place must be cleared within this new world for the preaching of the Gospel. We are bombarded by an unprecedented density of images and sounds today. The Gospel must be communicated in symbols, models, images, and words which are accessible to each culture and understood by it. Otherwise it does not get communicated at all. People today are fascinated by the image, by what is visible and concrete rather than by reason or abstract knowledge. This means we have to rediscover the image dimension of the Gospel. Since the word which moves, attracts, and empowers people today is not abstract doctrine but instead the word of story, metaphor and image, we must therefore recover that liberating word within all aspects of our religious experience.

Church communicators need to identify new perspectives and possibilities for retelling the stories of Scripture within the human stories of today, or, alternatively, for disclosing the spirituality of the human situation in the light of Scripture. Such storytelling may take the form of "narrowcasting," reaching out to a more defined, specialized audience, for example through a cable channel or group media. "Broadcasting" (radio and television) offers the Church an opportunity to reach mass audiences

---

7. Ibid., #114-125.

within the culture. Also the means of classical and contemporary literature, drama, poetry, music, film, photography, painting, video, and other
cultural forms offer support.

II. Evangelization

Paul VI's apostolic exhortation *Evangelii nuntiandi* ten years after
the Council aimed at making "the Church of the twentieth century better
fitted for proclaiming the Gospel to the people of the twentieth century."[8]
The document begins its reflections with three questions that had been
centerpieces for the discussion at the 1974 Synod of Bishops.

> 1. In our day, what has happened to that hidden energy of the Good
> News, which is able to have a powerful effect in man's conscience?
> 2. To what extent and in what way is the evangelical force capable of
> really transforming the people of this century?
> 3. What methods should be followed in order that the power of the
> Gospel may have its effect?[9]

These three questions show concern that the Gospel has not effectively engaged the world. Paul VI states that "the split between the Gospel and culture is without a doubt the drama of our time" and that "every
effort must be made to ensure a full evangelization of culture, or more
correctly, cultures."[10] He goes on to say that what really matters for the
Church now "is to evangelize human culture (not in a purely decorative
way as it were by applying a thin veneer, but a vital way, in depth, and
right to their very roots)."[11]

The most serious challenge, therefore, in the long term, to evangelization comes from radical secularism and a concomitant consumerism that
tends to exclude all forms of transcendence and religiosity from the dominant culture and from the public and civic life. Evangelization's most serious challenge, in short term, is the problem posed by those who evangelize in a spirit of Christian fundamentalism, fomenting an exclusivist and
escapist mentality, which is what the so-called sects represent.

In 1985, the European bishops focused on these issues in depth:

> Underlying the bishops' concern is awareness of an unprecedented and
> accelerating secularization: the family, the school and the community
> appear increasingly unable to provide a context in which the faith can
> be learned and lived; religion is privatized and marginalized in soci-
> ety; religion is no longer considered a 'natural' aspect of human life,

---

8. Paul VI, Apostolic Exhortation, *On Evangelization in the Modern World*
(*Evangelii nuntiandi*) (Washington: USCC, 1976), # 2, p. 6.

9. Ibid., #4, p. 7.

10. Ibid. , # 20, p. 16.

11. Ibid.

but a rather eccentric personal option. In essence, this means that as people arrive at a personal synthesis of values at some stage in their lives, it is less likely that they will take as central framework of ideals a belief in a transcendent God, Jesus Christ and the Gospel or other traditional motivating symbolism of the Christian community.[12]

This perspective makes it clear that evangelization must involve more than "getting people back to Church" or even converting the unbaptized. Paul VI had a broader view of evangelization.

For the Church, evangelizing means bringing the good news into all the strata of humanity, and through its influence transforming humanity from within and making it new.[13]

In speaking about the transformation of humanity and making creation new, Pope Paul envisioned the work of evangelization in its wider scope. The kind of renewal spoken of involves "interior renewal which the Gospel calls *metanoia*; it is a radical conversion, a profound change of mind and heart."[14] We are not merely talking about methods of organizing parishioners for the work of evangelization, but more essentially of ways of being open to God's grace which is at work in changing hearts.

The Culture Challenge

For Paul VI, evangelization has to do with culture: the Church's mission is to evangelize culture.[15] But since context and history are also essential features of human existence, culture is not monolithic; there is not one single culture, but a variety of cultures. This approach to evangelization has led to a new vocabulary in mission theology such as enculturation, acculturation, and inculturation. This perspective on the Church's mission has also sharpened the fundamental debate present in the major texts of Vatican II on the relation between evangelization and humanization, a debate which is basically about the nature of the religious and the secular.

What is at stake when the Church is called to insert itself into the contemporary cultures of six continents (North/South America, Europe, Asia, Africa, and Pacific)? This insertion process called *inculturation* first made its appearance in the 1977 international Synod of Bishops and further manifested itself in *Catechesis tradendae* (1979) and *Familiaris consortio* (1981), and in *Slavorum apostoli* (1985). Inculturation has been defined as "the process of a deep, sympathetic adaption to and appropriation

---

12. Robert White. Taken from the unpublished paper, "Communication and Evangelization in Europe," 1988.

13. Paul VI, *On Evangelization in the Modern World,* #18, p. 15.

14. Ibid., # 10, p. 11.

15. Ibid., # 20.

of a local cultural setting in which the Church finds itself in a way that
does not compromise its basic faith in Christ.[16] But why speak of inculturation today? Two key reasons come to mind. First, we are in an age of
mission which challenges the Church to proclaim the Gospel in a rapidly
changing technological world. Second, we are in an age of global awareness which includes the awareness of cultural diversity. The mass media
are making us more aware of the rich and basic differences which exits
between cultures.

Recent studies in education, sociology and psychology have demonstrated that peoples and cultures are different. The young child has different questions, outlooks, and needs from those of the aging. We know that
men view life and its problems and possibilities differently than women
do. And yet it is to this pluralistic world that the Gospel must be
preached. Hence, the need for reflection on how this can be done in particular situations, the need for inculturation.

Pope John Paul II in speaking to the African bishops assembled in
Nairobi, Kenya, in 1980, stated:

> By respecting, preserving, and fostering the particular values and rich-
> ness of your people's cultural heritage, you will be in a better position
> to lead them to a better understanding of the mystery of Christ, which
> is to be lived in the noble, concrete, and daily experience of African
> life. . . . It is a question of bringing Christ into the very center of
> African life, and lifting up all African life to Christ. Thus not only is
> Christianity relevant to Africa, but Christ in the members of his body
> is himself African.[17]

To gain some perspective on the issue of inculturation, on why it
has emerged as a new imperative for the Church today, Avery Dulles reflects on H. Richard Niebuhr's classic study *Christ and Culture*. He
streamlines Niebuhr's typology into three basic types: a confrontation
model, a synthesis model, and transformation model.[18]

The confrontation model creates an opposition between Christianity
and culture. This model is reflective of some modern Protestant theology,
such as, the thinking of Karl Barth who states that Christianity and culture must always be in conflict.[19] Yet, how can one proclaim the Gospel
without at least provisionally accepting the language and other cultural

---

16. Definition taken from William Reiser, "Inculturation and Doctrinal
Development," *Heythrop Journal* 22 (1981): 135.

17. John Paul II, Address to the Bishops of Kenya, May 7, 1980, "The African
Bishop's Challenge," in *Origins*, May 29, 1980, Vol. 10, no. 2: 29.

18. See Avery Dulles, *The Reshaping of Catholicism* (New York: Harper & Row,
1988), pp. 34-50.

19. See Karl Barth, *The Epistle of the Romans* (Oxford: Oxford University Press,
1977), pp. 267-68.

forms in which one is framing the message.[20] The reality of interrelationship of communication and culture becomes paramount in our discussion.

In the synthesis model culture is regarded as good in its own order offering Christianity a suitable cultural base for evangelization. This is demonstrated by the Eurocentric mentality of Christianity which dominated the evangelization efforts of the Church over the centuries. In more recent times, the identification of Christianity with European culture has come to be perceived by some as a form of cultural imperialism and has provoked hostile reactions in Asia, Africa, Latin America, and in some communities within the United States.[21]

The transformation model is more in tune with the Second Vatican Council and the spirit of the documents flowing from the Council. It is a balance of the previous two. Dulles identifies five points of the transformationist position: 1) In a certain sense, Christianity is supracultural; 2) Christianity has always been, and must be, culturally embodied: 3) Culture is broader than Christianity or any religion; 4) Christianity is not exclusively linked to any one culture; and, 5) The evangelization of cultures pertains to the mission of the Church.

This transformation model encourages evangelists, communicators, missionaries, and theologians to reach that naked *kenosis,* the mystical core, that supernatural faith which can be incarnated in any human culture. While the Gospel is compatible with all cultures, it poses a challenge to every culture and demands *metanoia,* conversion. Evangelization means the intimate transformation of authentic cultural values through their integration in Christianity in a process of "inculturation." Paul VI, in his address to the African bishops, described this process.

> The expression, that is, the language and mode of manifesting this one Faith, may be manifold; hence, it may be original, suited to the tongue, the style, the genius, and the culture, of the one who professes this one Faith. From this pint of view, a certain pluralism is not only legitimate, but desirable. An adaptation of the Christian life in the fields of pastoral, ritual, didactic and spiritual activities is not only possible, it is even favored by the Church. The liturgical renewal is a living example of this. And in this sense you may, and you must, have an African Christianity. Indeed, you possess human values and characteristic forms of culture which can rise up to perfection such as to find in Christianity, and for Christianity, a true superior fullness, and prove

---

20. See Paul Tillich, *Systematic Theology* (Chicago: University of Chicago Press, 1951), I: 7.

21. The celebration of the Fifth Centenary of Evangelization in the Americas caused problems for Native Americans, African Americans, and others in the United States. These groups questioned the reason for celebration when reconciliation and healing might be more appropriate. They challenged the Church to rethink the concept and process of indigenization and enculturation of the Gospel.

to be capable of a richness of expression all its own, and genuinely African. This may take time. It will require that your African soul become imbued to its depths with the secret charisms of Christianity, so that these charisms may then overflow freely, in beauty and wisdom, in the true African manner.[22]

A number of Asian and African Catholic theologians have been attempting to open new doors for identifying a more respective way for Christianity to be communicated in diverse cultures. Raimundo Panikkar repeatedly calls our attention to the fundamental idea that the Christian event is seen as a supracultural fact. If until now it has adopted and adapted a certain garb, this is due to historical contingencies and/or the predominance of a particular culture over others. But, in itself, nothing stands in the way of Christianity taking flesh in the most remote and, for Western tastes, most exotic cultures.[23]

During the 1990 UNDA/OCIC[24] World Congress in Bangkok, Thailand, the Catholic church of Thailand shared how video is used for evangelization and dialogue within their culture. Water was one integrating symbol. Beginning with the Thai and Buddhist symbolic understanding of water, the video presentation created a bridge in drawing on the strengths of the prevailing culture to explain the meaning of baptism and reconciliation in the Christian tradition. Such an approach—respects the traditions of the culture while speaking in the symbolic language of the people.

The symbolic representation of a Thai purification ritual was one of the highlights of the Congress. At the beginning and the end of the Buddhist season of Lent (Kao Pan Xa and Ock Pan Xa)—the special time of purification and of special religious training in the Buddhist tradition—the people (in particular, the young people) prepare with a great devotion, the bamboo sailboats covered with white paper. On the sides of the boat and on the mast, the people place, in order and in line, the white lighted candles. On the white paper, the people write their confessions, their promises, and their wishes. At nightfall, when a temple gong or drum signals the monks raising the prayer of Sayathro or the prayer of blessing, the boats, all lighted, are sailed down the river. The people applaud, cry aloud and pray in thanksgiving. As the Congress moved in procession down to the river to float our candles, we discussed at length how rich this symbolism is for our Christian understanding of baptism and reconciliation.

---

22. Paul VI, Address to the Bishops of the African Continent, July 31, 1969. See *L'osservatore romano,* August 1, 1969.

23. See Raimundo Panikkar, "Theology in a Culturally Diverse World," in *Pluralism and Oppression* (Lanham, Md.: University Press of America, 1988), p. 6.

24. UNDA is the International Association of Catholic Radio and Television Communicators. OCIC is the International Organization for Cinema and Audiovisual.

In *Christianity Rediscovered,* Vincent Donovan shares with us his experience of missiology and evangelization among the Massi in Africa. Initially he approached his missionary work with his Western mentality well fixed and directed. Over time he learned to trust the cultural experience of the Massi and the translation of the Word by the wisdom figures within the community.

> And there was almost always a man in each community who was notably eloquent. He always had been eloquent, and was frequently called on by the community for speeches. He was their preacher. And every community had one or two people who had the power to take old and familiar things and make them new and challenging, to stir the people to action, to make them move when moving could be the difference between life and death in a nomadic community. We would have a name for those persons. We would call them prophets.

He continues:

> Even before baptism I could see a pattern forming, a community of faith in the making, but not exactly the pattern of Christian community that I, from my background, had expected, or to which I was accustomed. All I would add to that already formed pagan community was the dimension of faith, and on the reception of baptism they would become, as they were and where they were, a fully formed and functional church.[25]

Authentic inculturation demands on the part of the Church a willingness to dialogue with all cultures. To the Greeks *dialogos* meant a freeflowing of meaning through a group, allowing the group to discover insights not attainable individually. Dialogue differs from the more common "discussion," which has its roots with "percussion" and "concussion," literally a heaving of ideas back and forth in a winner-takes-all competition. Dialogue demands concern and hospitality toward the other, as well as respectful acceptance of the other's identity, modes of expression and values. This is what my Native American friends taught me so well. They demonstrated that true dialogue does not invade; it does not manipulate, for dialogical manipulation is a contradiction in terms. Dialogue achieves a communion of horizons which leads to mutual self-disclosure and self-understanding.

The task of the Church in the coming decades is to be faithful to its mission of preaching the Christ event in such a way as to transform and penetrate the various existing cultures but to do so in such a manner as to be opened itself to transformation. The Second Vatican Council committed the Church in the contemporary world to dialogue that leads to "a feeling of deep solidarity with the human race and its history."[26] From the

---

25. Vincent Donovan, *Christianity Rediscovered*, 2nd ed., (Maryknoll, N..Y.: Orbis Books, 1983), pp. 144-45.

perspective of communication, the Church represents a public dialogue of faith.

Two pastoral letters of the United States' bishops demonstrates how dialogue can support the inculturation process in modern culture: *"The Challenge of Peace: God's Promise and Our Response,"* and *"Economic Justice for All: Catholic Social Teaching and the U.S. Economy."* These two letters are attempts to examine the issues of peace and economic justice and to bring Christian Gospel values to bear on these issues. The letter on the economy, we might note, could not have been written without the input, insight, and challenge that came to the United States Church from Latin American liberation theology. The bishops also engaged in a wide consultation process with the laity. It is to the laity in business and educational institutions, in the military and in government, that the bishops turned to carry out this process of inculturation.

Other attempts at inculturation are the many other varied letters of the United States' bishops or groups of bishops that address more particular questions and areas such as the Hispanic peoples, Black Catholics, the issue of the land in Appalachia or the Middle West, and the native American population.[27] Most recently, the draft of the pastoral letter on women, "Partners in the Mystery of Redemption," furthers the dialogue on ways in which women play essential roles in inculturating gospel values into American society through their personal witness and ministry.

The challenge of inculturation is immense. Yet, as the theory of inculturation reminds us, all inculturation is a two-way street. If the Church in the United States is to be truly Catholic, Christian, Roman, and American, then it must learn form the world Church. The insights of Latin America on the role of the Church in the work for justice, the insights of the African Church on the nature of celebration and on the healing power of the Church, and the insights of the Asian church on the mystery and transcendence of God must become part of the consciousness of the American Church. If inculturation is taken seriously, then every Church, including the American Church, is both a learning and a teaching Church. But as inculturation reminds us, priority must be given to listening and learning.

---

26. *Gaudium et spes* 1.

27. It is important that national conferences of bishops deal with problems that their regions face. Two examples of this approach: "Strangers and Guests: A Regional Catholic Bishops' Statement on Land Issues" (1980) and "This Land is Home to Me" from the bishops in Appalachia (1975).

III. Ecclesiology and Communications

Where we place ourselves regarding the Church will determine to a great extent the kind of communication we will judge to be most apropos for the proclamation of the Gospel. Ecclesiology dictates one's approach to ministry, one's sense of authority and leadership within the Church.

We all know that there are differences of opinion and differences of strategy here. A review of various understandings of the Church may help us to understand more clearly our styles of communication for evangelization. Avery Dulles in *The Reshaping of Catholicism* states states that we would search in vain in the documents of Vatican II for a single theology of communications. He reminds us that the bishops and theologians who were engaged in writing the sixteen documents represented a variety of theological perspectives. In light of this fact, Dulles believes one must understand their ecclesiological perspective if they wish to understand and analyze the forms of communications practiced by the Church. Dulles presents five models.

First, the hierarchical or institution model of ecclesiology is most familiar to us Catholics. As institution it is defined in terms of its visible structures and can be described in clear organizational terms. Membership categories are delineated; the Church has the primary functions of teaching, governing, and sanctifying its members. The mode of communication is the teaching of the church in clear, concise statements that have been issued by legitimate authority in proper form, and is widely available in printed text. The assumption seems to be that the traditional channels—such as papal encyclicals, decrees of Roman Congregations, pastoral letters, catechetical institution, formation programs and sermons are the key means of communication.

Second, the Church can also be described as a herald, as one who receives an official message and passes it on. In this light the Church so defines itself—especially when it gathers to listen to the Word of God, a Word which both vivifies it and commissions it to proclaim what it has heard. The proclaimed message, Paul VI points out in *Evangelii nuntiandi,* "does not reach its full development until it is listened to, accepted, and assimilated"[28] through adherence to the ecclesial community, through sacramental worship, and through a committed Christian life. The mass media may and should be used for a kind of "first proclamation" sometimes called "pre-evangelization." The herald model also reflects the kerygmatic model which has been revived in the twentieth century.

Thirdly, the Church finds an analogue in the notion of sacrament. The Church is defined in terms of the symbolic structure of existence. The members of the Church are visible and address each other and the world in witness, worship, and service. The chief function of the Church

---

28. Paul VI, *On Evangelization in the Modern World,* #23, p. 18.

is being a symbol which serves to bring about the reality it signifies. According to this model, religious communication occurs not only through words but equally through persons, events and ritual. This Church communicates both to the world and to its own members as a living symbol.

A fourth ecclesiological model is the Church as *communio* or communion of people who are bond by both interior and exterior bonds. It is composed of many types of persons, having their own distinct abilities and charisms, working together to build up the whole body in love. Such a community is not as visible as an institution because its primary manifestation occurs on the local level. This idea of *communio* which emerged from the Council was a promise of a new perspective that had not previously been thought possible or even desirable. Klaus Kienzler believes that the Church is still "dealing with an emerging conceptualization" of communio.[29] In many ways, the Council Fathers were reflecting a realization that the whole world was moving in a direction that even now in the middle of the 1990's is yet to come to full fruition. And so, the communication characteristic of such a Church is witness and dialogue.

Fifthly, Dulles sees the emergence of a secular-dialogic model. The image of the Church is not in opposition to the world but in dialogue with it exploring how the creative and redemptive will of God is mysteriously at work today. *Gaudium et spes* juxtaposes two communities—the Church and the modern world—and tries to set out ways in which these two communities can interact. Two major considerations for this kind of juxtaposition have to be that the two communities are not mutually exclusive and that interaction means that each is likely to influence the other. The Council Fathers seem to admit this, at the same time that they try to suggest that the Church is other-worldly, and that the influence should be more unidirectional than otherwise. Thus we read in the document:

> . . . the Council, as witness and guide to the faith of the whole people of God . . . can find no more eloquent expression of its solidarity and respectful affection for the whole human family . . . than to enter into dialogue with it about these different problems (namely, problems which arise form the discoveries and power of the modern world, the anxiety about the current trend of the world, the place and role of human beings in the world, etc.).[30]

The style of communication which emerges in the secular dialogic model calls for dialogue and cooperation. The mass media have no small part to play in this dialogue. Because no one can be excluded, the Church publicly manifests Christ's presence in the world. Communication implies this public quality: to communicate is to share, to overcome isolation and

---

29. Klaus Kienzler. Taken from the unpublished paper, "The Church as Communion and Communication," given at the 1989 Cavalletti Seminar.

30. *Gaudium et spes* 3.

individuality, and to become a community. I hope the foregoing glimpse of the relationship between ecclesiology and communications makes at least one thing apparent: as one imagines Church, so one does, lives, and communicates as Church. The dominant image dictates the praxis. We cannot ignore the reality that new images of the church are already on the horizon. These new images are already calling for a new understanding of communications in and with the church. Liberation theologians like Jon Sobrino, Juan Segundo, Guillermo Cook, and others have been advocates for a renewed, cleansed ecclesiology, one with universal principles but also admitting of much cultural adaptation and syncretism (in a positive sense), that is, building on the local customs and symbols of people. Gustavo Gutierrez calls for an "uncentering" of the Church over against ecclesiocentrism, and for a sacramental rather than a juridical understanding of salvation.[31] Leonardo Boff calls for the creation of a "communitarian spirit," and provides a sharply delineated comparison of the hierarchical and communal models of being Church.[32]

A feminist ecclesial vision is also contributing significantly to a new paradigm of Church: a discovery of the egalitarian and inclusive character of many of the early Christian communities; the changing role of women in Church leadership, including the emergence of the women-church movement; and the practice of inclusive language.[33] Aware of the limitations on the range of options open to women in the past, mainstream Christian feminists—both scholars and ministers—see the Church as a significant cultural force in forming the attitudes, self-understandings, and expectations of women—and of men—and of society itself. According to Catholic theologian Anne C. Carr the wider social concerns of today's Church women have brought them more solidly into national and local political life just as they have been active in bringing concerns for justice and equality into the life of the Church. They refuse to ignore the liberating, indeed revolutionary, message that the churches bear about the realm of justice, peace, and equality coming in the future but, as the Gospel proclaims, even now being born among us. The new ecclesiology calls for a new dialectical process which images the Church as a collaborator, networker, a Church in the round which encourages and supports an on-going transformation or birthing process for nurturing an authentic sense of *communio.*

---

31. Gustavo Gutierrez, *A Theology of Liberation* (Maryknoll, N.Y.: Orbis Books, 1973), Chapter 12.

32. Leonardo Boff, *Church: Charism and Power* (New York: Crossroad, 1985), Chapters 1 and 2.

33. See Rebecca Oxford-Carpenter, "Gender and Trinity," *Theology Today* 41 (1984-85): 7-25, and Susan B. Thistlethwaite, "Inclusive Language and Linguistic Blindness," *Theology Today* 43 (1986-87): 533-39.

The Church cannot, of course, exist without organizational structure, but hierarchy must not be allowed to establish the model or pattern. In place of a vertically linear model, we should think of a circular, interactive, or triangular one. Hierarchy is in fact so deeply imbedded in Western consciousness that it is difficult for us to think of an organizational structure of any kind in nonhierarchical terms, although clearly there are alternative possibilities which emerge waiting to be disclosed and acted upon.

IV. Pastoral Implications

A Sense of Communio

What might the evangelization and communication efforts we are discussing look like in the year 2000? The challenge of community that emerges from the Second Vatican Council, and especially from *Gaudium et spes,* is a call away from isolation to identification with all peoples. We are part of a global community; the world is one family, one people; and our survival on this planet will be as a world community or not at all. Paul Roy in speaking of a new sense of community states:

> The contemporary North American Church, twenty years after the Second Vatican Council, must become willing to look to the margins of its own institution if it is to rethink the Gospel in light of *Gaudium et spes.* What it will find there—at the margins—is a growing number of Christians who seek a kind of community that gets its life from reflection on human experience . . . It will be a collection of people who are becoming community because they choose relationships characterized by mutuality rather than by dominance of one over the other. It will be authentically Christian because its members will share Jesus' sense of indignation to oppression, his anger at those who would "lord it over" others . . . It will be a community of people who, in Cox's words, "have been excluded from or trampled by the modern world" victims of poverty, racism, and sexism.[34]

Now, twenty years after the Second Vatican Council, the Church must intensify its efforts to truly live its "worldly mission"—to make real its promise of *communio* and to contribute significantly to the humanizing of the human family and its history through each of its members and its community as a whole.

The uniqueness of Christ is his mission to reveal that "the divine life is trinitarian communion."[35] Evangelizers and proclaimers are "agents of communion and participation."[36] The Spirit, whom we confess in the

---

34. Paul Roy, "The Developing Sense of Community," in L. Richard et al., *Vatican II: The Unfinished Agenda* (New York: Paulist Press, 1987) , p. 201.

35. NCCB, *Puebla: Evangelization at Present and in the Future of Latin America* (Washington: USCC, 1979), #212.

Creed to be "the Lord and Giver of life," is that person in whom the Father through Christ has contact with history and the world. The Spirit, "creating communion and abundance," prompts the *communio* to reach out beyond the boundaries of believers to proclaim to all that eternal life is communion with the Father.[37] The Spirit also prompts the Church to become "servants of humanity."[38]

The Church "is a sacrament of communion."[39] Even eucharistic celebration at the parish level "makes the global reality of the Church" clear to all.[40] The local communion is linked with the universal communion by fidelity to the Gospel and eucharistic fellowship. At the diocesan level the Church is a complex of smaller "centers of communion and participation," which are also "preferential centers or locales of evangelization," especially the family and the basic Christian communities."[41]

Christian Base Communities

In 1979 the Episcopal Council of Latin America (CELAM) convened a conference of all Latin American bishops in Puebla, Mexico. Puebla tried to relate the task of evangelization to the Latin American social reality. This meant that some theological instrument had to be found that would integrate the goals of proclamation with the grave necessities of the socioeconomic situation and, at the same time, effect social and religious reconciliation between alienated and often traumatized populations. Puebla chose *koinonia/communio*. Because *communio* has many-leveled meaning, it could express sharing in a common good and mean participating at the same time in trinitarian life, in eucharistic community, and in human and material goods.

In reflecting on the above, it is proposed that small communities provide the most hopeful approach to evangelization. Small communities aid every aspect of the evangelization process. Brazil is popularly targeted or named as the womb in which basic ecclesial communities were conceived. Central in this movement was Dom Angelo Rossi, who used lay catechists to evangelize regions beyond Barra do Pirai that were not, could not be, reached by pastors. His movement was an attempt to undo the closing of churches and chapels because of the lack of clergy. Use of the radio became an efficient, unifying tool in both catechesis and celebration of the eucharist. By 1963, there were 1,410 centers connected via radio catechesis and also radio celebration of the eucharist with persons

36. Ibid., #658.
37. Ibid., #1294.
38. Ibid., #1295.
39. Ibid., #1302.
40. Ibid., #644.
41. Ibid.,#567.

participating at the sites of reception. Evangelical teams traveled Brazil. A nationwide pastoral plan, under the guidance of the Brazilian Bishops Conference, was implemented from 1965-1970, with the goal of renewing parishes and other natural gatherings of people for the purpose of generating small base communities. Cardinal Joseph Bernardin of Chicago in his Pentecost '87 address spoke to this reality:

> What can we do to take bold initiatives in evangelizing? How can we move away from merely reactive proclamation of the Word? A possible solution is to restructure the parish as a community of communities. In such a vision and structure, Catholics gather in small groups in order to pray, read Scripture, and share. Authentic community is vital to effective evangelization. It nurtures believers.[42]

Preaching

It's Sunday morning in America. At the local Catholic Church the organist intones the Alleluia. Accompanied by altar servers with lighted candles on either side, the congregation singing, the priest mounts the pulpit. After the proclamation of the Gospel, the congregation is seated and the homily begins. Now visualize the fast growing, local interdenominational Church in your community. A rousing choir sings while an enraptured congregation sways rhythmically to the music, clapping their hands and shouting "Amen" as the pastor prepares to preach. Given a choice between the above scenarios, which homily would you like to hear? Preaching the Gospel is the reason the Church exists. Today, more than ever, it is clear that preaching in the Catholic Church could be more powerful in promoting the Gospel. The greatest challenge to the growing spirit of evangelization is a spirit-filled message that is the responsibility of the preacher of the Word to deliver. Growing churches are churches where there is an evangelizing energy sweeping the Church community. The direction and formation of this energy finds its focus in the preaching event.

Preachers must process the Word as storytellers: "The more we can turn to the picture language of the poet and the storyteller, the more we will be able to preach in a way that invites people to respond from the heart as well as from the mind."[43] The preacher is sometimes an exegete, sometimes a teacher, but always must be an artist and poet. Rahner was convinced that "where the word of God says what is most sublime and plunges this most deeply into man's heart, there is also to be found a pregnant word of human poetry."[44] It is possible that the reason why

---

42. Cardinal Joseph Bernardin at Pentecost '87. Each year the Paulist Evangelization Center in Washington sponsors a tele-conference on evangelization. It is aired on the Catholic Telecommunications Network of America into all dioceses in the United States.

43. See NCCB Committee on Education, *To Teach as Jesus Did* (Washington: USCC, 1972), #44.

preachers today do not ignite hearts and read the signs of the times in light of the Gospel is because they have never become poets.[45]

A key understanding of *Fulfilled in Your Hearing* published by the NCCB in 1982 is that the homily is an interpretive rather than a catechetical event. This worthy little document goes beyond the restrictive definitions of the homily found in *Sacrosanctum concilium*. It incorporates the "reading of the signs of the times" motif from *Gaudium et spes* and insights from contemporary biblical and communication scholarship. The homily is a speaking event which attempts to speak the truth of God's presence in relation to a community's lived experience.[46]

Media Consciousness

I teach a graduate course on The Parish, Faith, and Contemporary Culture. During the course we discuss the importance of understanding and interpreting the "culture of the parish." One element in the process is insight into the media milieu of one's parishioners. If a minister is serious about knowing—really knowing—the people he/she serves, it is worth their time and effort to identify the types of mass media experiences which are predominant in their parishioners lives. This media investigation can enrich one's homilies, spiritual directions, evangelization, and catechetical efforts, as well as, strengthen informal dialogue. Let me give an example.

A friend of mine ministers in a parish with approximately 1,000 families. He believes he can best communicate with his parishioners by occasionally reflecting with them on mass media events which invite or challenge their faith commitment today.

He is beginning with a well-known principle in education known as "apperception," working from the known to the unknown. While visiting the Catholic school, religious education program, parish organization meetings or homes, he always takes the opportunity to discuss what has sparked his parishioners interest in the media during the week. This approach not only opens the door for quality conversations but offers great insights to weave into his Sunday homilies.

Media consciousness in our ministry is supported in *Communio et progressio*:

> If students for the priesthood and religious in training wish to be part of modern life and also to be at all effective in their apostolate, they should know how the media work upon the fabric of society, and also

---

44. K. Rahner "Priest and Poet," in *The Word: Readings in Theology* (New York : P . J . Kenedy & Sons, 1964), p. 24.

45. See NCCB Committee on Liturgy, *Fulfilled in Your Hearing: The Homily in the Sunday Assembly* (Washington: USCC, 1982).

46. Ibid., # 3-8.

the technique of their use. This knowledge should be an integral part of their ordinary education.[47]

The pastoral leadership of the Church and the theological disciplines have much to learn from communications technology. The effectiveness of the apostolate in every age has depended on the Church's ability to make use of the dominant forms of communication. In the words of Paul VI, "The Church would feel guilty before the Lord if she did not utilize these powerful means of communication that human skill is daily rendering more perfect."[48] Finally, in 1986 the Congregation for Catholic Education (Vatican) published the *Guide to the Training of Future Priests Concerning the Instruments of Social Communication*. In this directive the importance of stages of initiation and education in social communications is clearly defined.

The Use of the Mass Media

When Pope Paul VI issued *Evangelli nuntiandi,* he noted:

> When they (media) are put at the service of the Gospel, they are capable of increasing almost indefinitely the area in which the Word of God is heard; they enable the good news to reach millions of people. The Church would feel guilty before the Lord if she did not utilize these powerful means that human skill is daily rendering more perfect. It is through them that she proclaims, 'from the housetops' the message of which she is the depository. In them she finds a modern and effective version of the pulpit. Thanks to them she succeeds in speaking to the multitudes.[49]

The Medellin conference of the Latin American bishops included in its conclusions a chapter on the mass media, in which dialogue is centrally focused. The media are valued for their capacity to awaken the consciousness of the masses, to promote people's aspiration for a better life and to manifest the urgency of radical social change.[50] For reasons given by Vatican II, the Church must participate in this process:

> The involvement of Christians in today's world obliges them to work in the media of social communication external to the Church in keeping with the spirit of dialogue and service which marks the Constitution *Gaudium et spes*. The Catholic professional, called to be the leaven in the dough, will better perform (his) mission if (he) integrates (himself) in these media in order to broaden the contacts be-

---

47. *Communio et progressio,* #22.

48. Paul VI, *On Evangelization in the Modern World,* # 45.

49. Ibid.

50. Second General Conference of Latin American Bishops (Medellin, 1968), *The Church in the Present-Day Transformation of Latin America in the Light of the Council* (Washington: USCC, 1973), 16:12, p. 212.

tween the Church and the world, and at the same time contribute to the transformation of the latter.[51]

During the 1989 Cavalletti seminar, Jerry O'Sullivan of Venezuela spoke at length and with passion on the importance for the Church in all cultures to seriously look at the opportunities of the mass media for evangelization today. Aware of the potential negative impact of the mass media, O'Sullivan pointed to the Puebla and Medellin documents as encouragement to assume a more proactive role in the new media age. He stated:

> I personally consider that it is of urgent importance to rethink the attitude and role of the Church in relation to the mass media and in particular to television. . . . over twenty years almost all our efforts have gone towards the group media and interpersonal communication. Catholics working in the mass media have been marginalized, partly because of our bias against the TV . . . A genuine commitment to TV would oblige us to rethink our priorities not only from a personal point of view but also from the concept of our investments, pastoral strategies and so much more.[52]

V. Conclusion

Since evangelization is a form of communications and communications is at the heart of what the Church is all about, our vocation for working toward a 'new evangelization' cannot be taken lightly. Each and every program of formation for church ministry must include a solid foundation for understanding and appropriating the necessary communication skills to enable ministers to engage in a public dialogue of faith today.[53] The media can and should be instruments in the Church's program of re-evangelization and new evangelization in the contemporary world. Indeed, "the Church would feel guilty before the Lord if she did not utilize these powerful means (communication) that human skills is daily rendering more perfect."[54] It is important, however, not simply to instrumentalize the media for religious purposes. But "the first Areopagus of the modern age is the world of communications," and this points to a conclusion of great importance for the Church's approach to media and the culture they do so much to shape: "(it) is not enough to use the media simply to spread the Christian message and the Church's authentic teaching. It is also necessary to integrate that message into the 'new culture' created by

51. Ibid., 16:12, pp. 214-15.
52. Jerry Ryan O'Sullivan. From "Ecclesiology and Communication," an unpublished paper from 1989 Cavalletti Seminar.
53. Congregation for Catholic Education, *Guide to the Training of Future Priests Concerning the Instruments of Social Communication* (Rome, 1986).
54. Paul VI, *On the Evangelization of the Modern World*, #45, pp. 30-31.

modern communications . . . with new languages, new techniques and a new psychology."[55]

The pastoral instruction *Aetatis Novae* (1992) emphasizes that the evangelization efforts of today "ought to well up from the Church's active, sympathetic presence within the world of communications."[56]

We need to work toward a Catholic style of doing media, one which does not simply copy evangelical or fundamentalist models. We need to take up the authentic religious concerns of our contemporary culture with ongoing, unbounded communication insight and skills. Finally, we must reflect on the impact and correlation between image and word and the power of religious faith to awaken basic questions and offer challenge and consolation to the people of God. Let us ask ourselves whether we create a dynamic, two-way communication whereby the ministry we are engaged in and the programs we produce help people to change their lives, or do we leave people passively unresponsive to our message? In the age of the image, are we connecting with reality through our religious use of images? There are no straightforward solutions to the complexity of issues surrounding the challenges of a communications age for addressing a 'new evangelization' in our society today. "Faithful to the past and open to the future, we must accept the burden and welcome the opportunity of proclaiming the Gospel of Christ in our times. Where this is a summons to change, we must be willing to change. Where this is a call to stand firm, we must not yield."[57]   The spirit of the new age—of constant change and rapid saturation of secular images and sound—are not easily reconcilable with the demands of the Christian Gospel. The process of the transformation of our culture begins, however, with a deep reverence and respect for the dignity of each individual. As we concentrate on enhancing our skills for engaging in quality conversation and dialogue with one another, we will begin the process of transformation.

---

55. John Paul II, *Redemptoris missio*, # 37.

56. Pontifical Council for Social Communication, Pastoral Instruction *Aetatis novae* in *Origins*, March 26,1992, Vol. 21, no. 442: #11, p. 674.

57. *To Teach as Jesus Did*, #41.

11

Interactive Communications in the Church

Frances Forde Plude

On a foggy morning in Berlin a taxi dropped me at the Brandenburg Gate. Tears came to my eyes as I felt *communion* with people who had struggled to *participate*, to unite. I had been part of it through the mass media.

For many, the fall of the Berlin Wall remains a symbol of hope and enormous challenge. If this happened so quickly and dramatically—in Berlin and, later, in Moscow and the Middle East—then barriers can be minimized between local, regional, national, and global communities.

Unity in diversity is a challenge for churches and society in a post-modern world.

In *Lumen gentium*, the Second Vatican Council referred to a multiplicity of "the abilities, the resources, and customs of peoples," saying "each part contributes its own gifts to other parts and to the whole Church."[1] At the historical moment of the Council, we were called to communion and community,

The ideas that follow are an attempt to reflect on aspects of communications and the theology of *communio*. Specific questions guide our study:

1. What forms of participatory communications are emerging in churches? What is the role of authority in such forums?

2. How do we encourage collaboration—called "animating forms of cooperation" by the theologian Hermann Pottmeyer?[2]

3. Must participatory freedom lead to polarization and, in reaction, central control?

4. Can new communication and collaborative theories help churches become vital communities, to reanimate an apparent diminution of faith in some modern societies?

---

1. *Lumen gentium* 13.
2. Hermann J. Pottmeyer, "The Church: Its Self-Understanding and Structures." Unpublished manuscript.

I. Conceptual Framework

It is helpful to make some comments about the analytical perspective employed here. This is clearly an interdisciplinary investigation. Theology, specifically ecclesiology, and communications are involved in this inquiry, and the communication ideas will involve both theoretical reflections and practical guidelines.

Applicable too are insights from social theory and from the field of organizational communication since it is a challenge to coordinate dialogical responses within Church structures. Much study is required concerning the process and interrelatedness of those communicating.

Two theologians have noted that Vatican II should be considered "transitional"—a work in progress. Pottmeyer called the Council "an act of setting out . . . not as a single, once-and-for-all step, but as an example of a passage to be made over and over again, in every moment, the signs of which must be read in the light of the Gospel."[3] In a similar vein, Walter Kasper noted that "today there is not yet any way which leads fundamentally beyond the Council. . . . It is not only that we do not have the presuppositions and the preliminary work. We have not as yet nearly exhausted the potentialities of the last Council."[4]

I will draw substantially here from my own research on collaborative systems theory—reflections on cooperative strategies in a media/information world. These ideas supply a framework for analysis which can aid us in our understanding of emerging realities of communication and Church. Hopefully, such a framework will enable others to offer additional organizing principles, thus encouraging both unity and diversity.

We need to explore specific topics:

- participatory components of *communio* ecclesiology

- emerging communication theories of discourse

- how these two areas converge and interact in participatory communications

- practical applications and case study examples: collaborative communications; the implications of freedom and autonomy; new roles for laity

- specific suggestions and goals for the future

---

3. Hermann J. Pottmeyer, "A New Phase in the Reception of Vatican II: Twenty Years of Interpretation of the Council," in G. Alberigo, J. P. Jossua, and J. A. Komonchak, eds., *The Reception of Vatican II* (Washington: The Catholic University of America Press, 1987), p. 29.

4. Walter Kasper, *Theology and Church* (New York: Crossroad, 1989), p. 165.

Lonergan reminds us in *Method in Theology* that "A community . . . is an achievement of common meaning."[5] And we must recall the practical advice of Dulles, in 1971, in a prophetic document: "The Church cannot wall itself up in a cultural ghetto at a time when humanity as a whole is passing into the electronic age."[6]

II. Participatory Components of *Communio* Ecclesiology

There is a distinction, of course, between ecclesiology—the aspect of theology that examines the nature and mission of the Church—and what the Church is in practice. It is clear that historical diversity and the development of ecclesiology permit a richness in the Church's own self-understanding.

In the last century the Church was presented as a full and perfect society, on the same level as the state; at the same time, emphasis was placed on the hierarchical and juridical aspects of the Church as institution. Later the theme of the Mystical Body was stressed, integrating previous concepts of Church.

Various aspects of the Church's nature and mission have been made more understandable by the models of Church proposed by Avery Dulles.[7] The first model mentioned, the Church as institution, places exclusive emphasis on the hierarchical structure. This model notes that the Church descends from God through its hierarchy to others. The faithful are asked to assent to this and subordinate themselves. The hierarchy represent authoritative teachers (*ecclesia docens*), and the people are learners (*ecclesia discens*). This was the view of Church emphasized when the Second Vatican Council began.

Dulles identifies and explores other images of Church, including the Church as Herald (to proclaim its message), as Sacrament (Church as sign, personal witness) and the secular-dialogic metaphor.[8] In another work Dulles speaks of Discipleship as an appropriate image of Church.[9]

A clearly distinct model is the Church as *communio*—a fellowship animated by the Spirit, No one metaphor contains the totality of the Church's nature and each contributes to our understanding. Obviously different individuals will tend toward various aspects of Church. We should

---

5. Bernard J. F. Lonergan, *Method in Theology* (New York: Herder and Herder, 1972), p. 79.

6. Avery Dulles, "The Church Is Communications," *Catholic Mind* 69 (1971): p. 13.

7. Avery Dulles, *Models of the Church* (Garden City, N.Y.: Image Books, 1987).

8. Ibid.

9. Avery Dulles, *A Church to Believe In* (New York: Crossroad, 1982).

note that each model of Church has a different image and seems to have its own style of communication appropriate to it.

In the document *Lumen gentium* the Council sets forth the Church's revised understanding of her own nature. Dulles notes that *Lumen gentium*, "because of its central importance and its wealth of doctrine, probably deserves to be called the most imposing achievement of Vatican II."[10] Indeed, the very *process* of developing *Lumen gentium* is an example of a participatory forum. As Dulles notes: "The successive drafts of the Constitution, compared with one another, strikingly reveal the tremendous development in self-understanding of the Church which resulted from the *dialogue* within the Council."[11] (Emphasis added) The institutional and *communio* models of Church had supporters within the Council. Some tension between these diverse ecclesiologies continues as a result of Council efforts to express the nature of church. The Church, organic and graced, is—in the last analysis—a mystery because it is an embodiment of the essential mystery of God Incarnate.

Several participatory concepts do emerge in *Lumen gentium*, including a creative view of laity roles and the principle of bishops' collegiality. Both provide a balance to the earlier heavy emphasis on papal power and authority. The new self-understanding was based upon biblical scholarship and a reconnection with early Church history and practice.

Most consider graced the bold new direction in the Church's self-understanding and participatory vision. On the practical level, however, it did require compromise as the dialogue at the Council proceeded. As a result, several ecclesiologies exist side by side in Council documents; this has made subsequent application of Council teaching somewhat complicated and even contentious.

Pottmeyer notes: "The active reception of the Council's first steps toward a new ecclesial self-understanding is . . . a task that will take decades. . . . Would it not have been inherently contradictory to give a fixed legal formulation to what was in fact the expression of a desire for transition and mobility?"[12] Much participatory development has occurred since the Council; understandably, it has not been easy.

Shared Responsibility

The Council challenged *all* Church members to accept responsibility as a community specifically called—participating actively in the Church's life and mission by virtue of their sacramental entrance into the commu-

---

10. Avery Dulles, "Introduction" in W. M. Abbott and J. Gallagher, *The Documents of Vatican II* (New York: America Press, 1966), p. 13.

11. Ibid., p. 10.

12. Pottmeyer, "A New Phase," p. 29.

nity. Kasper notes that this marked the end of a pattern of a welfare Church.

> In hardly any sector since the Council have things moved so much as here. . . . Stimulated by the Council, bodies of common responsibility have come into being on all levels of the church's life: parish councils, diocesan councils, diocesan synods, episcopal synods. Lay interest, and the preparedness of lay people to take a share of responsibility, is perhaps the most valuable and most important contribution of the post-conciliar period.[13]

It is helpful to look briefly at the issue of "democracy" in the Church. Rahner notes:

> . . . many structures and institutions may be built into the Church which give the people of the Church a more active role than that which they have previously had in the life of the Church itself. In other words . . . these new structures and institutions may signify 'democratic' rights within the Church. In fact many changes in this direction have in practice already been achieved within the Church, even though we may hold the opinion that still more changes of the same kind will have to take place in the future.[14]

Schillebeeckx, in a recent book, gives extensive treatment to this issue in a chapter entitled "Towards Democratic Rule of the Church as a Community of God."[15] This work explores the impact of various historical developments: bishops as feudal princes; the Enlightenment; the French Revolution; bourgeois religion; and the Council's final "break with its feudal past."[16]

> The co-responsibility of all believers for the church . . . essentially includes the participation of all believers in decisions relating to church government (however this may be organized in practice). Vatican II also gave at least some institutional encouragement towards making this universal participation possible: the Roman synods, the national councils, the episcopal conferences, the councils of priests, the diocesan and parish councils of lay believers and the frameworks of many organizations.[17]

Schillebeeckx notes the danger of overemphasizing "our one-sidedly technological consumer society" and urges "the interplay of official teaching

---

13. Kasper, *Theology and Church*, p. 162.

14. Karl Rahner, "Basic Observations on the Subject of Changeable and Unchangeable Factors in the Church," in *Theological Investigations* (New York: Seabury Press, 1976), XIV: p. 19.

15. Edward Schillebeeckx, *Church: The Human Story of God* (New York: Crossroad, 1990).

16. Ibid., p. 206.

17. Ibid., p. 209.

authority and the teaching authority of believers and their theologians (always in some tension)."[18]

Obviously, the Church is not free to disregard Scripture and tradition; and it retains divine guidance. Kasper also notes that the term "'People of God' does not mean a political association of people or 'ordinary, simple people,' as distinct from the establishment. . . . It means the organic and structured whole of the church, the people gathered round their bishop, and attached to their shepherd, as Cyprian put it."[19]

III. An "Open Systems" View of Church

Many would agree on the concept of shared responsibility in the Church. The tensions arise when it is worked out in practice. Much of the difficulty relates to communication patterns and practices.

Another issue is the need to develop and build a theory of subsidiarity; it is not just a question of Rome implementing it. What is required is the *institutionalization* of subsidiarity. This needs to be developed organically, not simply from the top down, or one contradicts the principle of subsidiarity. These are some of the specific tasks when integrating practical applications of authority and co-responsibility in churches today.

Many of these issues are worked out at the local level. Thus, the Church at the parish and diocesan level is the focus of much current ecclesial inquiry and theological reflection. Joseph Komonchak notes reasons for the shift to the local Church. These include ". . . the revalidation of the bishop's role; the importance of regional episcopal collegiality; ecumenical reflection on the differences compatible with unity; challenges of inculturation; . . . (the need for) genuine community in a world of increased anonymity and bureaucracy . . ."[20]

The Church also exists in a society of advancing scientific inquiry. From an organizational or institutional viewpoint, it is helpful to examine the impact of one scientific perspective—systems theory.

Everett and Rekha Rogers have analyzed organizational communication. One can trace the history of organizational behavior studies from early "scientific management" days through the discovery of "human relations. Rogers notes the emergence of "a more eclectic and encompassing viewpoint" in the 1960's and 1970's—"the systems school."[21] Based on general systems theory, this work "conceptualizes an organization as a

---

18. Ibid., p. 233.

19. Kasper, *Theology and Church*, p. 162.

20. Joseph A. Komonchak, "The Local Church," *Chicago Studies* 28 (1989): p. 320.

21. Everett M. Rogers and Rekha Agarwala-Rogers, *Communication in Organizations* (New York: Free Press, 1976).

system of interrelated components, and stresses the orchestration of these parts as the key to maximizing performance. . . . This intellectual viewpoint has been the single most influential theory in contemporary scientific thought, especially in the social sciences."[22]

These theorists conceive of a system as a set of *interdependent* parts. Communication is one essential element of any system—linking the parts (subsystems) and facilitating their interdependence. The focus on *interaction* is very significant; the increasing interactivity of communication technologies, discussed below, parallels the emphasis on interactivity in systems theory. This theme of interdependence is reflected also, of course, in the ecclesiology of *communio*.

In describing an "open system" approach Rogers explains:

> A system is a set of units that has some degree of structure, and that is differentiated from the environment by a boundary. The system's boundary is defined by communication flows . . . any system that does not input matter, energy, and information from its environment will soon run down and eventually cease to exist. . . an *open system* continuously exchanges information with its environment.[23]

Research within organizations indicates that "the more turbulent environments require a more differentiated and decentralized organizational structure."[24] This may have interesting ramifications for churches today.

I have seen two interesting applications of systems concepts to ecclesiology and church governance. The first is a study of ecclesial cybernetics by Patrick Granfield.[25] This author uses case study analysis (of slavery, birth control, ecumenism, and celibacy) to examine concepts of democratic (interactive) communication, noting implications for ecclesiology.

In citing institutional conditions for improved church communication and responsive decision-making, Granfield lists:

- small communities fostering religious commitment;
- the principle of pluralism;
- greater local autonomy and flexibility;
- credible study commissions; and
- broad participation in the selection of leadership

Another study uses a systems approach to analyze shared responsibility in the educational system of the Church.[26] Olin J. Murdick has de-

---

22. Ibid., p. 48.

23. Ibid., pp. 50-51.

24. Ibid., p. 63.

25. Patrick Granfield, *Ecclesial Cybernetics: A Study of Democracy in the Church* (New York: Macmillan, 1973).

26. Olin J. Murdick, "Who Runs Catholic Schools? A Model for Shared Responsibility," *Notre Dame Journal of Education*, Vol. 6, Summer, 1975, pp. 105-190.

signed a systems approach "reality grid." In the Murdick dialectic, specific operational components—such as goals, policies, programs, and governance—move through systematic stages. This significant study provided much of the theoretical foundation for the development of participatory school boards for Catholic schools in the United States. Murdick's concept of the School Board as "the voice of the community" is almost a metaphor for other participatory forums within the Church.

The challenge is to respect the role of *authority* while facilitating dialogue. The sensitive leader knows that participation permits both information-sharing and human affirmation. We have reviewed the ecclesiology of *communio* and the significance of systems theory in the institutional Church. It is important to understand that—in parallel with these—dynamic developments have occurred in the field of communications.

IV. The Role of the Message and Stories in Our Lives

When we review human history and communication roles within it, we move back before the time of complex structures when oral cultures were smaller and communal. Linking these groups required communication channels, both oral and written. These patterns were present in both Judaic and early Christian communities or churches. Leaders emerged but much interaction occurred among local people because there were not complex infrastructures above them nor easy access to other groups. The storyteller represented data storage—like computer memory of today.

When the technology of print emerged in medieval Europe an upheaval occurred that eventually fractured the local and regional loyalties of feudal society. Other factors include the Reformation, the ascendancy of the arts, the Enlightenment, and the concept of absolutism—the idea that power could be centralized in a king or a state. Meanwhile, trade routes provided financial and communications infrastructures; later the Industrial Revolution and nation-state concept added complexities making communication channels more difficult to analyze.

This brings us quickly to modern history, but it is here that we must function. And it is in this context that the Church must discern how communication theory and tools can infuse its unique mission and service to others.

Complicating and enriching this modern context is the growth of natural sciences and social sciences. Included are varied specifics such as: economic theory; psychiatry; systems analysis; the growth of bureaucracies; the science of management; the development of the democratic ideal; striving for universal education; personalism (fulfilling the earlier promise of the Enlightenment); the rise and fall of colonialism; and modern liberation movements. No wonder all this seems impossible to control or understand! The fact is that "control"—at least "centralized control"—is much more difficult, if not completely impossible, in the light of the above developments and the advances of mass communication systems.

Two additional factors should be mentioned. At least in the United States, pressure groups have focused enormous energies, funds, and communication manipulation into special-interest arenas, causing the noted consultant Peter Drucker and others to speak of "gridlock" when describing it. In addition, communication/information overload is tending to induce fear and anxiety; this breeds conflict.

Where does hope reside? How can one trust in "animating forms of cooperation," as Pottmeyer uses the term above? Advances in communication theories help somewhat. Specialists in communication are more sophisticated in tracking information flows between individuals, among groups, and within organizations and societal structures. New communication theories arise, like the "public sphere" model discussed below. And information *technologies* can provide enabling infrastructures—electronic highways which parallel the trade routes, railroads, and canals of previous ages.

In a 1989 conference of theologians and communication scholars held in Rome, some efforts were made to link the ecclesial concept of *communio* with communication sciences. One participant, Ricardo Antoncich, noted that theology (as reflection about the faith of the Church), should enter into dialogue with other forms of thought that rationally explain the life of the human being in the world. He noted: "Methodologically, the contribution of communication to ecclesiology does not refer exclusively to the analysis of how the Church lives its internal or external communication; rather it refers to the total contribution that communication sciences offer to the understanding of the human person, the world, and history."[27]

A corresponding communication/*communio* model was offered by Pottmeyer. He spoke of *communio* as a leitmotif—a norm or criterion—for the Church, her structures and relations. Rather than a concrete single concept, it has a theological and anthropological meaning. Pottmeyer noted that *communio* has three corresponding communications dimensions:

1. communication within the church (*communio fidelium, communio ecclesiarum*);

2. extra-ecclesial communication (Church as sacrament of the Kingdom within the unity of mankind); and

3. the self-communication of God (history of salvation).

All Church communication converges within the framework of divine self-communication, thus the Church's role as sign or witness.[28]

---

27. Ricardo Antoncich. From unpublished paper given at the Cavalletti Seminar in 1989.

28. Hermann J. Pottmeyer. From unpublished paper given at the Cavalletti Seminar

V. Communication Forums

In speaking of the emerging models of communication we need to move toward the concept of *participative communication forums*. Our first guide toward this path is Bernard Häring's thoughtful essay entitled "Ethics of Communication" in his volume on moral theology for priests and laity. Häring speaks in this work about mass media (TV, films, advertising), but we also see here the early traces of a sensitive awareness of communication as *interactive* and *dialogic*. He speaks of The Word as "listener;" he says the "Spirit *is* sharing;" (his emphasis). He notes: "A teaching Church that is not, above all, a learning, listening Church, is not on the wave-length of divine communication."[29]

In this work, written almost two decades ago, Häring says that a new dimension of today's communication is its "public forum" role. "The public forum in which information and opinions are exchanged is not something static . . . it is the sum of various 'worlds'" and he reminds us: "Vatican II considers the awareness of this changing world as fundamental for understanding our task."[30]

Häring moves then to a rich appreciation of pluralism.

> Pluralism is not at all anarchy of ideas and a structureless society. Democracy needs mutual respect and agreement on basic values. But tolerance does not imply neutrality of thought . . . a legitimate pluralism is never a threat but rather an indispensable condition for catholicity in truth and truth in catholicity. . . .

As one of the outstanding "signs of the times," pluralism invites a courageous and generous ecumenical spirit and action.[31]
He concludes:

> . . . the full recognition of pluralism and methods of dialogue, the common search for truth, and reciprocal communication not only do not threaten the consistency and unity of a united Christianity but can greatly help to strengthen and deepen them.[32]

Häring confronts realistically the pathologies of modern communication, the dark side. He bemoans technology-for-its-own-sake, the lack of access, the manipulation.

> One of the most serious threats to human integrity is the constant exposure to scenes of excessive cruelty. This abuse of mass media, which suggests that the normal solution of human conflict is violence

in 1989.

29. Bernard Häring, *Free and Faithful in Christ* (New York: Seabury Press, 1979), II: p. 155.

30. Ibid., p. 158.

31. Ibid., pp. 161-62.

32. Ibid., p. 163.

and even cruelty, is called by Haseldon "the most monstrous obscenity of our time." Particularly dangerous to humankind is the glorification of war and "the glamorizing of the military tradition."[33]

In an overview of Church documents on media, Häring concludes that evangelization through mass media should involve a prudent limitation of any media that make dialogue difficult. "Churches have to develop a dialogical style that invites everyone to participate trustfully."[34]

Culture and the Public Sphere

The concept of communication as *forum* (thereby dialogical) is a bold move in a field that has tended to focus on the model of a message moving from a source to a receiver (with much passivity). Under the influence of studies in cultural anthropology and linguistics, scholars now realize the significant interaction between communication and popular culture. We know that the common currency of any culture is deeply integrated into the communication channels existing within that culture.

A significant analysis of this, applied to developing nations, has been done by Robert White at The Gregorian University. White uses a concept stressed by other scholars—"the public sphere."

> Descriptively, the public sphere refers to that aspect of social action, cultural institutions, and collective decision-making that affects all people in the society and engages the interests of all people in the national body. . . . a nation may be said to exist insofar as it has a core of social interaction that is truly common and public.[35]

White explains the need to move away from emphasis on mass media to "the way that different groups construct discourses of meaning." The issue of a *participatory conception of the public sphere* leads communication experts to study group media instead of focusing on mass media only. We note once again the significance of *community* in public culture and participative media.

My own conviction is that we need to expand our communication horizon *beyond* group media (generally understood as audio and video "programs") to include what I would term *interconnecting* or *interactive* or *link* communication technologies. This interaction is participatory and connects quite naturally with the theology of *communio*.

---

33. Ibid., p. 181.

34. Ibid., p. 196.

35. Robert A. White, "Cultural Analysis in Communication for Development." Unpublished manuscript.

Interactivity: An Epistemological Turning Point

Driving an epistemological revolution is the interactivity of new communication technologies. To date much social science research in communication has focused on either the message *content* or media *effects*—linear models. We are now facing a totally new direction in our analytical focus, moving to "communication-as-exchange," to the *process* of interaction.

This new direction is analyzed by the communications scholar Everett Rogers who has researched how innovation is diffused. His own personal story shows an early antitechnology attitude. However, through the influence of Ed Parker, a Stanford colleague, Rogers began to realize the significance of the diffusion and social impacts of new communication technologies.[36]

My own growing commitment to the study of interactive technologies involved a trip to Stanford to talk with Parker; this resulted in an awareness of the emerging impact of communication satellites, telephony, and computer technologies, and the integration of communications and computers. After this "conversion," I moved from work in TV production to doctoral studies in telecommunications at Harvard and MIT.

Figure 1
INFORMATION TECHNOLOGIES

Design	*Storage*	*Distribution*
Development of Creative or Informational Concepts	Film	Broadcast Radio (AM, FM)
Design of Mediated Materials by Technology Professionals and Content Creators (Informational and/or Entertainment Materials)	Audio Tapes, Cassettes, Compact Discs Videocassettes Computor Software Telephone Answering Systems Videodiscs and CD Roms	Broadcast TV (UHF, VHF) Cable Systems Microwave Technology Satellites Telephone Technology (Including Mobile Phones, Paging, Cellular)

↕   ↕   ↕

Interactive
(These modes involve Design, Storage, and Distribution technologies)

Teleconferencing	Teletext, Videotext
Video Stores	Interactive Cable Mechanisms
Computer-Based Interactive Systems	Off-Site Audio/Video Feeds

Source: *Syracuse Scholar* **10 (1990): 36.**

---

36. Everett M. Rogers, *Communication Technology* (New York: Free Press, 1986).

Communication and computer technologies are now so integrated that it is impossible to distinguish between them in many media. I have developed a model to clarify relationships among components of information technologies. (Figure 1) This model disinguishes between *design, storage, distribution,* and *interactive* technologies.

It has always seemed necessary to me to separate the components or roles of communication/information technologies. Some are obviously storage technologies and some involve distribution. In fact, most of our attention is focused on only a few of the components: film, audio and video tapes/cassettes (storage technologies); and broadcast radio and TV and cable (distribution technologies).

New types of technologies have emerged in each of these areas. Newer storage tools include computer software, telephone answering systems, videodiscs, and CD-ROM, for example. Newer distribution technologies include microwave improvements, satellites, optical fiber, and technologies such as paging and cellular telephony. Facsimile messages also represent an exploding use of a practical tool.

Our conceptual analysis and management of the current terrain is enriched, I think, if we pay more attention than we have in the past to both design technologies and interactive technologies. As Figure 1 indicates, the design and development of content to be stored and distributed is a technology all its own. I suppose most of us call this "writing."

And then there is *interactivity.* This category actually involves or integrates all of the other groups—design, storage, and distribution. As these technologies converge we are reminded of Shakespeare's description of a "brave new world that has such creatures in it": video stores (allowing us to interact with program choice more vigorously), facsimile, conferencing, varied computer-based interactive systems, and off-site audio-video feeds, which permit the aggressive interactivity of world-wide news broadcasts.

Technological tools challenge both individuals and institutions to reach for new ideas, for exploratory skills, for higher-order thinking. A strategic tool needed for this task is *collaboration.*

VI. Institutionalizing Collaboration

The intellectual marketplace has become more of a challenge due to the increasing amounts of information (data) and the complexity of the technological systems for processing the data. When you add the factor of decreasing resources, it seems as if the only way to respond to the converging pressures is through fierce competition—often resulting in polarization within institutions.

Another way to view the situation, however, is that working smarter, not harder, can often involve working *with* others. Computer technology itself provides a metaphor for this approach in *time sharing,* a procedure allowing many people to use computer technology virtually simultaneously.

Other metaphors for this situation include the destruction of the Berlin Wall, the dissolution of the Soviet Union, and the growing peace accord between Israel and her Arab neighbors. It is possible that we are approaching the end of the concept and the reality of the nation-state. Part of the defining nature of the nation-state is that it has been the source, inspirer and container of information. Now, however, media images and computer networks override geographical boundaries. Regulatory mechanisms, like parliaments of the nation-state, no longer rule exclusively. Another reality is the ethnic enclave; communication technologies homogenize, but ethnicity—a type of family link—will probably be increasingly significant in the coming decades.

Today global economic challenges, while making people aware of the need for competitive advantage, also seem to be the direct cause of bold new collaboratives like the European Community—emerging with certainty albeit with difficulty. Even a noted authority like Peter Drucker states that we are in need of new economic models; the old theories are feeling the weight of increasing complexities, most of them technological. It may be that the new theoretical constructs will reflect a more conjoined world.

Technologies seem to be having a decentralizing effect on the bureaucracies of modern culture—the system or "technique" that the French philosopher, Jacques Ellul, critiqued in his writings. Drucker sees a new kind of organization emerging—one with more horizontal operational structures. Replacing most of the mid-level management will be task-force teams that are fluid and comprised of experts from various areas collaborating on tasks.

On the factory floor and in major corporate offices the team is already being institutionalized; *Fortune* magazine, in a cover story, said "the (team) phenomenon is spreading. It may be *the* productivity breakthrough of the 1990s."[37] The challenge is to *use* technological tools that facilitate interactivity and collaboration, thus leading to greater productivity (and community).

Communication forums mean we *plug in* to tools such as computer-based messaging systems. The studies of California analyst Jacques Vallee demonstrate that technological forums are productive. Such forums substitute for many face-to-face meetings and allow quick response when emergency changes are required.

After the Three Mile Island nuclear accident in the United States, messages were continually available on computer bulletin boards like

---

37. *Fortune*, May 7, 1990.

"emergency hotline," "emergency planner information," and "operations and maintenance information," and many others.[38]

Mundane messages are integral to our daily planning and often the message provides greater information precision and thus improves decision-making. This also keeps us connected as individuals, as community.

Our marketplace of ideas is more complex; information and machinery keep changing. The pace of change is staggering and this requires new tools; many of these enabling technologies involve the telephone and computer, often linked by satellites. More important than the technology is the *institutionalization* of collaboration in utilizing the tools in effective ways. In an Aspen Institute study, David Bollier notes:

> The concept of *information sharing* is what characterizes the current situation. . . . That is the most noteworthy trend in the dissemination of information technologies. It's the nature of information as a resource that it's going to be shared.[39]

I have undertaken a series of research projects in communication and collaboration, constructing a theory and related case study analysis in the telecommunications sector.

My hypothesis is that:

1. Communication/computer technologies are changing rapidly;

2. Entrepreneurial opportunities in this market sector are vast; and

3. To keep pace with the technological changes and market forces, we need new strategic planning and operational tools.

I have formulated a theoretical perspective which emphasizes the role of collaboration or cooperative efforts in meeting telecommunications needs and pressures. I call this concept Interactive Strategic Alliances (ISAs). Case studies under analysis from this theoretical perspective include: direct broadcast satellite development; teleconferencing for meetings; international negotiations for satellite use by many nations; the cooperative communications efforts among European Community nations; and others.

One dramatic forum has emerged in the increasing demand for liberation politically throughout the world. Viewers connected by mass media globally have watched "people power" emerge in Manila, in Poland, and on the streets of Moscow. Behind the television coverage, however, large numbers of people on the street are nodes in a communication network, using telephones, computers, and fax machines, where messages cannot be controlled. This communication pattern empowers individuals and groups; authority, whether legitimate or not, seems to move from "the top" to "the

---

38. Jacques Vallee, *Computer Message Systems* (New York: McGraw-Hill, 1984).
39. David Bollier, *The Social Impact of Widespread Computer Use* (Aspen, Colorado: Aspen Institute), p. 7.

grass roots." Pyramid organizational and authority structures are under seige (both in Moscow and in centralized church structures in Rome); this happens, to a large degree, because people communicate easily in new and interactive ways. There are many aspects of interactive communications and collaborative structures that require more analysis and more field-work, both in political societies and in churches.

One interesting question concerns gender differences. Are women socialized to be more collaborative than men?[40] Is there a connection be-tween the competitive nature of society and the fact that women have lim-ited leadership roles to date within that society? We may begin to see the collaborative model employed more by males, thus enabling joint owner-ship, with increased societal effectiveness because of a greater commit-ment to this *mutuality* by both the female and the male.

We need to study patterns of collaborative activity within groups and institutions and the regional economic collaboratives emerging throughout the world. We must identify the barriers to collaboration that will be troublesome in this decade when large empires will have disap-peared but regional and ethnic strife will have probably continued.

More information is needed on economies of scale within collabora-tives. We need current analysis of the uses of power and its impact on cooperatives (the concept of power-with instead of power-over). We must ask how we can design incentives for cooperative action, but we must also learn how to communicate through adversarial positions honestly ar-rived at. Mary Parker Follett, an organizational specialist involved in es-tablishing the Harvard Business School early in this century, noted: "We should never allow ourselves to be bullied by an 'either-or.' There is often the possibility of something better than either of two given alternatives."[41]

A Collaborative and Mediated Church

It is a challenge that our struggle to clarify models of Church is oc-curing at a time of enormous technological change. It is a challenge, but it is perhaps also a grace. A sign of this grace for me is the fact that a leading theologian like Avery Dulles began saying several decades ago that "the Church *is* communication."[42] As more members of the Church community throughout the world use and understand the varied technolo-gies of information-sharing and interconnecting we may well empower new communities—i.e., new forms of *communio*.

---

40. Mary Field Belenky et al., *Women's Ways of Knowing* (New York: Basic Books, 1986).

41. Mary Parker Follett, *Dynamic Administration*, edited by Elliot M. Fox (London: Pitman, 1973), p. 20.

42. Avery Dulles, "The Church Is Communication," p. 6.

A major theme of this document has been that *interactivity* inevitably and effectively removes passivity—in communications, in society, in churches. One-way structures are crumbling. Hopefully, the participatory *communio* ecclesiology of Vatican II documents will become more evident, instead of a pyramidal structure; otherwise, the Church will have difficulty communicating credibly in a collaborative, mediated world.

Our metaphor for this communion has been the reality that, even at great cost, people have taken down a Wall in Berlin. Perhaps it is appropriate, therefore, to conclude with reflections by two German theologians.

Bishop Walter Kasper has written in *Theology and Church*:

> To understand the church in a new way as a communion, to live it better, and to realize it more profoundly is . . . more than a programme for church reform. The church as a communion is a message and a promise for the people and the world of today.[43]

And Hermann Pottmeyer adds:

> The task that must be faced . . . is to incorporate what is still binding in preconciliar theology into the newly acquired foundation . . . into a *communio* ecclesiology and a Christian anthropology that calls for commitment to human dignity. . . . The decisive question . . . is whether we are giving the Spirit of God enough freedom to lead the church along new paths.[44]

---

43. Kasper, *Theology and Church,* p. 164.
44. Pottmeyer, "A New Phase," p. 34.

12

The Ecclesial Status of Catholic Communicators

John T. Catoir

Some communicators in the Church are highly skilled professionals, but they lack ecclesial status; while other communicators have ecclesial status but little or no expertise in their given field. If Catholic communicators can be defined as those who teach, share, or impart the faith, then ecclesial status has little to do with it.

On the other hand, one can see the practicality of identifying those who claim to represent the Church. There is the question of accountability and fidelity to the truth of the Gospel as it is taught and interpreted by the Church's Magisterium. And so I formed the two following propositions, both of which I believe capture an element of the truth.

Ecclesial status has little to do with communicating the faith.

Ecclesial status has everything to do with communicating the faith.

Communicating effectively is a skill. One's ecclesial status has little to do with one's expertise in that skill or craft. According to Webster a communicator is one who imparts or shares knowledge or information. The majority of Catholic writers are without any ecclesial status, and yet many of them are among the finest communicators of the faith. Here is a Christmas Poem by poet Catherine de Vinck. I leave the reader to decide if ecclesial status would enhance this gifted expression of faith.

And the Word was made flesh . . .

The stars speak
in their Christmas tongues
hang their cold silver overhead.
How can this be taught:
what the water says
in its transparent running
what the earth hums
in the labyrinth of its roots?

How can this be heard
these hosannahs

    sustained from age to age:
voices of elephants and sparrows
alleluias of luminous flowers
white canticles of snowflakes, or moonlight
and the ever-rising chorus of leaves
shaking green sounds into the air?

How can this be understood?
She who has never known man
    —singular woman yet like any other
    rich in flesh and blood—
she breaks open: the child bursts forth
wild and free, hearing within himself
the chant of the seven seas
the song of the whales
the tumult of angels unrolling
great banners of praise
and the immense concert of all the hosts
heavenly and others, shepherds, wise men.
fools on every continent singing
day after day as the blue planet turns
on the spindle of time.
      Holy, Holy, Holy Lord
        God of Power
          God of might.[1]

Can anyone deny that poets are Catholic communicators or that the gifts of the best among them transcend the whole discussion of ecclesial status. The same is true for good writers as well.

On the other hand there are some practical considerations. The term "ecclesial status" refers to a condition or position with regard to church law, even though this is only one aspect of a complex subject. However, legally speaking, the whole idea of "ecclesial status" has undergone significant revision since Vatican Council II. In the 1917 Code of Canon Law, categories such as states of life, canonical offices, precedence, positions of honor, etc., received more attention than they do in the 1983 Code of Canon Law which is now in force. For instance, the new Code simply names one general category of persons in the Church: the Christian Faithful; and within that heading, two states of life: the clergy and the laity.

---

1. "The Word Made Flesh," by Catherine de Vinck in *God of a Thousand Names* (Allendale, N.J.: Alleluia Press, 1993). Used with the permission of the author.

Canon 207, #1. Among the Christian Faithful by divine institution there exists in the Church sacred ministers, who are also called clerics in law, and other Christian faithful, who are called laity.

#2. From both groups there exist Christian Faithful who are consecrated to God in their own special manner and serve the salvific mission of the Church through the profession of the evangelical counsels by means of vows. . . ."

According to the new Code, therefore, members of religious communities do not form a third canonical state of life between clergy and laity, even though they may practice a distinct lifestyle. They are simply part of the faithful.

The word "status" does not appear in the 1983 Code of Canon Law at all, except in Canon 1643 where it refers to an obscure point in Book VII on Judicial Processes. The question of a person's marital status is discussed in relation to a *res judicata* that is, a final judicial decision in a matrimonial case. Needless to say, this paper is not concerned with a person's marital status.

The word "ministry" is important. One could write a separate book about the ministries of the laity which are operative in today's Church, jobs that were once the exclusive domain of the clergy. In the twenty five years since Vatican II, a dynamic spirit has breathed new life into the Roman Catholic Church. That Council called the Church "The People of God," and there have been amazing ministerial shifts taking place. Before Vatican II ministry was basically considered an individual calling, primarily for clerics, secondarily for religious in vows. The few remaining areas of ministerial service were given to the laity provided they had special permission. Their activities were viewed as a participation in the mission of the hierarchy, and they generally needed the proper delegation to be considered in ministry.

Since Vatican Council II the focus has moved away from the hierarchy, to the community. The emerging lay ministries like Eucharistic ministers, directors of religious education and the like, are now a routine part of parish life. The traditional role of priests is being reevaluated. Clerics who once performed nearly all the available ministries themselves, now look to the laity for support and help.

Consequently the meaning of ecclesial status needs reevaluation. Since some Catholic communicators are clerics, some are lay, and some are religious, their ecclesial status does not come from these categories. A lay woman might be a Diocesan Director of Communications, holding authority over a priest who works in her office. She would have ecclesial status by virtue of her position, and he would not. Even though he might be the most gifted writer on the staff, he does not hold a position with "status," because in day-to-day life "ecclesial status" belongs to those who have been given some form of authority in the Church.

A canonical office confers status. The Pope. the bishops, and the pastors all hold a canonical office. A Catholic communicator—for example, the editor of a Catholic newspaper—does not hold such an office, even though he or she might have ecclesial status by virtue of a non-canonical office.

The premise of this paper rests on the assumption that some communicators in the Church have more status than others. I do not mean to imply that some have more prestige than others, prestige is not the issue.

Some might say that a secretary working for the bishop in the chancery office has more status than a secretary in a local parish. It's true, one job might have more prestige connected to it than the other, but strictly speaking neither has "ecclesial status," because neither one has real authority. Although in all honesty, I have known some bishops' secretaries who have more power than their job description indicates. Access to the bishop gives one considerable influence in the decision-making process. But we are talking here about something else.

I was once the Chief Judge (Judicial Vicar) of the marriage tribunal in the Diocese of Paterson, New Jersey. That position confers what is called ordinary power, i.e., authority that is not delegated but rests in the office itself. In running the tribunal I had judicial power in my own right and ecclesial status. Theoretically the Judicial Vicar ranks third in the diocese after the bishop and the vicar general. I say theoretically, because, generally speaking, the chief judge is out of the administrative loop and knows little of what's going on from day to day in the bishop's office.

Most positions of authority in the Church do not have ordinary power but they do have delegated authority. In the field of communications, a Diocesan Director of Communications (hereafter: DDC) often has delegated authority over the editor of the diocesan newspaper. As a rule editors do not like an intermediary person blocking direct access to the bishop. The bishop after all is also their publisher. Editors certainly have ecclesial status in their own right, but it is of a lesser nature in the chain of command, especially in places where the DDC supervises them. There is much confusion in dioceses where two different people fill these two positions (in some places the editor is also the DCC). The editor's position does not lend itself easily to having two bosses, the bishop and a DCC.

Editors have a professional job to do. There are papal documents urging bishops to respect the principles of professional journalism which protects the readers' right to information presented honestly and completely. Bishops, in their position as publishers of the diocesan newspapers, usually respect the editors' professionalism, but conflicts inevitably arise when it comes to prudential judgments about how much information should be given in cases involving Church scandals and the like. Heavy handed newspaper censorship by a bishop does happen, but it usually is counter-effective since the secular press tells all while the Catholic press is accused of white-washing the story. Heavy-handed censorship destroys credibility, which in turn leads to financial disaster. A lack of reader-interest is the death knell of any paper.

What difference does ecclesial status make when it comes to Church communications?

It does make a difference. Ecclesial status is important to Catholic communications in determining an individual's qualifications and accountability to those in authority. The Pope and bishops are obviously concerned about orthodoxy. Faulty teaching cannot be ignored. When a communicator gains power over public opinion, serious problems can arise if that person should teach error. The messenger may appear to have the Church's stamp of approval. Those who want to avoid such abuses are inclined to try to tighten their control over communicators, but this is easier said than done since so much depends on mutual trust.

Times have changed. There has been a gradual evolution in the Church regarding the need for stronger control over the faithful particularly over communicators. Certainly in matters of faith and morals, control is needed to preserve the deposit of faith. And yet, communication admits of such a variety of functions that it is difficult to elaborate a set of rules to cover all eventualities. Accountability to the community is not easily rendered juridically. Bishops have to rely on a communicator's knowledge and good will.

To protect the faith handed down to us from the Apostles, those in authority want to be sure that the official teachings of the Church are being faithfully transmitted. Is the one teaching authorized to teach? Is the one teaching, communicating beliefs that have the official approval of the Church? Who is accountable to whom?

This paper will not deal with the educational dimension of this problem. Teachers in Catholic schools, on every level, have worked out their own professional standards for accountability. My focus will be on the accountability of those working directly in the communications ministry.

To elaborate further, I have divided this paper into four general topics:

    I.   The Mystery of Church Communications
    II. The Accountability Issue
    III. Catholic Communicators With Ecclesial Status
    IV. Conclusion

I. The Mystery of Church Communications

Since God is infinite, one must admit with due humility that He is not limited to the Roman Catholic Church in communicating Himself. Though he has blessed the Church, and made it a privileged channel of communication between Himself and the human family, He is in no way restricted by our Church structures. In other words He communicates

Himself to whomever he chooses, whenever He chooses—ecclesial status notwithstanding.

To some extent all communications between persons is a mystery. Language itself is a fascinating but inexact human tool which at times defies the passion for clarity. More often than not, we communicate imperfectly, creating more confusion than light.

One of my early experiences with communications in the Church goes back to 1960. A few weeks after ordination, my classmates and I were brought before our bishop to be given our first assignments. Each one was told which parish he would go to, and when my turn came the bishop said, "Fr. Catoir you will go to The Catholic University of America to study for your doctorate in canon law." The news hit me like an electric shock. Prior to that moment, no one had said a word to me about it. I didn't like canon law. The Code was in Latin which I barely understood, and at age 29, the thought of three more years of schooling made me nauseous. To compound the misery, I envisioned myself as a slave behind a desk in some musty chancery office for the rest of my life.

When I tried to persuade the bishop to send me to a parish, he would hear none of it. And so with my life predetermined without so much as a hint of preparation or polite inquiry about my thoughts on the matter, I accepted my fate. I learned the hard way that the Church can fall short of the mark when it comes to human relations, the most basic component of communications.

Ultimately, all human communication is personal. Even on the divine level, everything that emanates from the life of God is personal. God communicated himself to us in the Person of Jesus Christ, and Jesus communicates Himself to us in the Eucharist and in the living Word of Scripture. This is mystery pure and simple. Some communicators are more effective in penetrating the veil of mystery than others; and some excel in giving expression to it.

In an effort to be more clear myself, a few definitions are in order.

"Church doctrines" are those beliefs that have received the official approval of the highest teaching authority of the Church which is called the "Magisterium." Beliefs are expressions of faith. Since people communicate their beliefs according to their own understanding of revealed truths, there is a need for some agreement on these interpretations.

Theology is the interpretation of one's beliefs. Catholic theology is the Catholic interpretation of divine revelation. There are many theological specialties: Patristic theology, for instance, is the interpretation of the Deposit of Faith based on the insights of the early Fathers of the Church. Dogmatic theology is the interpretation of the Faith as clarified and taught by the Magisterium. Scriptural theology is the interpretation of Faith based on scripture. Systematic theology is an orderly systemization of the various branches of theology within one theological perspective.

Theological disagreements have been going on in the Church from its earliest days. Ever since Saint Paul challenged St. Peter on the circumcision issue, controversies of all kinds have raged over one theological problem or another.

The Magisterium has always settled these controversies authoritatively, and the resultant doctrine became a starting point for a new debate. For instance, in the early Church some theologians interpreted the humanity of Christ incorrectly, saying that Jesus was divine and therefore not a real human being. The Magisterium said, no, Jesus was true man and true God. Once these parameters were established theologians could then try to go forward and make sense out of the underlying mystery.

The Church depends on the correct use of authority to achieve its goals. Consequently there are those who favor strong central control, and those who hope for shared authority and a greater diffusion of power. This type of conflict has produced much tension in the Church down through the centuries.

In fact, the current crisis in Roman Catholicism seems to be related to efforts either to implement the principle of collegiality which was endorsed by the Second Vatican Council or to undermine it. At least that is the way it is perceived by most observers on this side of the Atlantic.

The question of ecclesial status in the Church takes on a new meaning when seen in this context. Those who favor stricter controls differ from those who favor more freedom and greater trust. A great deal depends on how one views the Catholic communicator.

If a Catholic communicator is defined as one who is a spokesperson for the hierarchy, then the mandate will be quite different from one who has a charism for proclaiming the Gospel through preaching. Preserving orthodoxy is essential in both cases, of course, but one approach is more formal than the other.

The Holy Spirit comes as a fire upon the earth in the pursuit of souls. Canon law recognizes the primacy of the Church's mission as the salvation of souls. (Canon 1752)

This is a great mystery, and the challenge for those in authority is to protect orthodoxy while at the same time creating an atmosphere of emotional comfort that will enable communicators to follow their grace in proclaiming the truth of Christ to the world. That challenge requires the skillful blending of charisms.

There are two main charisms in the Church, the charism of office and the personal charisms of individuals. The problem for those in authority is the intelligent blending of the two for the good of all.

When the control factor is emphasized too strongly it can suppress creativity. It sometimes happens that a person in authority with little experience in the art of communicating might crush the spirit of a gifted communicator who knows how to touch the lives of people in need of the

Gospel. The communicator's knowledge and experience can confer an authority that actually exceeds the competence of a superior.

An example taken from the secular world might be helpful here. There is an axiom in commercial television which asserts that all marketing decisions must precede production decisions. This means that the target audience must be clearly identified before production begins. Even before the script is finalized there must be a complete plan to attract and engage the target audience. Even 30-second radio or TV spots are aimed at a particular audience. A boss who does not know the ground rules of effective communication would not be useful in a position of authority. The same type of thing can happen in the Church. Even if the superior has ecclesial status, it will not serve the Church well if he does not possess basic communication skills.

When there is a lack of professionalism in the Church's use of the print or electronic media, ecclesial status will not make up for it. If an obedient but totally unimaginative priest was given the job of Director of Communications in a diocese, would the Church be better off because he has ecclesial standing? Clearly this is a complex question.

The ecclesial status of a Catholic communicator has little relevance when it comes to media expertise. Whether it be an editor of a diocesan newspaper or a priest in the pulpit, communication skills have to be honed and sharpened until the communicator becomes a specialist.

I will return to the topic of ecclesial status in part three, but first I would like to explore the use of control and accountability in the Church. A consideration of modern papal history might be helpful in gaining a better understanding of the current political climate.

II. The Accountability Issue

For centuries the Church boldly asserted that it was the supreme society on earth. Theoretically this is understandable, but the political implications of such an idea could be frightening, especially if a pope happened to have despotic tendencies.

The ancient dictum, "error has no rights," which led to inquisitions and other horrible abuses, has been replaced by the acknowledgment that people have rights even when they are in error. As a result of this shift, "*Communicatio in sacris*," the once forbidden practice of attending the worship services of non-Catholics, is no longer considered sinful.

In modern times a gradual change has been taking place in Church thinking. "A new ecclesiology was slowly being formulated that sought to integrate the ecclesiology of the Church's visible structure into a more complete and vital understanding of the mystery as found in the Scriptures and Fathers."[2] The evolution was very slow in developing.

The accountability issue is essentially an authority problem, and it might be helpful to examine the records of some recent Popes to determine the current trends in Vatican policies.[3] This review will serve as a prelude to a particular Vatican intervention in the life of Father James Keller, one of the leading Catholic communicators of this century.

Pius VI (1775-1799) resisted the new American concept of the separation of Church and state. During this period, the world was experiencing the collapse of many European monarchies, and Rome feared the revolutionary spirit.

Pius VII (1800-1823) regarded himself as the protector of sound doctrine. He stressed the importance of the Church as a supra-national authority, since it was the supreme society on earth. Imagine how Napoleon felt about that.

Leo XII (1823-1829) tried to be less political and more religious than his predecessors. He regarded himself as a champion of orthodoxy.

Pius VIII (1829-1830) died shortly after ascending to the papacy, but he lived long enough to approve the American bishop's first Provincial Council of Baltimore in 1829, which strengthened the ties of the U.S. Church with Rome.

Gregory XVI (1831-1846) was uncompromising in matters of doctrine. In his encyclical *Mirari vos* (1832) he denounced the notions of freedom of conscience, and freedom of the press. He also rejected the idea of the separation of Church and state.

Pope Pius IX (1846-1878) had the longest reign in papal history. He was a strong authoritarian who increased Vatican control in all areas of Church life. During the American Civil War he wrote the "Syllabus of Errors" (1864) which condemned many errors prevalent at the time. He rejected the idea that "the Pope should reconcile himself to or agree with progress, liberalism and modern civilization." In reaction to the 19th Century Rationalists who insisted that faith required rational analysis, he summoned the First Vatican Council (1869-1870). More about this will follow, let it suffice to say here that he declared the infallibility of the pope, thus removing all conciliarist interpretations of the role of the papacy.

Pope Leo XIII (1878-1903) attempted to bring the Church in closer harmony with the modern world. He gave a grudging approval to democracy in his encyclical *Diuturnum illud* (1881), but later, in an encyclical entitled, *Longinqua oceani* (1895) he stated that the Catholic Church in America

2. J. R. Lerch, "Ecclesiology" in *New Catholic Encylopedia* 5: 34.

3. The information on the Popes is taken from J. N. D. Kelly, *The Oxford Dictionary of Popes* (Oxford and New York: Oxford University Press, 1986).

would be healthier if it was the official Church of the American government. In 1899, he censured a trend called 'Americanism,' the name given to a movement seeking to adapt Catholicism to contemporary ideas and practices. His most famous manifesto was *Rerum novarum* (1891) which unheld the right to private property, the right to a just wage, and the right of workers to join trade unions. He became known as "the worker's Pope."

Pius X (1903-1914) was a compromise candidate. After Leo XIII's death, it took seven ballots to elect him. He made it clear from the start that he wanted a more religious papacy than a political one. To do this he tightened controls. He imposed on the clergy the Oath Against Modernism. Modernism was a liberalizing movement in the Church which was seen by the Holy See as an attempt to redefine dogmatic and biblical theology. In many ways it was a dangerous movement, but some of the feared danger signs turned out to be trends which led to the Second Vatican Council. Pius X revised and codified the canon law, updated the curia, and reformed seminaries. He was also a promoter of Catholic Action, which called upon the laity to serve under the hierarchy in addressing the apostolic tasks of the Church.

Benedict XV (1914-1922) reigned during World War I. The isolation of the Vatican during those years put him on the sidelines of the world stage. He supported the idea of the League of Nations, but was generally excluded from the peace settlement of 1919. He was a peace-maker who called a halt to the witch-hunting and bitterness between diehard traditionalists and modernists which was the legacy of Pius X's suppression of Modernism.

Pius XI (1922-1939) took as his motto "Christ's peace in Christ's kingdom" which he interpreted as a call to action. He thought that the Church and Christianity in general should be active in and not insulated from the world. In his first encyclical *Ubi arcano* (1922) he encouraged the laity to collaborate with the hierarchy in the Church's mission; this was an echo of Leo XIII's Catholic Action concept. He eventually denounced the Nazi government as fundamentally anti-Christian in 1937, after discovering that his earlier attempts to placate Hitler were naive. He was firmly against ecumenism and forbade Catholics to take part in conferences with Protestants. However he did ease the Modernist controversy rehabilitating some leading figures who had been chastised earlier.

Pius XII (1939-1958) saw himself as a Pope of peace, but in his attempt to remain strictly neutral during World War II, he ran into sharp criticism for failing to speak out firmly against Nazi atrocities. In 1943 he wrote *Divino afflante Spiritu* which permitted the use of modern historical methods by Catholic exegetes of Scripture. This was something that was condemned by earlier popes. He acted as his own Secretary of State from 1944 on, and increasingly diminished the role of cardinals. His spirit of isolation made his papacy seem more imperial than those of his predecessors. There were many Vatican investigations of perceived abuses during his reign. I am familiar with one investigation, and it involved Fr. James Keller, founder of The Christophers.

A young Maryknoll missionary named Father James Keller began formulating an approach to missionary work which caught the attention of Church authorities. He was assigned to vocational promotion in California, and he began telling people they didn't have to be foreign missionaries to spread the Gospel, each one could be a missionary right at home, at school, or at work. It seems harmless enough now but what was disturbing for the Vatican was his use of the mass media to challenge not only Catholics but non-Catholics as well.

Keller would say, "You have a job to do in this world that nobody else can do. God has a task for you to perform that He has assigned to no one else." He encouraged people of all faiths to use their gifts and talents to help make this a better world. He advised them to enter professions where they could make the most of their personal influence to bring about positive constructive changes for the common good. He encouraged them to consult their own consciences for the assignment God had in mind for them. This was a far cry from the teachings of Leo XIII in his encyclical *Testem benevolentiae* (1899), in which he rebuked American bishops for a lack of control of the laity. According to the Church's teaching up to that time, all Catholic action had to be seen as a participation in the work of the hierarchy. Encouraging Catholics to act on their own conscience was viewed as a Protestant abuse.

Fr. Keller was an obedient priest and an effective Catholic communicator. He submitted to the authorities dutifully, and was allowed to continue to use the media to get his message across. At this time TV was in its infancy. His decision to include non-Catholics in his radio and TV broadcasts made sense to a communicator, but those in the highest authority considered his approach to be a blurring of the lines.

On May 20, 1952, a letter of inquiry came to Cardinal Spellman, the Archbishop of New York, from Rome by way of the Apostolic Delegate, Archbishop Cicognani. It read: "Father Keller is known at the Vatican as priest of zeal and his work is looked upon favorably; however, a complaint has been received by the Holy Father (Pius XII), that Father Keller issues an invitation to all to join him regardless of religious confession."

Fortunately, Cardinal Spellman's friendship with Pope Pius XII carried enough weight to dispel needless fear. Here is what the Cardinal wrote in reply to Cicognani: "I wish to say that I can see no valid objection to the Christopher movement and I know personally that through the example, personality, and preaching of Father Keller many indifferent Catholics have become good Catholics and many good Catholics have become truly apostolic."

He then went on to explain what might be regarded as Father Keller's ecclesial status. Actually he had no status per se, but he was under the control of Church authorities. Cardinal Spellman wrote:

> Father Keller is a Maryknoll priest, and he serves under the supervision of the Vicar General of his own Order, Father Walsh the Rector of our Seminary, who reviews the books and other literature published by The Christophers; and Monsignor Maguire, the Chancellor of the Archdiocese of New York, who supervises the financial aspects of The Christopher activities. . . . I do not know the purpose of this query but, to avoid possible misunderstanding, I would say that, if there is any idea of the Holy See issuing any document concerning The Christophers, I would like to be heard before any action is taken to avoid the sensational and harmful repercussions to the Church which were occasioned by the general condemnation of membership in Rotary Clubs.

It must have pleased James Keller M.M. to have a Cardinal fight his battle for him. He was described as a priest in good standing whose charism was respected by his superiors. Keller was a communicator, but not by official appointment. He never had ecclesial status in the sense that he was part of the structure, he was assigned by Maryknoll to promote vocations and to raise money for the missions. And later he expanded his outreach using the mass media to reach people of all faiths and people of no particular faith. When that shift occurred, his message became less parochial and more generic. His motto was, "It's better to light one candle than curse the darkness."

Keller became a professional communicator in the transition. Perhaps it just proves that nearly every assignment in the Church involves communication in one way or another. Fr. Keller had the talent and imagination to energize his audience to aspire to new levels of Christian living. He chose the word "Christopher" as the name of his organization because the Greek word "*christophorus*" meant Christbearer. That is precisely what he wanted to make everyone, a Christbearer in the highways and byways of modern life. "Go out into the world and carry Christ with you wherever you go," he insisted.

Keller knew how to reach audiences and point them in the direction of a faith-filled life, but he never once suggested that their work should be seen as a participation in the mission of the hierarchy. This writer is the current director of the Christophers. I am happy to say we have never had any further inquiries from the Holy See about our work or our *modus operandi*.

After the death of Pius XII, the climate was ripe for a change of style in leadership. Pope John XXIII was soon elected and a few years later he convened the Second Vatican Council (1962-1965).

Vatican II continued the tradition of Vatican I (1869-1870) which had denounced the 19th century Rationalists, liberal Protestant theologians who virtually eliminated the supernatural nature of the act of faith, asserting the belief that nothing can be accepted as true unless reason can perceive it to be true. The Catholic Church in the First Vatican Council said "No" to that proposition—Catholics believe in the revelation of scripture not because of its intrinsic truth as seen by the light of reason, but because of the authority of the One revealing these truths to us, Jesus Christ.

Ninety-two years later, Vatican II repeated this same theme, asserting that in the act of faith, its supernatural character notwithstanding, our response is a free act which cannot be coerced. Faith is a free gift and our response must be free, therefore we must respect the faith of others as being subjectively sincere, even if we differ with them theologically. This paved the way for a new religious freedom and a new ecumenical era.

The second major contribution of Vatican II evolved in the form of a willingness to respect the diversity of opinion within the Church. Richard McBrien said: "Just as the Church has grown to respect the diversity in the human community at large, so has it grown to respect diversity within the Body of Christ itself."[4] *The Dogmatic Constitution on the Church* (n.15) and the *Decree on Ecumenism* (n.3) both acknowledge that the Christian faith exists outside the Catholic Church, that it is a justifying faith and that it relates one not only to Christ, but to the Church as well.

Paul VI (1963-1978) continued Vatican II after John's death and began implementing the council's decisions with great courage. He reorganized the curia and advanced the cause of ecumenism. Under his leadership, the Council Fathers wrote a *Pastoral Constitution of the Church in the Modern World*, and summoned the Church to a greater dialogue with the world, urging all Catholics to see God in the structures and experiences of contemporary life. The *Dogmatic Constitution on the Church* mentioned above, called for a renewed Church, one which must be reformed over and over again. The Council Fathers also adopted the principle of collegiality which had to do with the diffusion of power and the sharing of authority on all levels in the life of the Church.

John Paul I (Aug 26-Sept 28, 1978) is almost unknown outside of Italy due to his short reign; after his death, John Paul II (1978-   ) was elected Pope. He is an intellectual with a strong commitment to implementing the Second Vatican Council, but on his own terms. For instance, the idea that a plurality of theologies can exist in the Church was clarified by our present Holy Father to mean that a rich catholicity with a wide variety of cultures, languages, and life-styles does not mean that a pluralism of conflicting theologies can coexist in the Church. This would only divide and destroy Church unity. His belief in a strong centrist Church government is evident in many ways. Under his rule throughout the 1980's and into the 1990's we have had an untrembling center in the Church. He is a personalist, an intellectual, and a strong-willed leader who wants to keep the Church from falling apart.

---

4. Richard P. McBrien, *Catholicism* (Minneapolis: Winston Press, 1980), I: 45.

In an age of volatile change, where the exaggerated individualism of many Catholics finds them extolling the privatization of religion, there is need for a strong pope.

In 1983 Pope John Paul II endorsed the present Code of Canon Law which stated: "The Roman pontiff . . . possesses . . . power over all individual Churches . . . There is neither appeal nor recourse against a decision or decree of the Roman Pontiff." (Canon 333). That belief was the constant teaching of the Church down through the centuries. How a Pope chooses to implement his power, however, is a matter of personal style. One of the leading characteristics of John Paul II's papacy has been his awareness of the power of the media, and his willingness to create media events all over the world by his widespread travels.

John Paul II issued an apostolic exhortation entitled, *Christifideles laici* (1989) which reaffirmed the laity's secular mission to become actively engaged for Christ in the world. He urged the laity to accept their responsibility to exert a Christian influence in the "professional, social, cultural, and political world." This statement carries essentially the same message which was preached by Father Keller nearly fifty years ago.

Catholic initiatives in evangelization need not originate with the hierarchy. Fr. Keller's thinking has finally been given the authoritative approbation it deserved. Thank God for prophets in the Church. When an idea comes of age even the Popes surrender to it. This kind of intellectual evolution has a direct bearing on our topic: the ecclesial status of Catholic communicators.

III. Catholic Communicators with Ecclesial Status

Who has ecclesial status among Catholic communicators? The answer to this question depends on how you define the term itself. For our purposes "ecclesial status" shall refer to all those who are an integral part of the ecclesiastical structure. Apply this to the field of communications, and you can follow a descending order from Pope to all those individuals and institutions under the Pope; which includes the Pontifical Council for Social Communications presently headed by Archbishop John P. Foley, a former editor of Philadelphia's diocesan newspaper, *The Catholic Standard and Times*.

Under the aegis of this Pontifical Council we find a network of international Catholic organizations: UNDA (an association of electronic communicators. The word is not an acronym but a Latin word meaning "wave"), OCIC (an association concerned with film. The title is taken from the French, "Organization Catholique Internationale du Cinema"), and UCIP (an association of print journalists, in English it means "International Catholic Union of the Press").

The presidents of these three international associations are full members of Archbishop Foley's Pontifical Council, and one might argue that they thereby possess ecclesial status even though they were elected by their peers.

Under the UCIP umbrella for instance there are now seven regions, UCLAP (Latin American Union of the Press), UCAP (African Catholic Union of the Press), SACPA (South Asian Catholic Union of the Press), SEACPA (South East Asian Catholic Union of the Press), EACPA (East Asian Catholic Union of the Press), ECAP (European Catholic Union of the Press), and the most recent addition NACAP (North American Catholic Union of the Press). The presidents of these groups have quasi-official status in ecclsiastical circles.

Within the various national hierarchies, there are episcopal conferences which are represented in the field of communications by an officer in charge. In the U.S., Richard Daw currently holds this position and is called the "Secretary of the Office of Communications." He has the highest level of ecclesial status in the field of communications in America, but Mr. Daw will quite readily admit that his specialty is in print not in electronic communications. Nevertheless, he manages a unit called CTNA, the Catholic Television Network of America, and he is an expert manager. The priest in charge of CTNA answers to him and the relationship has been mutually supportive. That priest might be considered as having ecclesial status to a lesser degree that Mr. Daw.

However another more famous Catholic cable network in the United States called EWTN (Eternal Word TV Network) has a founder/president named Mother Angelica who has no ecclesial status. Though she is nationally known and a powerful figure in Catholic communications, she is not part of the official Church communication structure, and therefore, technically, does not enjoy ecclesial status in the strict sense of the term.

Fortunately, the official Church welcomes and encourages private ventures to flourish. Perhaps a review of my own position in the Church might help to elucidate this puzzling use of terms. I am a priest of the Diocese of Paterson, New Jersey. My bishop, the Most Rev. Frank J. Rodimer, gave me permission to accept the invitation of the board of directors of The Christophers to serve as the Director of The Christophers for a five-year term. My term has been renewed several times, and I have been in this assignment for the last 15 years, and will step down in 1995, God willing, on the 50th Anniversary of The Christophers. I have no ecclesial status because of my current position, even though we have been leaders in the field with a TV program that has aired for over 42 consecutive years.

For all these years The Christophers have been producing radio and TV programs, reaching millions of people all over the world. Currently our TV show is aired on forty-nine commercial TV stations, and about

450 cable outlets, as well as Armed Forces Radio and TV, which brings us to over 100 nations, wherever U.S. military personnel are stationed. Our radio outreach goes to nearly 1000 stations worldwide. We also have a print division, i.e., a publishing company which produces books and leaflets. We distribute, free of charge, approximately 5 million leaflets each year to people in 126 nations.

In 1983 I was elected president of a national Catholic organization called ACTRS (Assn. of Catholic TV and Radio Syndicators). This brought prestige but not ecclesial status. For one fleeting moment I attained ecclesial status in 1988, when I was elected president of the Catholic Press Association of the United States and Canada. With that title I was automatically made a non-voting, ex-officio member of the Bishops' Committee for Communications. Membership on the bishops' committee conferred some ecclesial status, the presidency of the CPA did not. The Catholic Press Association is an international professional association, but it is a private corporation outside the Church structure.

What is interesting and I think quite wonderful is that the official Church has never made much of a point of ecclesial status. As director of The Christophers, I have been trusted and allowed to operate freely, without interference throughout my entire tenure. We have a representative of the Cardinal Archbishop of New York on our board of directors, so there is a control factor in place, but the board generally speaking does not get involved in the day to day running of the organization.

Never once did Cardinal O'Connor or Cardinal Cooke or Cardinal Spellman impose their wills concerning any phase of our print or electronic ministry, a remarkable record of trust and mutual respect. We are allowed to operate in a climate of freedom that has enhanced our creativity and effectiveness for nearly fifty years. Our budget is now $3,000,000 a year, 98% of which comes from individual donors, the rest from private foundations. We think this says something about the trust we receive from our listeners and readers. Our product is the Gospel message translated into today's language. Jesus Christ is at the heart of all we do.

IV. Conclusion

Ecclesial status has little to do with communicating the faith. The Holy Spirit is in charge of the Church, Christ is the Head of the Church. Communication is a mysterious process that has divine implications transcending human legalities.

Professionalism is the first law of effectiveness. A Catholic communicator with legal standing in the ecclesiastical structure, a position with a formal title and clear lines of accountability to those in authority, is in a position of authority. This function is needed to coordinate Church activity, but it is often a management function.

Those who hold management positions from the Pope on down, have to be competent professionals in what they do, and one of the most important characteristics of a good manager is the ability to trust his or her employees and volunteers. Trust is an essential part of management.

Ecclesial status can be said to have everything to do with communicating the faith, because individuals who hold highly visible positions in the Church actually set the direction and tone of the communication effort. They have the power to touch millions of lives for better or worse and their responsibility is awesome.

In a talk addressed to a group of secular professionals, mainly from the movie industry, Pope John Paul II had this to say:

> Certainly your profession subjects you to a great measure of accountability—accountability to God, to the community, and before the witness of history. And yet at times it seems that everything is left in your hands. Precisely because your responsibility is so great and your accountability to the community is not easily rendered juridically, society relies so much on your good will. In a sense the world is at your mercy. Errors in judgment, mistakes in evaluating the propriety and justice of what is transmitted, and wrong criteria in art can offend and wound consciences and human dignity. They can encroach on sacred and fundamental rights. The confidence the community has in you honors you deeply and challenges you mightily.[5]

These words apply to Church communicators as well.

In conclusion, ecclesial status, in the strict sense, is important as a management function; it has little relevance in the day-to-day work of communicating the faith. Trust is the key to good communications. Today the bishops of most nations do trust their communicators. They are right to do so.

One can understand the apprehension of bishops in times such as these, but if we think about it, communication itself is the answer. We have to talk openly and honestly with one another to resolve the areas of difficulty that arise from time to time.

We Catholics all have the same goals: to save souls and give glory to Almighty God. In a spirit of obedience we try to advance the Kingdom of God in order to bring Jesus Christ to the world, and make His Gospel known and loved from East to West; from North to South. We are the People of God, and as such we are all called to be Catholic communicators. We are all carriers of divine love and truth. This is the task of evangelization: to communicate Christ and to proclaim His Kingdom.

---

5. John Paul II, Address to Communications Leaders, September 15, 1987, Los Angeles. *Origins*, October 8, 1987, Vol. 17, no. 17: 299.

Contributors

RICARDO ANTONCICH, S.J. Peruvian theologian. Specialist in the social teaching of the Church and its relationship to Latin America.

HENRI BOURGEOIS. Professor of Dogmatic and Pastoral Theology at the Catholic University of Lyons. Former director of the Adult Catechumenate in the diocese of Lyons.

JOHN T. CATOIR. Director of The Christophers since 1978. Canonist, columnist, and past president of The Catholic Press Association.

GREGOR GOETHALS. Artist and professor at the Rhode Island School of Design.

PATRICK GRANFIELD. Professor of Systematic Theology at The Catholic University of America.

PETER HENRICI, S.J. Auxiliary bishop of Chur, Switzerland. Former Dean of the Faculty of Philosophy at the Gregorian University.

KLAUS KIENZLER. Professor of Fundamental Theology at the University of Augusburg, Germany.

FRANCES FORDE PLUDE. Associate Professor at the Newhouse School of Public Communications at Syracuse University.

HERMANN J. POTTMEYER. Professor of Fundamental Theology in the Department of Catholic Theology at the University of Bochum, Germany.

FRANCIS A. SULLIVAN, S.J. After thirty-six years as Professor of Ecclesiology at the Gregorian University, now teaching at Boston College.

ROBERT A. WHITE, S.J. Director of the Center for Interdisciplinary Study of Communications at the Gregorian University and former director of the Centre for the Study of Communication and Culture in London.

ANGELA ANN ZUKOWSKI, M.H.S.H. Founder and Executive Director of the Center for Religious Communications at the University of Dayton. Former President of UNDA-North America (the North American Catholic Association of Radio and Television Communicators).

Abbreviations

Sacrosanctum concilium	Constitution on the Sacred Liturgy
Inter mirifica	Decree on the Instruments of Social Communication
Lumen gentium	Dogmatic Constitution on the Church
Orientalium ecclesiarum	Decree on Eastern Catholic Churches
Unitatis redintegratio	Decree on Ecumenism
Christus Dominus	Decree on the Bishops' Pastoral Office in the Church
Perfectae caritatis	Decree on the Appropriate Renewal of the Religious Life
Optatam totius	Decree on Priestly Formation
Gravissimum educationis	Declaration on Christian Education
Nostra aetate	Declaration on the Relationship of the Church to Non-Christian Religions
Dei Verbum	Dogmatic Constitution on Divine Revelation
Apostolicam actuositatem	Decree on the Apostolate of the Laity
Dignitatis humanae	Declaration on Religious Freedom
Ad gentes	Decree on the Church's Missionary Activity
Presbyterorum ordinis	Decree on the Ministry and Life of Priests
Gaudium et spes	Pastoral Constitution on the Church in the Modern World

Pastoral Instruction "Aetatis Novae": On Social Communications

Pontifical Council for Social Communications (1992)

Introduction: A Revolution in Human Communications

1. At the dawn of a new era, a vast expansion of human communications is profoundly influencing culture everywhere. Revolutionary technological changes are only part of what is happening. Nowhere today are people untouched by the impact of media upon religious and moral attitudes, political and social systems, and education.

It is impossible to ignore, for instance, that geographical and political boundaries were both of very little avail in view of the role played by communications during the "radical transformations" of 1989 and 1990, on whose historical significance the pope reflects in *Centesimus Annus.*[1]

It becomes equally evident that "the first Areopagus of the modern age is the world of communications which is unifying humanity and turning it into what is known as a 'global village.' The means of social communications have become so important as to be for many the chief means of information and education, of guidance and inspiration in their behavior as individuals, families and within society at large."[2]

More than a quarter century after the promulgation of the Second Vatican Council's decree on social communications, *Inter Mirifca,* and two decades after the pastoral instruction *Communio et Progressio,* the Pontifical Council for Social Communications wishes to reflect on the pastoral implications of this situation.

We do so in the spirit expressed by the closing words of *Communio et Progressio*: "The people of God walk in history. As they . . . advance with their times, they look forward with confidence and even with enthusiasm to whatever the development of communications in a space age may have to offer."[3]

Taking for granted the continued validity of the principles and insights of these conciliar and post-conciliar documents, we wish to apply

---

1. Cf. John Paul II, *Centesimus Annus,* 12-13, in *Acta Apostolicae Sedis,* 1991, pp. 807-821.

2. Ibid., *Redemptoris Missio,* 37, in AAS, 1991, p. 285.

3. *Communio et Progressio,* 187, in AAS 1971, pp. 655-656.

them to new and emerging realities. We do not pretend to say the final word on a complex, fluid, rapidly changing situation, but simply wish to provide a working tool and a measure of encouragement to those confronting the pastoral implications of the new realities.

2. In the years since *Inter Mirifica* and *Communio et Progressio* appeared, people have grown accustomed to expressions like *information society, mass-media culture* and *media generation.* Terms like these underline a remarkable fact: Today, much that men and women know and think about life is conditioned by the media; to a considerable extent, human experience itself is an experience of media.

Recent decades also have witnessed remarkable developments in the technology of communicating. These include both the rapid evolution of previously existing technologies and the emergence of new telecommunications and media technologies: satellites, cable television fiber optics, videocassettes, compact disks, computerized image making and other computer and digital technology, and much else. The use of new media gives rise to what some speak of as "new languages" and has given birth to new possibilities for the mission of the church as well as to new pastoral problems.

3. Against this background we encourage the pastors and people of the Church to deepen their understanding of issues relating to communications and media, and to translate the understanding into practical policies and workable programs.

"As the council fathers looked to the future and tried to discern the context in which the church would be called upon to carry out her mission, they could clearly see that the progress of technology was already 'transforming the face of the earth' and even reaching out to conquer space. They recognized that developments in communications technology, in particular, were likely to set off chain reactions with unforeseen consequences."[4]

"Far from suggesting that the church should stand aloof or try to isolate herself from the mainstream of these events, the council fathers saw the church as being in the very midst of human progress, sharing the experiences of the rest of humanity, seeking to understand them and to interpret them in the light of faith. It was for God's faithful people to make creative use of the new discoveries and technologies for the benefit of humanity and the fulfillment of God's plan for the world . . . employing the full potential of the 'computer age' to serve the human and transcendent vocation of every person, and thus to give glory to the Father from whom all good things come.'"[5]

---

4. John Paul II, Message for 1990 World Communications Day, *L'Osservatore Romano,* Jan. 25, 1990, p. 6; cf. *Gaudium et Spes,* 5.

5. Ibid.

We express our gratitude to those responsible for the creative communications work under way in the church everywhere. Despite difficulties—arising from limited resources, from the obstacles sometimes placed in the way of the church's access to media and from a constant reshaping of culture, values and attitudes brought about by the pervasive presence of media—much has been and continues to be accomplished. The dedicated bishops, clergy, religious and lay people engaged in this critically important apostolate deserve the thanks of all.

Also welcome are those positive ventures in media-related ecumenical cooperation involving Catholics and their brothers and sisters of other churches and ecclesial communities, as well as interreligious cooperation with those of other world religions. It is not only appropriate but "necessary for Christians to work together more effectively in their communications efforts and to act in more direct cooperation with other religions to ensure a united religious presence in the very heart of mass communications."[6]

I. The Context of Social Communications

A. Cultural and Social Context

4. As more than just a technological revolution, today's revolution in social communications involves a fundamental reshaping of the elements by which people comprehend the world about them and verify and express what they comprehend. The constant availability of images and ideas, and their rapid transmission even from continent to continent, have profound consequences, both positive and negative, for the psychological, moral and social development of persons, the structure and functioning of societies, intercultural communications and the perception and transmission of values, worldviews, ideologies and religious beliefs. The communications revolution affects perceptions even of the church, and has a significant impact on the church's own structures and modes of functioning.

All this has striking pastoral implications. The media can be used to proclaim the Gospel or to reduce it to silence in human hearts. As media become ever more intertwined with people's daily lives, they influence how people understand the meaning of life itself.

Indeed the power of media extends to defining not only what people will think but even what they will think about. Reality, for many, is what the media recognize as real; what media do not acknowledge seems of little importance. Thus de facto silence can be imposed upon individuals and

---

6. Pontifical Council for Social Communications, "Criteria for Ecumenical and Interreligious Cooperation in Communications," 1, Vatican City, 1989.

groups whom the media ignore, and even the voice of the Gospel can be muted, though not entirely stilled, in this way.

It is important therefore that Christians find ways to furnish the missing information to those deprived of it and also to give a voice to the voiceless.

The power of media either to reinforce or override the traditional reference points of religion, culture and family underlines the continued relevance of the council's words: "If the media are to be correctly employed, it is essential that all who use them know the principles of the moral order and apply them faithfully in this domain."[7]

B. Political and Economic Context

5. The economic structures of nations are inextricably linked to contemporary communications systems. National investment in an efficient communications infrastructure is widely regarded as necessary to economic and political development, and the growing cost of such investment has been a major factor leading governments in a number of countries to adopt policies aimed at increasing market competition. For this and other reasons, public telecommunications and broadcasting systems in many instances have been subject to policies of deregulation and privatization.

While public systems can clearly be misused for purposes of ideological and political manipulation, unregulated commercialization and privatization in broadcasting can also have far-reaching consequences. In practice, and often as a matter of public policy, public accountability for the use of the airwaves is devalued. Profit, not service, tends to become the most important measure of success. Profit motives and advertisers' interests exert undue influence on media content: Popularity is preferred over quality, and the lowest common denominator prevails. Advertisers move beyond their legitimate role of identifying genuine needs and responding to them, and, driven by profit motives, strive to create artificial needs and patterns of consumption.

Commercial pressures also operate across national boundaries at the expense of particular peoples and their cultures. Faced with increasing competition and the need to develop new markets, communications firms become ever more "multinational" in character; at the same time, lack of local production capabilities makes some countries increasingly dependent on foreign material. Thus, the products of the popular media of one culture spread into another, often to the detriment of established art forms and media and the values which they embody.

Even so, the solution to problems arising from unregulated commercialization and privatization does not lie in state control of media but in more regulation according to criteria of public service and in greater pub-

---

7. *Inter Mirifica*, 4.

lic accountability. It should be noted in this connection that, although the legal and political frameworks within which media operate in some countries are currently changing strikingly for the better, elsewhere government intervention remains an instrument of oppression and exclusion.

II. The Work of the Means of Social Communications

6. *Communio et Progressio* is rooted in a vision of communication as a way toward communion. For "more than the expression of ideas and the indication of emotion," it declares, communication is "the giving of self in love."[8] In this respect, communication mirrors the church's own communion and is capable of contributing to it.

Indeed, the communication of truth can have a redemptive power, which comes from the person of Christ. He is God's Word made flesh and the image of the invisible God. In and through him God's own life is communicated to humanity by the Spirit's action. "Since the creation of the world, invisible realities, God's eternal power and divinity have become visible, recognized through the things he has made";[9] and now "the Word has become flesh and made his dwelling among us, and we have seen his glory: the glory of an only Son coming from the Father, filled with enduring love."[10]

Here, in the Word made flesh, God's self-communication is definitive. In Jesus' words and deeds the Word is liberating, redemptive, for all humankind. This loving self-revelation of God, combined with humanity's response of faith, constitutes a profound dialogue.

Human history and all human relationships exist within the framework established by this self-communication of God in Christ. History itself is ordered toward becoming a kind of word of God, and it is part of the human vocation to contribute to bringing this about by living out the ongoing, unlimited communication of God's reconciling love in creative new ways. We are to do this through words of hope and deeds of love, that is, through our very way of life. Thus, communication must lie at the heart of the church community.

Christ is both the content and the dynamic source of the church's communications in proclaiming the Gospel. For the church itself is "Christ's mystical body—the hidden completion of Christ glorified—who 'fills the whole creation.'"[11] As a result we move, within the church and with the help of the word and the sacraments, toward the hope of that last unity where "God will be all in all."[12]

---

8. *Communio et Progressio*, 11.
9. Rom. 1:20.
10. Jn. 1:14.
11. Eph. 3:23; 4:10.

A. Media at the Service of Persons and Cultures

7. For all the good which they do and are capable of doing, mass media, "which can be such effective instruments of unity and understanding, can also sometimes be the vehicles of a deformed outlook on life, on the family, on religion and on morality—an outlook that does not respect the true dignity and destiny of the human person."[13] It is imperative that media respect and contribute to that integral development of the person which embraces "the cultural, transcendent and religious dimensions of man and society."[14]

One also finds the source of certain individual and social problems in the replacement of human interaction by increased media use and intense attachment to fictitious media characters. Media, after all, cannot take the place of immediate personal contact and interaction among family members and friends. But the solution to this difficulty also may lie largely in the media: through their use in ways—dialogue groups, discussions of films and broadcasts—which stimulate interpersonal communication rather than substituting for it.

B. Media at the Service of Dialogue With the World

8. The Second Vatican Council underlined the awareness of the people of God that they are "truly and intimately linked with mankind and its history."[15] Those who proclaim God's word are obligated to heed and seek to understand the "words" of diverse peoples and cultures in order not only to learn from them but to help them recognize and accept the Word of God.[16] The church therefore must maintain an active, listening presence in relation to the world—a kind of presence which both nurtures community and supports people in seeking acceptable solutions to personal and social problems.

Moreover, as the church always must communicate its message in a manner suited to each age and to the cultures of particular nations and peoples, so today it must communicate in and to the emerging media culture.[17] This is a basic condition for responding to a crucial point made by the Second Vatican Council: The emergence of "social, technical and cultural bonds" linking people ever more closely lends "special urgency" to the church's task of bringing all to "full union with Christ."[18] Considering

---

12. I Cor. 15:28; *Communio et Progressio*, 11.

13. Pontifical Council for Social Communications, "Pornography and Violence in the Media: A Pastoral Response," 7, Vatican City, 1989.

14. John Paul 11, *Sollicitudo Rei Socialis*, 46, in AAS, 1988, p. 579.

15. *Gaudium et Spes*, 11.

16. Cf. Paul VI, *Evangelii Nuntiandi*, 20, in AAS, 1976, pp. 18-19.

17. Cf. *Inter Mirifica*, 3.

18. *Lumen Gentium*, 1.

how important a contribution the media of social communications can make to its efforts to foster this unity, the church views them as means "devised under God's providence" for the promotion of communication and communion among human beings during their earthly pilgrimage.[19]

Thus, in seeking to enter into dialogue with the modern world, the church necessarily desires honest and respectful dialogue with those responsible for the communications media. On the church's side this dialogue involves effort to understand the media—their purposes, procedures, forms and genres, internal structures and modalities—and to offer support and encouragement to those involved in media work. On the basis of this sympathetic understanding and support, it becomes possible to offer meaningful proposals for removing obstacles to human progress and the proclamation of the Gospel.

Such dialogue therefore requires that the church be actively concerned with the secular media and especially with the shaping of media policy. Christians have in effect a responsibility to make their voice heard in all the media, and their task is not confined merely to the giving out of church news. The dialogue also involves support for media artists; it requires the development of an anthropology and a theology of communication—not least so that theology itself may be more communicative, more successful in disclosing Gospel values and applying them to the contemporary realities of the human condition; it requires that church leaders and pastoral workers respond willingly and prudently to media when requested, while seeking to establish relationships of mutual confidence and respect, based on fundamental common values, with those who are not of our faith.

C. Media at the Service of Human Community and Progress

9. Communications in and by the church is essentially communication of the good news of Jesus Christ. It is the proclamation of the Gospel as a prophetic, liberating word to the men and women of our times; it is testimony, in the face of radical secularization, to divine truth and to the transcendent destiny of the human person; it is the witness given in solidarity with all believers against conflict and division, to justice and communion among peoples, nations and cultures.

This understanding of communication on the part of the church sheds a unique light on social communications and on the role which, in the providential plan of God, the media are intended to play in promoting the integral development of human persons and societies.

---

19. Cf. *Communio et Progressio,* 12.

D. Media at the Service of Ecclesial Communion

10. Along with all this, it is necessary constantly to recall the importance of the fundamental right of dialogue and information within the church, as described in *Communio et Progressio*,[20] and to continue to seek effective means, including a responsible use of media of social communications for realizing and protecting this right In this connection we also have in mind the affirmations of the Code of Canon Law that, besides showing obedience to the pastors of the church, the faithful "are at liberty to make known their needs, especially their spiritual needs and their wishes" to these pastors,[21] and that the faithful, in keeping with their knowledge, competence and position have "the right, indeed at times the duty," to express to the pastors their views on matters concerning the good of the church.[22]

Partly this is a matter of maintaining and enhancing the church's credibility and effectiveness. But more fundamentally, it is one of the ways of realizing in a concrete manner the church's character as *communio,* rooted in and mirroring the intimate communion of the Trinity. Among the members of the community of persons who make up the church, there is a radical equality in dignity and mission which arises from baptism and underlies hierarchical structure and diversity of office and function; and this equality necessarily will express itself in an honest and respectful sharing of information and opinions.

It will be well to bear in mind however, in cases of dissent, that "it is not by seeking to exert the pressure of public opinion that one contributes to the clarification of doctrinal issues and renders service to the truth."[23] In fact "not all ideas which circulate among the people of God" are to be "simply and purely identified with the 'sense of the faith. '"[24]

Why does the church insist that people have the right to receive correct information? Why does the church emphasize its right to proclaim authentic Gospel truth? Why does the church stress the responsibility of its pastors to communicate the truth and to form the faithful to do the same? It is because the whole understanding of what communication in the church means is based upon the realization that the Word of God communicates himself.

E. Media at the Service of a New Evangelization

11. Along with traditional means such as witness of life, catechetics, personal contact, popular piety, the liturgy and similar celebrations, the use of

---

20. Ibid., 114-121.

21. Cf. Canon 212.2.

22. Cf. Canon 212.3.

23. Congregation for the Doctrine of the Faith, "Instruction on the Ecclesial Vocation of the Theologian," 30, in AAS, 1990, p. 1562.

24. Cf. ibid., 35.

media is now essential in evangelization and catechesis. Indeed, "the church would feel guilty before the Lord if she did not utilize these powerful means that human skill is daily rendering more perfect."[25] The media of social communications can and should be instruments in the church's program of reevangelization and new evangelization in the contemporary world. In view of the proven efficacy of the old principle "see, judge, act," the audiovisual aspect of media in evangelization should be given due attention.

But it will also be of great importance in the church's approach to media and the culture they do so much to shape always to bear in mind that: "It is not enough to use the media simply to spread the Christian message and the church's authentic teaching. It is also necessary to integrate that message into the 'new culture' created by modern communications . . . with new languages, new techniques and a new psychology."[26] Today's evangelization ought to well up from the church's active, sympathetic presence within the world of communications.

III. Current Challenges

A. Need for a Critical Evaluation

12. But even as the church takes a positive, sympathetic approach to media, seeking to enter into the culture created by modern communications in order to evangelize effectively, it is necessary at the very same time that the church offer a critical evaluation of mass media and their impact upon culture.

As we have said repeatedly, communications technology is a marvelous expression of human genius, and the media confer innumerable benefits upon society. But as we have also pointed out, the application of communications technology has been a mixed blessing, and its use for good purposes requires sound values and wise choices on the part of individuals, the private sector, governments and society as a whole. The church does not presume to dictate these decisions and choices, but it does seek to be of help by indicating ethical and moral criteria which are relevant to the process—criteria which are to be found in both human and Christian values.

B. Solidarity and Integral Development

13. As matters stand, mass media at times exacerbate individual and social problems which stand in the way of human solidarity and the integral development of the human person. These obstacles include secularism, con-

---

25. *Evangelii Nuntiandi*, 45.
26. *Redemptoris Missio*, 37.

sumerism, materialism, dehumanization and lack of concern for the plight of the poor and neglected.[27]

It is against this background that the church, recognizing the media of social communications as "the privileged way" today for the creation and transmission of culture,[28] acknowledges its own duty to offer formation to communications professionals and to the public so that they will approach media with "a critical sense which is animated by a passion for the truth"; it likewise acknowledges its duty to engage in "a work of defense of liberty, respect for the dignity of individuals and the elevation of the authentic culture of peoples which occurs through a firm and courageous rejection of every form of monopoly and manipulation."[29]

C. Policies and Structures

14. Certain problems in this regard arise specifically from media policies and structures: for example, the unjust exclusion of some groups and classes from access to the means of communications, the systematic abridgment of the fundamental right to information, which is practiced in some places, the widespread domination of media by economic, social and political elites.

These things are contrary to the principal purposes and indeed to the very nature of the media, whose proper and essential social role consists in contributing to the realization of the human right to information, promoting justice in the pursuit of the common good and assisting individuals, groups and peoples in their search for truth. The media carry out these crucial tasks when they foster the exchange of ideas and information among all classes and sectors of society and offer to all responsible voices opportunities to be heard.

D. Defense of the Right to Information and Communications

15. It is not acceptable that the exercise of the freedom of communication should depend upon wealth, education or political power. The right to communicate is the right of all.

This calls for special national and international efforts, not only to give those who are poor and less powerful access to the information which they need for their individual and social development, but to ensure that they are able to play an effective, responsible role in deciding media content and determining the structures and policies of their national institutions of social communications.

Where legal and political structures foster the domination of the media by elites, the church for its part must urge respect for the right to

---

27. *Centesimus Annus,* 41.
28. John Paul II, *Christifideles Laici,* in AAS, 1989, p. 480.
29. Ibid., p. 481.

communicate, including its own right of access to media, while at the same time seeking alternative models of communications for its own members and for people at large. The right to communicate is part also of the right to religious freedom, which should not be confined to freedom of worship.

IV. Pastoral Priorities and Responses

A. Defense of Human Cultures

16. Considering the situation in many places, sensitivity to the rights and interests of individuals may often call for the church to promote alternative community media. Often, too, for the sake of evangelization and catechesis the church must take steps to preserve and promote folk media and other traditional forms of expression, recognizing that in particular societies these can be more effective than newer media in spreading the Gospel because they make possible greater personal participation and reach deeper levels of human feeling and motivation.

The overwhelming presence of mass media in the contemporary world by no means detracts from the importance of alternative media which are open to people's involvement and allow them to be active in production and even in designing the process of communications itself. Then, too, grassroots and traditional media not only provide an important forum for local cultural expression but develop competence for active participation in shaping and using mass media.

Similarly, we view with sympathy the desire of many peoples and groups for more just, equitable systems of communications and information which safeguard them against domination and manipulation, whether from abroad or at the hands of their fellow countrymen. This is a concern of developing nations in relation to developed ones, and often, too, it is a concern of minorities within particular nations, both developed and developing. In all cases people ought to be able to participate actively, autonomously and responsibly in the process of communications which in so many ways helps to shape the conditions of their lives.

B. Development and Promotion of the Church's Own Media of Social Communications

17. Along with its other commitments in the area of communications and media, the church must continue, in spite of the many difficulties involved, to develop, maintain and foster its own specifically Catholic instruments and programs for social communications. These include the Catholic press and Catholic publishing houses, Catholic radio and television, offices for public information and media relations, institutes and programs for training in and about media, media research and church-related organizations of

communications professionals—including especially the international Catholic communications organizations—whose members are knowledgeable and competent collaborators with the episcopal conferences as well as with the bishops individually.

Catholic media work is not simply one more program alongside all the rest of the church's activities: social communications have a role to play in every aspect of the church's mission. Thus, not only should there be a pastoral plan for communications, but communications should be an integral part of every pastoral plan, for it has something to contribute to virtually every other apostolate, ministry and program.

C. Formation of Christian Communicators

18. Education and training in communications should be an integral part of the formation of pastoral workers and priests.[30] There are several distinct elements and aspects to the education and training which are required. For example, in today's world so strongly influenced by media, church personnel require at least a working grasp of the impact which new information technologies and mass media are having upon individuals and society. They must likewise be prepared to minister both to the "information-rich" and to the "information-poor." They need to know how to invite others into dialogue, avoiding a style of communicating which suggests domination, manipulation or personal gain. As for those who will be actively engaged in media work for the church, they need to acquire professional skills in media along with doctrinal and spiritual formation.

D. Pastoral Care of Communications Personnel

19. Media work involves special psychological pressures and ethical dilemmas. Considering how important a role the media play in forming contemporary culture and shaping the lives of countless individuals and whole societies, it is essential that those professionally involved in secular media and the communications industries approach their responsibilities imbued with high ideals and a commitment to the service of humanity.

The church has a corresponding responsibility to develop and offer programs of pastoral care which are specifically responsive to the peculiar working conditions and moral challenges facing communications professionals. Typically, pastoral programs of this sort should include ongoing formation which will help these men and women—many of whom sincerely wish to know and do what is ethically and morally right—to integrate moral norms ever more fully into their professional work as well as their private lives.

---

30. Cf. Congregation for Catholic Education, "Guide to the Training of Future Priests Concerning the Instruments of Social Communications," Vatican City, 1986.

V. The Need for Pastoral Planning

A. Responsibilities of Bishops

20. Recognizing the validity, and indeed the urgency, of the claims advanced by communications work bishops and others responsible for decisions about allocating the church's limited human and material resources should assign it an appropriate high priority, taking into account the circumstances of their particular nations regions and dioceses.

This need may be even greater now than previously, precisely because, to some degree at least, the great contemporary "Areopagus" of mass media has more or less been neglected by the church up to this time.[31] As the Holy Father remarks: "Generally, preference has been given to other means of preaching the Gospel and of Christian education, while the mass media are left to the initiative of individuals or small groups and enter into pastoral planning only in a secondary way."[32] This situation needs correcting.

B. Urgency of a Pastoral Plan for Social Communications

21. We therefore strongly recommend that dioceses and episcopal conferences or assemblies include a communications component in every pastoral plan. We further recommend that they develop specific pastoral plans for social communications itself, or else review and bring up to date those plans which already exist, in this way fostering the desirable process of periodic reexamination and adaptation. In doing so, bishops should seek the collaboration of professionals in secular media and of the church's own media-related organizations, including especially the international and national organizations for film, radio-television, and the press.

Episcopal conferences in some regions already have been well served by pastoral plans which concretely identify needs and goals and encourage the coordination of efforts. The results of the study, assessment and consultation involved in preparing these documents can and should be shared at all levels in the church, as useful data for pastoral workers. Practical, realistic plans of this sort also can be adapted to the needs of local churches. They should of course be constantly open to revision and adaptation in light of changing needs.

This document itself concludes with elements of a pastoral plan, which also indicate issues for possible treatment in pastoral letters and episcopal statements at the national and local levels. These elements reflect suggestions received from episcopal conferences and media professionals.

---

31. Cf. *Redemptoris Missio*, 37.
32. Ibid.

Conclusion

22. We affirm once again that the church "sees these media as 'gifts of God,' which in accordance with his providential design unite men in brotherhood and so help them to cooperate with his plan for their salvation."[33] As the Spirit helped the prophets of old to see the divine plan in the signs of their times, so today the Spirit helps the church interpret the signs of our times and carry out its prophetic tasks, among which the study, evaluation and right use of communications technology and the media of social communications are now fundamental.

Appendix

Elements of a Pastoral Plan for Social Communications

23. Media conditions and the opportunities presented to the church in the field of social communications differ from nation to nation and even from diocese to diocese within the same country. It naturally follows that the church's approach to media and the cultural environment they help to form will differ from place to place, and that its plans and participation will be tailored to local situations.

Every episcopal conference and diocese should therefore develop an integrated pastoral plan for communications, preferably in consultation with representatives of international and national Catholic communications organizations and with local media professionals. Furthermore, communications ought to be taken into account in formulating and carrying out all other pastoral plans, including those concerning social service, education and evangelization. A number of episcopal conferences and dioceses already have developed such plans in which communications needs are identified, goals are articulated, realistic provision is made for financing and a variety of communications efforts is coordinated.

The following guidelines are offered as assistance to those formulating such pastoral plans or engaged in reassessing plans which exist.

Guidelines for Designing Pastoral Plans for Social Communications in a Diocese, Episcopal Conference or Patriarchal Assembly

24. A pastoral plan for social communications should include the following elements:

> a) The statement of a vision, based on extensive consultation, which identifies communications strategies for all church ministries and responds to contemporary issues and conditions.

---

33. *Communio et Progressio*, 2.

b) An inventory or assessment which describes the media environment in the territory under consideration, including audiences, public and commercial media producers and directors financial and technical resources delivery systems, ecumenical and educational resources, and Catholic media organizations and communications personnel, including those of religious communities.

c) A proposed structure for church-related social communications in support of evangelization, catechesis and education, social service and ecumenical cooperation, and including, as far as possible, public relations, press, radio, television, cinema, cassettes, computer networks, facsimile services and related forms of telecommunications.

d) Media education, with special emphasis on the relationship of media and values.

e) Pastoral outreach to, and dialogue with, media professionals, with particular attention to their faith development and spiritual growth.

f) Means of obtaining and maintaining financial support adequate to the carrying-out of the pastoral plan.

Process for Designing a Pastoral Plan for Social Communications

25. The plan should offer guidelines and suggestions helpful to church communicators in establishing realistic goals and priorities for their work. It is recommended that a planning team including church personnel and media professionals be involved in this process, whose two phases are: 1. research, and 2. design.

Research Phase

26. The elements of the research phase are needs assessment, information gathering and an exploration of alternative models of a pastoral plan. It includes an analysis of the internal communications environment, including the strengths and weaknesses of the church's current structures and programs for communications as well as the opportunities and challenges these face.

Three types of research will assist in gathering the required information: a needs assessment, a communications audit and a resource inventory. The first identifies areas of ministry requiring particular attention on the part of the episcopal conference or diocese. The second considers what is now being done—including its effectiveness—so as to identify strengths and weaknesses of existing communications structures and procedures. The third identifies communications resources, technology and personnel available to the church—including not only the church's "own" resources but those to which it may have access in the business community, the media industries and ecumenical settings.

Design Phase

27. After gathering and studying these data, the planning team should identify conference or diocesan communications goals and priorities. This is the beginning of the design phase. The planning team should then proceed to address each of the following issues as it relates to local circumstances.

28. *Education.* Communications issues and mass communications are relevant to every level of pastoral ministry, including education. A pastoral social communications plan should attempt:

> a) To offer educational opportunities in communications as essential components of the formation of all persons who are engaged in the work of the church: seminarians, priests, religious brothers and sisters, and lay leaders.

> b) To encourage Catholic schools and universities to offer programs and courses related to the communications needs of the church and society.

> c) To offer courses, workshops and seminars in technology, management and communication ethics and policy issues for church communicators seminarians, religious and clergy.

> d) To plan and carry out programs in media education and media literacy for teachers, parents and students.

> e) To encourage creative artists and writers accurately to reflect Gospel values as they share their gifts through the written word, legitimate theater, radio, television and film for entertainment and education.

> f) To identify new strategies for evangelization and catechesis through the application of communications technology and mass communications.

29. *Spiritual formation and pastoral care.* Lay Catholic professionals and others working in either the church apostolate of social communications or the secular media often look to the church for spiritual guidance and pastoral care. A pastoral plan for social communications therefore should seek:

> a) To offer opportunities for professional enrichment to lay Catholic and other professional communicators through days of recollection, retreats, seminars and professional support groups.

> b) To offer pastoral care which will provide the necessary support, nourish the communicators' faith and keep alive their sense of dedication in the difficult task of communicating Gospel values and authentic human values to the world.

30. *Cooperation.* Cooperation involves sharing resources among conferences and/or dioceses and between dioceses and other institutions, such as religious communities, universities and health-care facilities. A pastoral plan for social communications should be designed:

a) To enhance relations and encourage mutual consultation between church representatives and media professionals, who have much to teach the church about the use of media.

b) To explore cooperative productions through regional and national centers and to encourage the development of joint promotion, marketing and distribution networks.

c) To promote cooperation with religious congregations working in social communications.

d) To collaborate with ecumenical organizations and with other churches and religious groups regarding ways of securing and guaranteeing access to the media by religion, and to collaborate in "the more recently developed media: especially in regard to the common use of satellites, data banks and cable networks, and in informatics generally, beginning with system compatibility."[34]

e) To cooperate with secular media, especially in regard to common concerns on religious, moral, ethical, cultural, educational and social issues.

31. *Public relations.* Public relations by the church means active communication with the community through both secular and religious media. Involving readiness to communicate Gospel values and to publicize the ministries and programs of the church, it requires that the church do all in its power to ensure that its own true image reflects Christ. A pastoral plan for social communication should seek:

a) To maintain public relations offices with adequate human an material resources to make possible effective communication between the church and the community as a whole.

b) To produce publications and radio, television and video programs of excellent quality which give high visibility to the message of the Gospel and the mission of the church.

c) To promote media awards and other means of recognition in order to encourage and support media professionals.

d) To celebrate World Communications Day as a means of fostering awareness of the importance of social communications and supporting the communications initiatives of the church.

32. *Research.* The church's strategies in the field of social communications must be based on the results of sound media research which have been subjected to informed analysis and evaluation. It is important that communications research include topics and issues of particular relevance to the mission of the church in the particular nation and region involved. A pastoral plan for social communications should be designed:

---

34. "Criteria for Ecumenical and Interreligious Cooperation in Communications," 14.

a) To encourage institutes of higher studies, research centers and universities to engage in both applied and fundamental research related to communications needs and concerns of the church and society.

b) To identify practical ways of interpreting current communication research and applying it to the mission of the church.

c) To support ongoing theological reflection upon the processes and instruments of social communication and their role in the church and society.

33. *Communications and development of peoples.* Accessible point-to-point communication and mass media offer many people a more adequate opportunity to participate in the modern world economy, to experience freedom of expression and to contribute to the emergence of peace and justice in the world. A pastoral plan for social communications should be designed:

a) To bring Gospel values to bear upon the broad range of contemporary media activities—from book publishing to satellite communications—so as to contribute to the growth of international solidarity.

b) To defend the public interest and to safeguard religious access to the media by taking informed, responsible positions on matters of communications law and policy, and on the development of communications systems.

c) To analyze the social impact of advanced communications technology and to help prevent undue social disruption and cultural destabilization.

d) To assist professional communicators in articulating and observing ethical standards, especially in regard to the issues of fairness, accuracy, justice, decency and respect for life.

e) To develop strategies for encouraging more widespread, representative, responsible access to the media.

f) To exercise a prophetic role by speaking out in timely fashion from a Gospel perspective concerning the moral dimensions of significant public issues.

Vatican City, February 22, 1992, Feast of the Chair of St. Peter the Apostle.

+John P. Foley

President

Msgr. Pierfranco Pastore
Secretary

Index